TORONTO

The Place of Meeting · Frederick H. Armstrong

TORONTO

The Place of Meeting · Frederick H. Armstrong

FOREWORD BY J.M.S. CARELESS • PICTURE RESEARCH BY ROGER HALL • "PARTNERS IN PROGRESS" BY GORDON PITTS, ASSISTED BY GEOFFREY SIMMINS

PRODUCED IN COOPERATION WITH THE ONTARIO HISTORICAL SOCIETY
WINDSOR PUBLICATIONS

TO THE MEMORY OF MY GRANDFATHER,
FREDERICK JOHN GOODE (1873-1941),
AN ADOPTED TORONTONIAN
WHOSE INTEREST IN HISTORY
KINDLED MY OWN

All colour photographs appear courtesy of the Ontario Ministry of Industry and Tourism unless otherwise indicated.

Windsor Publications
History Books Division
Publisher: John M. Phillips
Editorial Director: Lissa Sanders
Production Supervisor: Katherine Cooper
Senior Picture Editor: Teri Davis Greenberg
Senior Corporate History Editor: Karen Story
Corporate History Editor: Phyllis Gray
Marketing Director: Ellen Kettenbeil
Production Manager: James Burke
Art Director: Alexander D'Anca
Art Production Manager: Dee Cooper
Typesetting Manager: E. Beryl Myers
Proofreading Manager: Doris R. Malkin

Staff for *Toronto: The Place of Meeting*
Editor: Annette Igra
Picture Editor: Laurel H. Paley
Assistant Editor: Elaine Linden
Editorial Assistants: Susan Block, Patricia Buzard, Judith Hunter, Gladys McKnight, Patricia Morris, Pat Pittman, Susan Wells
Proofreaders: Henriette Henderson, Jeff Leckrone, Kaylene Ohman
Typesetters: Barbara Neiman, Cynthia B. Pinter
Layout Artist: Karen McBride
Production Artists: Beth Bowman, Ellen Hazeltine, Julie Sloto
Sales Manager: Paul Pender

Published 1983
Printed in Canada

First Edition

0-89781-077-5

Frontispiece: James Gray's York from Gibraltar Point *includes a romanticized scene of Indians cooking amidst the leafy wilderness of what would become the Toronto Islands. The city appears in the distance, its harbour dominated by the steamship, symbol of 1820s progress. Courtesy, Picture Division, Public Archives of Canada, Ottawa (PAC), C2046*

For almost one hundred years the Ontario Historical Society has encouraged and publicized local and provincial history. These efforts have included assisting research, writing, and publishing for both general and specified audiences. The Society's participation in the publication of *Toronto: The Place of Meeting* is in keeping with our tradition. I am pleased that two of the contributors, J.M.S. Careless and Frederick H. Armstrong, are past presidents of the Society. They are both eminent scholars in the field of Canadian urban studies.

This book commemorates the sesquicentennial of Toronto as a city and should, therefore, appeal to Torontonians everywhere. But it has a wider interest, for it contributes to our understanding of this great Ontario urban centre. I am sure *Toronto: The Place of Meeting* will provide informative and pleasurable reading to anyone interested in our past.

Wesley B. Turner
President,
Ontario Historical Society

CONTENTS

FOREWORD

Toronto was made a city in 1834, and so can celebrate 150 years of city-hood in Canada. But it was first founded as the British colonial town of York in 1793; it was a French fur trade post in the 1720s; its site was known to French explorers from the early 1600s, and to native Indian peoples far back into prehistoric times. Its story in North America, then, is neither short nor dull. Still, the greatest changes—and pace of change—have come within the last 200 years, when it grew from a small British base of garrison and government to a leading North American metro-politan community. Progressively, it became a provincial capital, a com-mercial Great Lakes port, a railway focus, an industrial and financial power-centre, and a dominant Canadian metropolis, massed with people, cultural facilities, and decision-making authority. All this is in Toronto's many-sided history; and all this is in this book.

The backwater town of "muddy little York" was growing so fast by the early 1830s, thanks largely to British immigration and land settlement in fertile southern Ontario, that in 1834 it was incorporated as the city of Toronto, the older name for the site. It never looked back thereafter, as continued migration and economic advances sped its growth forward. And successive migrations, in the 20th century increasingly from non-British sources, went on swelling its numbers, complexity of organiza-tion, and outreaching cityscape. Today, as a result, it has a notably cos-mopolitan society with varied ethnic pluralisms, a sweep of residential areas, highrises, and central skyscrapers, all organized under a metropolitan government in which the original city of Toronto is only one unit along with other highly populous boroughs. And that, too, is succinctly dealt with in this volume.

This volume comprises, in fact, an admirably informed and no less informative account of the rise of Canada's now-largest city. The author knows his Toronto, after years of scholarly research into aspects of its history. He appreciates it—whether it be reviled as "Hogtown" or hailed as "Queen City"—but does not oversell it. His clear perceptions regularly produce sound judgements. Furthermore, while he packs a wealth of knowledge into the pages, he finds room, too, for painting in the setting, the human personalities, and the living colour of their community; the work is not overloaded either. It is a bright, interesting story throughout, one that smoothly carries the reader onward. Quite obviously, I hold it in high regard.

And I am glad to be able to say so, though not at all surprised. I have known the author, Fred Armstrong, for many years, and equally know his quality: first, long ago if not far away, as my graduate student (I am happy to note) who did his doctoral history thesis on the early city of Toronto; then, as a colleague and friend who taught me a good deal as his wider studies proceeded, and who still is doing just that. Besides, I have just finished my own book on Toronto down to 1918, and can't help comparing the two volumes, which are naturally different but essentially complementary—which of course makes me happy too. Fred had to cover right to the present, which means that he could say less on the 19th century city than I did: the 20th-century metropolis is a pretty sizeable order in itself. But what he does provide on the younger Toronto I notably agree with, and if I'm not astonished, I am equally pleased that he did manage to fit in so much. It is a skillful, well-conceived piece of work indeed.

Thus his book stays duly authoritative while being a popular, broader treatment. Both general readers and students of urban history will discover plenty to enjoy and commend here. For, from French trading post or British garrison base to Canadian world-city of three million, the complex growth and transformations of Toronto are most lucidly depicted and explained in this welcome volume, by an eminently qualified writer on Canada's urban past.

J.M.S. Careless
University Professor of History
University of Toronto

Previous page: August Köllner's 1851 lithotint of Toronto shows a more genteel side of 19th-century North American urban life than most contemporary cityscapes. Instead of illustrating the frantic bustle of industry along the waterfront, Köllner has chosen to view the city from the north, on the escarpment. From the I.N. Phelps Stokes collection. Courtesy, The New York Public Library, Astor, Lenox, and Tilden foundations

Following page: It seems likely that Elizabeth Hale (wife of an important government official at Quebec and sister of Lord Amherst, governor-general of India) based her 1804 watercolour of York on a sketch by Surgeon Edward Walsh of the 49th Regiment. The view shows the principal establishments of the 10-year-old town crammed onto the lake's shore alongside the yet unvanquished forest. The military structure to the far right is the town blockhouse. PAC C34334

INTRODUCTION

A CITY OF CONTRASTS

Cities do not grow and prosper by chance; yet establishing rigid formulae for development can lead to more headaches than insights. Rather, what is needed are some general guiding themes that can be used to examine a city's evolution. One is geography, including the economic geography behind urban growth. The land dictates the activities of the people who dwell on it; without the right geographic factors, a great centre cannot arise.

Toronto is well provided for in this regard: the harbour is good, the land flat and reasonably healthy, the water supply apparently inexhaustible, and the climate sufficiently mild. A current from the Don River runs through the harbour to wash away waste, and the Don and other rivers flowing into the lake provided mill sites. As well, there were clay beds for brick, the endless forest supplied building material, and once the forest was cleared, there was excellent agricultural land for market gardens.

More broadly, Toronto was central both to the developing province and later to the continent, and it had good potential communication routes. Also, there was that necessary complement to a great city: a prosperous, extensive hinterland. The successful urban-hinterland inter-relationship led to success in business; Toronto was to develop as a commercial, manufacturing, and finally a financial centre because of this base. As the city's power grew, its hinterland spread wider; Ontario became its local region, its inner hinterland, and Canada beyond was shared unwillingly with Montreal as a broader hinterland for resources, a consumer base for the metropolitan centres' industries, and a market for their trade.

Political geography has been yet another factor in the city's growth. As both the capital and the economic centre of Upper Canada-Ontario,

Toronto is in a special position. It can protect its interests from outside rivals by legislation, and the tale of urban advance is naturally one of clashing rivalries. Here again the city that becomes rich is the one that is well located. Provincially, Toronto's rivals lacked either its early start, its geographical advantages, or its political clout. Although Hamilton possessed a good harbour, Toronto pulled far ahead because in the crucial early years, access to Hamilton's harbour was blocked by the sand bar. The immediate hinterlands of Kingston and Montreal are inadequate as a good growth base, and both were eventually bypassed by the routes of commerce as the canals and railways evolved.

Rivalry has served Toronto more broadly in another way; it has played the rival ports of Montreal and New York against each other and successfully disengaged itself from Montreal's dominance in the process. Before 1914 transatlantic trade with London was the road to wealth and prosperity. Toronto was in the happy position of having two routes available; it used both.

Beyond geography, a second factor in the rise of the cities, especially since the Industrial Revolution, has been the advance of technology. Cities like Toronto were quick to exploit new means of communication to expand their metropolitan areas. In transportation and communication, from the appearance of steamships to the building of canals, from improved surfacing of roads to that revolutionary means of transportation, the railway, Toronto was among the forerunners.

The people of the city are themselves a third reason for Toronto's urban development. A successful city with a good hinterland attracts men and women of ambition from satellite centres, as well as providing a stopping place for settlers. The variety of people who have come to Toronto has created a city of contrasts, which can be a key to success. The English, Scottish, Protestant Anglo-Irish, Catholic Irish, and German immigrants, along with those from the United States of many ethnic backgrounds, early brought a cultural diversity to Toronto that became more complex with each new wave of immigrants. The arrival and melding of minority groups has always been a major theme in the city's development: for old residents and new arrivals, Toronto has been a "place of meeting," true to the meaning of its Iroquoian name.

Socially, to see just the stuffiness and the puritanical outlook of the late 19th and early 20th centuries is to overlook the many other facets of Toronto's character. Toronto, like most cities, has always been an amalgam of contrasts, not just the monolithic bastion of Canadian Waspish "virtues" that has been depicted. Behind the churches and charities of Toronto the Good were the taverns and brothels of Toronto the questionable, or even the downright wicked; behind the establishment, be it the

Family Compact, or the later business elite, has been the large, British middle-class who really carried the ball for puritanism and most of Toronto's other "virtues." Underlying both the establishment and the middle-class there has always been a much vaster poor population, frequently without the time or money to care beyond its immediate needs.

An old joke, also attributed to other cities, ran that the first prize for a contest was one week in Toronto, the second prize two weeks, and the third prize three weeks. "Old Hogtown" was long the butt of such ridicule and humour. But somehow Canada's dismal dowager, the "Good City," the home of the perpetual Sunday, the rallying point of temperance crusades, Orange parades, and narrow Imperial patriotism, has burst forth from its cocoon, which everyone outside mistakenly perceived as its true self, and has become Canada's largest metropolis, the centre of Canadian finance, a centre for fun, a shopping mecca for the nation and tourists, and a thoroughly international city.

The major turning point in the city's history came early when the British refounded it in 1793 as the provincial capital with all the power and dignity that distinction implies. However, more gradual trends greatly influenced the building of the metropolis, such as the creation of a basic railway network, which took more than 20 years. The growth of manufacturing and the spread of Toronto's control over the North were also gradual developments. Yet in these lie the riches of the city.

On the other hand, many of the most often retold events in the history of the city really did little to affect its growth. Toronto endured two captures in war and two great fires. It has been attacked in a rebellion, been hit by a hurricane, had its share of riots, witnessed ship and rail disasters, and even suffered some good scandals, many financial—as behooves a great business centre. Some of these events have provided legends that have helped shape the outlook of the city. They may prove that it has not always been a dull place, but they did not change the course of its evolution. Toronto's rise to metropolitan status has been the result of steadily moving forces, not sudden upheavals.

The 150th anniversary of incorporation of a city is a good time to look at both its present status and its future possibilities. But to do this, it is first necessary to establish a sense of development of the city, to decide what was really important in its past, what was just coincidental, and finally what is unique in both time and place. Any such selections will of necessity have some focus, a point of view, and in a Torontonian examining Toronto such a focus may be a bit biased toward the positive side. Whatever the perspective, however, to approach and gain any understanding of today's Toronto calls for an examination of its evolution through the years.

CHAPTER I

A HARBOUR AND A HINTERLAND

THE SETTING AND THE SETTLEMENTS

Underlying the growth of every great city is a good geographical setting. People may build the city, yet nature must provide them with the site. Defensibility, a good harbour, and easy communication with a potentially rich hinterland are basic criteria. Add to these an adequate supply of drinkable water, ready sources of building materials, reasonable soil, and a moderate climate, and metropolitan growth becomes almost certain.

In southern Ontario, Toronto alone possesses all these characteristics: it has no real rival. In addition, the city has been fortunate in enjoying the advantages of the lake shore while being reasonably remote from the threat of attack from below the lake. Given any of the luck that can sometimes be said to accompany human progress, Toronto's rise to metropolitan status was almost inevitable.

THE SETTING

The Toronto harbour, or bay as it is also called, is the best natural harbour on Lake Ontario. It is nearly circular, three square miles in area, and protected by a long, low, narrow spit of land jutting out from the east: the Island or Islands of today. Created over the last 7,000 years by the erosion of the Scarborough Bluffs to the east, this spit has been constantly but gradually renewed. Originally a peninsula, it was long a source of sand for the city contractors who so depleted it that by 1858 storms had broken through, creating the Eastern Gap, making the peninsula into an island, and providing better water circulation in the bay.

Inside the protecting spit, the Don River provides a flow of water which ensured that the harbour did not become a swamp, despite the fact that originally it had only one entrance, and from the first the city used it for garbage disposal. The east end of the harbour past the junction of the Don River was long an extensive marsh, later called Ashbridge's Bay, which gradually developed into a major shipping centre.

At the western end of the harbour, the Island curves inward toward the shore, forming what was first known as Gibralter Point and is now Hanlan's Point. Between this promontory and the mainland there was a wide opening (now partly filled to form the Island Airport), but shifting sand shoals forced ships into a narrow 300-foot-wide channel along the shore—the modern Western Gap. Aside from these shoals, the channel presented another problem: it was at the wrong end of the bay. Departing sailing ships had to "beat out" westward against the prevailing winds, and Montreal shipping lost an hour detouring around the peninsula.

Opposite the Western Gap on the mainland, near the foot of present Bathurst Street, was the mouth of a small, swampy stream later named Garrison Creek, which flowed eastward into the harbour at a sharp angle creating a triangle of land with only the narrowest, westward side unprotected by water. This was something of a defensive point, although not one over which any military engineer would enthuse. Here, dominating the entrance to the harbour, Old Fort York was to rise on much the same site as it occupies today.

Stretching eastward from the fort, a low ridge to the north of the railway represents the original north shore of the harbour before landfill began. The embankment is high enough to prevent flooding, yet not sufficiently high to present a communications problem. Beyond this bank stretches the wide, gradually rising plain that begins at Scarborough Bluffs to the east of the city and stretches westward to Burlington Bay and around the head of the lake to the Niagara fruit belt. The plain once formed the northern edge of the bed of the glacial Lake Iroquois, which was considerably larger than Lake Ontario. When European settlement began, its sand and clay soil supported an endless dark forest composed of large oaks and maples intermixed with hickories and some poplars, an excellent source of building material, and, after the forest was cleared, extensive agriculture developed.

Flowing across the plain from north to south are Toronto's two moderately large rivers, the Don, which became the eastern boundary of the early settlement, and the Humber, originally far beyond the western outskirts of the city. The plain is also intersected by the many streams now relegated to sewers, such as Garrison Creek and Taddle Creek, which flowed south through the university grounds. These provided a further source of water supply and waste disposal for the city, as well as power for mills, particularly in such areas as Todmorden on the Don River to the northeast. Bridging them has been a constant problem for road builders, from the pioneer pathmaster to the planning departments of today.

The actual town site that was selected in the 1790s was slightly inland and near the eastern end of the harbour. It did not provide a pleasant haven during much of the year. Stagnant water sometimes backed up the Don and the creeks, particularly during the spring and autumn; moreover, there were extensive swamps adjacent to the Don, at the eastern end of the harbour, and in small pockets throughout the town. These produced swarms of mosquitoes, which were responsible for frequent outbreaks of malaria in the hot summers. In the spring and autumn the Iroquois clay, which underlies the town, turned into a sea of mud, as it still does during Toronto's endless street reconstructions. Then, too, there were pockets of quicksand. Miserable as it was, however, Toronto did not present a greatly different picture from most nascent towns in the North American Midwest; pioneer life was anything but easy.

THE HINTERLAND

Behind the lakefront the coastal plain gradually rises for some three miles inland, although it extends further northward at the river valleys, particularly where the Humber River and Black Creek flow in from the west. While the plain spreads unimpeded westward toward Hamilton, to the east it is interrupted by higher land that stretches down to the lake to form the impressive Scarborough Bluffs. This ridge is a very old feature, being the delta of a preglacial river. Along its front, instead of the gentle shoreline, the bluffs rise stark and spectacular from 170 to 360 feet above the lake.

Directly to the north of the harbour beyond the coastal plain rises a 75-foot-high escarpment formed by the wave action of ancient Lake Iroquois. This terrace runs to the south of present St. Clair Avenue and is clearly seen on such streets as Yonge Street and Avenue Road. North of the one-time Iroquois shoreline stretches the rich, undulating agricultural land of York and Simcoe counties extending 60 miles northward to Lake Simcoe. This fine agricultural land sweeps westward without break or impediment into southwestern Ontario; to the east, gradually narrowing because of the Canadian Shield, it stretches nearly to Kingston. This inner hinterland was one of the greatest sources of Toronto's wealth throughout the early years, although it was not until the railway era that the city secured control of the entire area.

Still another geographical advantage for early Toronto was its site at one end of the narrowing of land that separates Lake Ontario and Georgian Bay, forming one of the three early portage routes to the Northwest and the fur trade. For the traveller passing westward from the St. Lawrence River or New York State, this was a possible short cut that eliminated the need for the long boat trip around the southwestern Ontario peninsula via the Great Lakes. The advantages of the Toronto Portage, however, were more imaginary than real. Indians used the portage and the North West Company tried to develop it for the fur trade, but the Ottawa-French River system remained by far the most popular route. Nevertheless, the Toronto passage had certain strategic military advantages. Also the idea of an important portage was perhaps as useful as its actuality. Its existence was one of the reasons for the siting of the town.

Toronto has yet another advantage—its central position on the continent. The well-cherished legends that Canadians are hardy Northerners sometimes obscure the fact that the most densely occupied parts of Canada are not really northern at all. The southern Ontario peninsula cuts far down into the American heartland. Toronto itself at 43.48 degrees north latitude is farther south than Minneapolis-St. Paul and Portland, Maine, and Portland, Oregon. It is a relatively central node on a continental transportation system. For New Yorkers or New Englanders, communications to the West could be effected just as easily through British territory. Conversely, for British emigrants the Hudson-Mohawk River Valley through New York State could be more convenient than the St. Lawrence River. For trade from the American West via Chicago or other Great Lakes ports, the route past Toronto to the St. Lawrence holds definite promise. Settlement and trade have naturally followed the easiest, least expensive routes. Toronto's central position meant that it always benefitted and frequently prospered from its location on these transportation networks.

Thus the site of Toronto was, and is, ideal: well connected for trade and possessed of an excellent harbour, a more than adequate water supply, mill power, and plenty of good land for market gardens and eventual produce export. The advantages of geography have been compounded by the effects of politics, defence, and national economic interest. In these again Toronto has done very well.

THE INDIAN PEOPLES

Long before there were any permanent Indian settlements in the Toronto area, the region was traversed by nomadic hunters. From 9000 to 5000 B.C., Paleo-Indian groups hunted caribou and possibly mammoths and mastodons where the city now rises. The Paleo-Indians were followed by the Laurentian Archaic peoples, who occupied the river valleys of the Toronto plain between 5000 and 1000 B.C. These people, too, were predominantly big game hunters, not agriculturalists. They lived off elk, bears, and beaver, supplementing their diet with smaller game when necessary.

It was only after 1000 B.C. that these earlier migrating groups were succeeded by the first settlers, the ancestors of the Iroquois, or Six Nations Confederacy, which was not actually formed until the 16th century. These agricultural groups basically cultivated corn, supplemented by squash, beans, and pumpkins. They also raised tobacco. In all, 191 of their settlement sites have been found in the Toronto area. Their type of village, which began to develop about 900 A.D., attained its final form about 1500 to 1600, just before the period of European contact. Villages were located on defensible, well-drained ground, with a surrounding forest of mixed growth and a reliable water supply, preferably a spring that would flow all year located within 500 feet. Even with such a carefully selected site, depletion of the soil and the need for firewood meant the

Indians had to move their settlements three to six miles every eight to twelve years.

The villages, which were circular, palisaded, and up to 10 acres in extent, consisted of elongated "longhouses" built of saplings covered with bark. These buildings could extend for as much as 150 to 175 feet, and were frequently aligned to present the least surface to the prevailing winds. They were heated by several open hearths situated in a line down the center of the house, the smoke rising through holes in the roof. Inside and around the longhouses, large numbers of pits were dug for everything from food storage to burials. The most famous settlement, and one of the longest lasting, was located on the east bank of the Humber River near the mouth. It appears in the early records as Teiaiagon or Tayagon ("The Crossing"). Another village, Ganestiquiagon, was sited near the mouth of the Rouge River at Metro Toronto's eastern boundary with Pickering. Through these villages the Senecas, the local Iroquois, controlled the portage routes to Lake Simcoe.

THE PERIOD OF EUROPEAN CONTACT, 1615-1720

In the years after 1600 the French and British, moving inward from their Atlantic and St. Lawrence bases, extended their empires to the north and west in their search for new sources of furs. This expansion drew the region into the worldwide struggle for hegemony that was being waged between the two 18th-century superpowers. The French came to the Lake Ontario area first. The trading companies that administered New France established Quebec in 1608, Three Rivers in 1634, and Montreal in 1642. The French thus gained control of the St. Lawrence River basin and then began opening up the St. Lawrence and Ottawa river routes to what they called the *pays d'en haut,* today's southern Ontario, and the lands beyond, although the process of expansion was sporadic.

Samuel de Champlain, governor of New France from 1608 until his death in 1635, except for a brief period of English occupation, was deeply interested in trade, exploration, and the conversion of the natives of the *pays d'en haut.* In September 1615, while exploring the Georgian Bay area via the Ottawa River route, he found the French-allied Hurons about to contact the Andastes, their allies to the south of Lake Ontario, for aid in their conflict with the Iroquois. Accordingly he instructed one of his interpreters, Etienne Brûlé, to accompany 12 Huron braves down the Toronto Portage to make the contact. The expedition was a failure from a military standpoint, as the Andastes' help did not arrive in time. However, with it the Toronto Portage enters recorded history for the first time, and Brûlé was the first white man to visit Toronto.

In the years following, the political situation in the area changed considerably. In the 1630s the Huron-Iroquois wars heated up; by 1649 the Iroquois were victorious over the Hurons and their French allies. In 1650 the Neutral Indians of southwestern Ontario were also conquered and Iroquoian power greatly expanded. But the Iroquois themselves were soon to face new problems as the English moved into upstate New York. At the same time French strength was growing. By 1665 the newly

No portrait of Samuel de Champlain has survived. However, this engraving from a painting by Théophile Hamel suggests Champlain as the competent, temperate man he was, as much reflective scholar as audacious explorer, dedicated to stabilizing and extending the French foothold in Canada. PAC C14305

Blustering, bad-tempered, and not a little pompous, Louis de Baude, Comte de Pallau et de Frontenac, was a poor civil administrator but a brilliant soldier. Under his prodding New France consolidated its armed grip on Lake Ontario. Sculptor Philippe Hébert has rendered him most heroic in this soldierly stance; a less kind critic might argue that his raids against the Indians often were counterproductive. PAC C7183

appointed intendant, or chief administrative official, of New France, the extremely able Jean Talon, was anxious to stop England from expanding its power and also to gain control over independent French fur traders. The result was an intensification of French activity in the West, which inevitably led to the destruction of much of the Iroquois power and a French-English fort-building race to gain control of the West. Lake Ontario was one of the focal points of this race and the establishment of Toronto one of its results. By 1671 Talon was writing Louis XIV recommending the establishment of posts on Lake Ontario; and then the Comte de Frontenac, the governor of New France, established Fort Frontenac on the site of Kingston in 1673. Five years later he founded the first, short-lived, Fort Niagara.

It is during this period that the name Toronto first appears on maps, applied rather vaguely to Lake Simcoe, the Severn River, and the southern Georgian Bay region, but gradually extended southward to include the Humber River portage, which naturally provided a convenient route between Fort Frontenac and Georgian Bay.

With trade increasing there was soon a suggestion that a post be established at Toronto. On June 6, 1686, the Marquis de Denonville, then the governor, recommended the establishment of posts at both Detroit and Toronto when writing to his commandant at Michilimackinac on Lake Superior. No action was taken at that time. However, with a resurgence of Iroquois hostilities, it became apparent that tighter French control was needed. In 1696 Frontenac, again the governor, led an expedition against the Iroquois, and, although he died in 1698, the Six Nations were pacified by 1701. They then retreated to the south of the lakes, concentrating their strength in upstate New York. The way was open for French consolidation of power on the lakes.

THE FIRST FRENCH POST, 1720-1730

By the beginning of the 18th century, *le fond du lac* ("the bottom of the lake"), as the French called the west end of Lake Ontario, was rapidly becoming the scene of increased European activity. In 1701 Detroit was founded to strengthen the French hold, and by 1715 a stream of settlers had begun to pass to the West. In 1720 Governor Philippe de Rigaud de Vaudreuil decided to counter English influence by rebuilding the French posts at the Bay of Quinte and Niagara, which had been destroyed, and by constructing a new post at Toronto. These *magasins Royaux*, or King's shops, were to be more like Hudson's Bay Company trading posts than full forts; they were not intended as centres of settlement but as posts for non-military commercial activities. While it was hoped that they could protect the King's goods and furs against Indian marauders, they were not designed to deflect English sorties.

The man ordered to build the post at Toronto, which was probably at the mouth of the Humber River on the east bank, was Alexandre Dagneau Douville, a cadet in the colonial regulars who had been born in 1698, had already spent considerable time in the West, and knew the territory well. (The Douville family played a strangely dual role in the histo-

ry of Toronto: one was the builder of the first French post and another the final commandant of the last one.) There is little information about Alexandre's structure, which was probably basically little more than a store. Like the later Toronto posts, it was intended as a branch of the more important fort at Niagara, which was reconstructed simultaneously.

The post's life was a short one. French charges for goods were not competitive with the English ones at Albany, and their purchasing evaluations of furs were lower. Trade languished, and the revenues that were intended to cover the costs of the construction and upkeep of the post remained insufficient. By 1730 the fort was allowed to lapse. Although traders continued to pass through the area, the Toronto Portage was to be deserted for almost two decades before the French again asserted their control.

Failure to retain the post did not indicate French intention to retreat from the north shore of the lake. In 1744 the French chief engineer, Gaspard Chaussegros de Léry, made the first survey of the area, the Humber River appearing on his map as the Toronto River. In the late 1740s the idea of restoring Toronto to cancel the effects of the first English trading house at Oswego near the southeast corner of Lake Ontario was revived, apparently in the hope that trade could be redirected and new trading habits instilled in the Indians by keeping prices low for two or three years. Perhaps more significant, the French could now trade in rum and brandy, formerly blocked by the priests, and the trade at Toronto would therefore be more attractive to the Indians.

THE SECOND POST AND FORT ROUILLÉ, 1750-1759

In April 1750 Minister of the Marine Antoine-Louis Rouillé, who was in charge of the colonies, approved the recommendation of the acting governor, the Marquis de La Galissionière, for the building of the fort at Toronto. This was the last French post built in what is now southern Ontario. The man placed in charge of the construction was Pierre Robineau, Chevalier de Portneuf, an ensign of the marines who was sent out from Fort Frontenac with a sergeant and four soldiers and arrived on May 20, 1750. The site chosen was probably again the east side of the Humber River near Baby Point. The structure, known as Fort Toronto, took about two months to erect. Governor the Marquis de La Jonquière reported it was a "small stockaded fort and a small house for safekeeping of His Majesty's effects."

A brisk trade rapidly developed, which frightened the French who, while pleased with the volume, feared the Indians might easily get out of control in the summer when large numbers converged on the fort and the stockade might not be strong enough to prevent the plunder of goods. The presence of a village of Mississaugas, who replaced the Iroquois, may have intensified these fears. As a result, in the summer of 1750, La Jonquière decided on the construction of a third Toronto fort located considerably farther to the east, near the harbour, on what are now the grounds of the Canadian National Exhibition. At the same time he

Jacques René de Brisay, Marquis de Denonville, might well be considered European Toronto's real founder since he gave the orders, as governor of New France, to establish a military presence there in 1686. The initiative was part of his plan finally to have done with the Iroquois "menace." PAC C9625

Extensive archaeological investigations are now being conducted on the site of Toronto's Fort Rouillé of 1749. When they are completed, a fuller understanding of the appearance of the building will be possible. In the meantime this illustration gives a rough idea of the simple stockade located in the centre of the present Canadian National Exhibition grounds. Preliminary findings show the fort to have had wood and not stone foundations; moreover, it appears that the rear walls of the five interior buildings were part of the fort's defensive perimeter.
PAC C116794

decided to retain the just-completed post as an auxiliary fort. Trade continued there through the 1750s, and the building may have survived the destruction of the main fort in 1759 and been used as a residence by the Rousseau family of traders in the early British period.

Completed in 1751, the new fort, officially Fort Rouillé, but locally called Fort Toronto, was erected beside the shore in a spot where rocky shoals prevented attack by water. Built with squared logs, it was a much more elaborate structure than the other two. To cite La Jonquière:

To avoid any risk I shall have built a double-staked fort with curtains of eighty feet not including the gorge of the bastions, with a lodge for the officer on the right side of the gate of the fort, and a guardhouse for twelve or fifteen soldiers on the left.

The complement was never large: in 1754 it totalled one officer, two sergeants, four soldiers, and a storekeeper; at the end, even with war raging, there were only 15 men in the garrison. In addition, some labourers and boatmen lived near the fort. Because of this small number of men and the fort's store of valuable trading goods, once again the possiblity of an Indian ambush to loot the storehouse was ever present. This nearly happened in 1757 during the Seven Years War when a group of France's Mississauga allies decided to seize the fort while on their way to Montreal. Fortunately Commandant Charles-Joseph de Noyelles heard of the proposed attack and sent a canoe to Fort Niagara to enlist aid. As a result, the would-be plunderers suddenly found themselves faced with two bateaux with swivel guns in the bows, manned by 61 soldiers. The would-be raiders quickly passed on toward Montreal without raising further difficulties.

Clashes with the Indians occurred periodically, largely because the French, like the English, used brandy as one of their principal trade goods. Also, the post was subject to constant illnesses, partly caused by the swamp environment, a problem that would continue well into the British colonial period. As the fort began operations in the summer of 1751, it was struck by a "fever," blamed on the "bad air," which incapacitated all but three soldiers and three French civilians and forced the commandant to send to Niagara to obtain a doctor.

Trade prospered, however, despite the perennial shortages caused both by the distances and by the difficulties of bringing in many types of goods. The resident soldiers at the fort were kept busy with maintenance and clearing the bush around the post, as well as with defence; by 1759 there were some 300 acres of open land surrounding the fort. This greatly decreased the chances of ambush and also provided space for a market garden.

THE SEVEN YEARS WAR AND THE END OF THE FRENCH REGIME, 1756-1759

Yet the life of the fort was to be short. By the mid-1750s France and England were drifting into their final war for North America—the Seven Years War, as it is called from its European engagements. After a series of initial successes by the French, in 1758 Britain organized its forces, captured Fort Duquesne (Pittsburgh), and then carried the war to the Lake Ontario theatre where Colonel John Bradstreet and 3,000 men from Lake George fell on Fort Frontenac, capturing and destroying it. In 1759 came the great disaster of the Battle of the Plains of Abraham and the fall of Quebec.

On the Great Lakes, the British under Sir William Johnson began the siege of Fort Niagara on June 6, 1759. This brought the war directly to the subsidiary post of Toronto, which had up to that time been reasonably well insulated from the battles, although it had been a way station for troops passing from Fort Frontenac to Niagara. As the siege of Niagara opened, the French schooner *Iroquoise* warned the commandant at Toronto, Captain Alexandre Dagneau Douville. When Niagara fell on June 25, Johnson quickly sent a force to take Toronto. All they found were smouldering embers; Douville had burned the post and fled with his 15 men to Montreal. On August 2 the Mississauga chief, Tequakareigh, was interviewed by Sir William and surrendered to the British Crown. Montreal was not to fall until in September 1760, but the French regime at Toronto was ended. The ruins of the fort remained as a memento until cleared to make way for the Toronto Exhibition grounds in 1878.

Toronto had ceased to be part of one empire, but the new empire that had seized Lake Ontario was not yet ready to occupy the north shore, for the settlement frontier was still remote. The English fur trade, now without a rival, could be redirected to such new British posts as Fort Niagara. The former outposts at Toronto and Kingston were virtually deserted.

CHAPTER II

FOUNDING THE CITY

1759-1793

With the Peace of Paris in 1763, New France was transferred to Great Britain; Lake Ontario became a British sea, and the Indians on its shores had only one power with which to trade. Settlement was as yet remote from the area; and Britain, to control the trade and keep peace with the Indians, as well as to reduce the territory under control of its possibly untrustworthy province of Quebec, cut back the former western boundary of New France. By the Proclamation of 1763, the former French Western territories became Indian lands excluded from settlement. The forts at Niagara and Detroit, with their surrounding small nuclei of settlement, remained; the sites of Forts Frontenac and Rouillé were deserted.

This system lasted for a decade only. The rapidly increasing populations of the established colonies demanded expansion room, and the Eastern colonial governments wanted control of the Indian lands. In 1774 the Quebec Act again extended the territory of Quebec. The Lake Ontario shores became part of the judiciary district of Montreal for local administration, and French civil law and French customs became mandatory.

Fortunately the Lake Ontario area was left in relative peace during the American Revolutionary War, and when the war was over Britain still retained control. Then came the second Peace of Paris in 1783 where British diplomatic blundering ceded the entire Old Northwest, although their armies still held much of upstate New York and all the Western territory. The unity of the lakes was shattered again. Along with the Old Northwest what is now southern Ontario lost its two "urban nuclei" at

Fort Niagara and Detroit, which were both on the wrong side of their rivers.

Settlement of the Lake Ontario area received its main impetus from the Loyalists who moved into surviving British territory partly via the St. Lawrence route, settling what were to become the eastern counties of modern Ontario, and partly across the Niagara River into the Niagara Peninsula. With them they brought their ideas of elected assemblies, township meetings, and local officials, and a desire for British-type government and institutions, not French ones. Thus western Quebec was becoming Anglicized. With the territorial transfer it would again become a front-line area; new forts would be needed to defend it, particularly since the Loyalists had to be protected. The Indian trade centres and the French forts had grown up because of their geographic positions; the same factors would now direct the British toward reestablishing a fort-cum-urban network on the same sites. Toronto was to arise from its ashes.

The man who supervised this reawakening of the north shore of the lake was Guy Carleton who, as governor, had drafted the Quebec Act of 1774 and after successfully superintending the evacuation of New York in 1782-1783, had returned, now ennobled as Baron Dorchester, for a second term as governor of British North America. His task was to sort out the postwar problems, particularly completing Loyalist resettlement and reorganizing the administration of the Western territories.

The refounding of Fort Frontenac, renamed Kingston, in the direct path of Loyalist settlement, had come quickly in 1783, but Toronto was at the very northwest end of the lake, well out of the direct line of both trade and settlement for the immediate future. Still, Dorchester saw the importance of the harbour and portage route even if immediate action was premature. By 1786 he was studying the site and expressing concern with the lack of navigability of the Humber River. He also began to take steps to legally acquire the area from the Mississaugas. As early as 1764 the British had purchased a small tract of land near Fort Niagara. This policy was continued with the Kingston purchase in 1781, and from these two focuses the Crown gradually extended its interests inward to acquire the north shore of Lake Ontario. The actual Toronto purchase of much of present Metro Toronto and York was arranged between Deputy Surveyor General John Collins and three Mississauga chiefs in 1787, for an estimated £1,700 in goods and cash. As the boundaries were uncertain, a second purchase was made in 1805, by which time the Mississaugas had been provided with reserves.

As development began many prominent citizens of Quebec cast their eyes westward to a potential source of profit. In the year of the first purchase, Philippe, Chevalier de Rocheblave, asked for a grant of 1,000 acres at the mouth of the Humber and the monopoly on the Toronto Portage carrying trade to Lake Simcoe. Several grants were made to leading French Canadian figures connected with Dorchester. Simultaneously Collins surveyed the harbour in 1788, noting that, while it was "capacious, safe, and well sheltered," there was the problem of entering by the west end because of the prevailing winds. Thus, although Dorchester may not have felt the portage route was very important, he liked the site itself and was making plans for the development of a town. In the same year four local judiciary districts were created in Montreal's western lands, with the District of Nassau (later renamed Home) covering the western end of Lake Ontario.

CREATING THE PROVINCE OF UPPER CANADA

Meanwhile, the Loyalists who had settled the Lake Ontario area were becoming increasingly restive under French law. Loyal they might be; that did not mean they were willing to give up British rights and institutions. By the end of the 1780s, despairing of a solution by Dorchester, William Grenville, the responsible minister in England, drew up a colonial constitution based on dividing Quebec into two colonies: Upper and Lower Canada, the southern parts of Ontario and Quebec of today.

This 1791 document provided for new colonial governments based on that of Great Britain, which became the ancestor of the present system. Under an overall governor at Quebec, in each colony there was a lieutenant-governor, an appointed upper house, the Legislative Council, and an elected lower house, the House of Assembly. Power rested with the governor and upper house, as well as with the Executive Council, a separately appointed body, which gradually evolved into the modern Cabinet. From 1794 there was also a provincial high court, the Court of King's Bench. Most of the offices were occupied by the major officials or merchant-landowners of the province. The governors were usually military men who were sometimes closed-minded martinets but in other cases were extremely competent administrators with considerable imagination. Inevitably, with Britain reeling from the American and French revolutions, the councils long stood as firm bastions of monarchy, the established church, and the interests of the ruling classes.

The new Upper Canadian administration faced major problems. The area was vast, very lightly populated, and immediately endangered by the impending cession of the Old Northwest to the United States, negotiated in 1794, to be effective in two years. The choice of a capital for the colony had to be directed by defence considerations to a large extent. Whichever site was chosen as the capital was bound to prosper; if it had good connecting routes and a good hinterland, its chances of completely dominating the province were excellent.

THE ARRIVAL OF COLONEL AND MRS. SIMCOE

Developing a colony in such a problem-beset wilderness called for a governor of unusual energy and ambition; Upper Canada and Toronto were fortunate in the selection of Lieutenant-Colonel John Graves Simcoe. Son of a naval officer who had fought with James Wolfe at Quebec, trained at Eton and Oxford, a soldier from age 19 and lieutenant colonel of the Queen's Rangers in the Revolutionary War, Simcoe had the necessary knowledge of North America. Invalided home in 1781, he had married a wealthy heiress, Elizabeth Gwillim, settled on estates in Devon-

William Wyndham Grenville was the chief architect of the Constitutional Act of 1791, which established Upper Canada as a separate province. Although the legislation did not guarantee Toronto prominence, it assured that a distinctive Loyalist society would be well-rooted on the northern shores of Lake Ontario: Toronto's strategic position would do the rest. PAC C945

John Graves Simcoe, founder of Upper Canada, originally hoped to build his small colonial capital inland at London on the fork of the Thames, safe from Yankee marauding. When Toronto was finally chosen, he consoled himself that at least the salmon fishing was good. Courtesy, Metropolitan Toronto Library (MTL), 927.1

Opposite page, top: Mrs. Simcoe, née Elizabeth Posthuma Gwillim, was both orphan and heiress. Her father, aide-de-camp to General Wolfe, died at Quebec, and her mother succumbed giving birth to her. Raised by her mother's sister, the aptly named Posthuma fell in love with Queen's Rangers commander John Graves Simcoe when she was 16. They married in 1782. The second great romance of her life seems to have been with Toronto, for which she possessed unalloyed and perpetual affection. She is pictured here in Welsh dress. Courtesy, Archives of Ontario (AO), S1072

shire, and been elected to Parliament. Ambitious and energetic, he immediately threw himself into the task of planning his new domain. Elizabeth Simcoe was a fit companion to her husband, active and interested in everything she saw, delighted with the New World despite its hardships. She was possibly the first person to fall in love with Toronto, a task that many, both then and later, would have thought impossible. Her lively diaries and talented water colours give a clear picture of the founding of the city.

In 1792, when the Simcoes arrived at Kingston, the problem of where to locate the capital required immediate attention. Niagara would do as an interim seat of government, but some safer locale had to be found. Simcoe had already carefully examined the maps available in England and was impressed with the need for developing the colony's far west. Governor Dorchester would have been happy with Kingston; the centre of commerce, gateway between the St. Lawrence system and the Great Lakes, and the colony's most populous town, it had the further advantage of being close to Quebec and thus more easily controlled.

Placing the need for a defensible location above all, Simcoe noted the value of the Toronto harbour as a naval station and temporary capital that was far from the American shore. For the ultimate capital, the site of London, Ontario, seemed ideal, in the centre of the southwestern peninsula with good water connections via the La Tranche (now Thames) River to the far west. It was, of course, inaccessible to the Americans—and to virtually everyone else. Richard Cartwright, possibly biased as the chief merchant of Kingston, commented that access would have to be by the newly invented balloon.

Dorchester, though not pleased, accepted Simcoe's Toronto as a naval base and temporary capital with Niagara-on-the-Lake across the river from Fort Niagara as an interim seat of administration while Toronto was being prepared. In human affairs there is little that is more permanent than something that is supposedly temporary; in one compromise decision Toronto's happy fate as capital of Upper Canada was decided. Eventually, with the settlement of the province's central and western areas, Toronto's geographical location paid off, and it became both the province's commercial and administrative metropolis. The most significant decision in the city's history had been made.

FOUNDING THE CITY

Simcoe's first months in Upper Canada were occupied with establishing the new government at Niagara-on-the-Lake and exploring his new province, including the London and Toronto sites. In the summer of 1793 he had made arrangements for the founding, or refounding—to give the French governors and traders credit—of his "temporary" capital. As a student of Roman history at Eton, he had studied Tacitus' *De Britannica* and understood the Roman method of using military camps both for defence and as an agent for civilizing their colonies. Regarding Upper Canada as a bastion of the British Empire in North America surrounded in all directions by hostile or potentially hostile foes, Simcoe conceived the idea of repeating the Roman experience in his colony. When appointed he had insisted on the reestablishment of his American Revolutionary War regiment, the Queen's Rangers, which has played such a long and distinguished role in Toronto's history. These troops were to be used for public works, as well as for defence and to provide a civilizing influence.

In late July 1793 some men of the Queen's Rangers were sent ahead by bateaux, the flat-bottomed carrying boats, to cut down trees and build huts for the coming winter. Then, to the music of the Queen's Rangers' band at Niagara, the Simcoe family boarded the schooner *Mississauga*, a craft of 120 tons with 6 guns and a crew of 14. With Captain Jean-Baptiste Bouchette of the Provincial Marine as a guide, they sailed across the lake. In the cargo was a rather remarkable object that was to become Toronto's first Government House—a large canvas tent made for Captain Cook's Pacific explorations and acquired by Simcoe after Cook's murder in Hawaii. The "canvas house" was a type of early prefabricated structure with canvas walls, wooden floors, and an outer shell of boards for insulation. It was fitted with doors and windows and had lean-to outbuildings.

At the end of August 1793, Toronto was ceremoniously refounded and renamed in honour of Frederick, Duke of York, a son of George III who had just trounced the revolutionary French in the Netherlands. To celebrate the victory, a 21-gun salute was fired on shore and answered by the guns of the ships in the harbour. Then the proclamation was read. Present were Mrs. Simcoe, young Francis Simcoe, who was to be killed in a much later campaign of the same wars being honoured that day, first Chief Justice William Osgoode, Attorney-General John White, who was

Below: Mrs. Simcoe's sketches are among the first permanent visual records of Indian life in and near the Toronto site. The location of this bark lodge, drawn around the 1790s, is not precisely known, but it would not have appeared out of place in Teiaiagon. AO Simcoe Sketches 175g

shortly to feature fatally in one of York's few duels, other aides, and 22 Indians, most of them chiefs. Toronto, or York as it would be called for the next 41 years, was duly established. The Simcoes settled into the semirural life that Elizabeth Simcoe has described so well in her diary. State duties were varied with horse rides on the Island and expeditions up the Don. There the Simcoes later built their summer residence, Castle Frank, named after Francis and now commemorated by a Bloor Street East subway station near its site.

Now lands could be granted to Simcoe's officials and the French Canadian claims conveniently forgotten. The site was surveyed by Alexander Aitken, who was responsible for much of the survey work done on the north shore of Lake Ontario from Kingston to Burlington Bay, including parts of Dundas Street and Yonge Street up to Lake Simcoe. For anyone who has wondered at the often strange surveys of southern Ontario, which seem to ignore topography, Aitken's reports exemplify the difficulties faced and the methods used. They paint a rather different picture from Mrs. Simcoe's diary. A North Englander, trained by apprenticeship, Aitken came to Canada about 1784. Like all surveyors he found the physical conditions dreadful. There was little relief from these hardships except the bottle, to which many surveyors became addicted, possibly explaining some of the jogs in the concession roads today.

Aitken himself often complained about the damp, the ague fevers that resulted, the "intermitting fever," possibly malaria, which was prevalent in the swampy areas, and the rheumatism. He also contracted tuberculosis. At times he had to supervise his none-too-competent assistants from a sick pallet in a tent. Such problems of health were compounded by the complexities of surveying the virgin forest, the lack of trained help, a shortage of equipment, and little overall coordination. In each township concessions were surveyed a few at a time as they were needed for settlement.

At York itself Aitken laid out what became known as the Old Town,

Alexander Aitken's 1793 Plan of York Harbour *was based on extensive surveys of the region initiated by Lieutenant-Governor Simcoe. The map might well be labelled Toronto's first official plan, and, indeed, residents live with its chief premises today: dull city blocks which hug the shoreline and ignore the site's picturesque land forms. PAC NMC 26071*

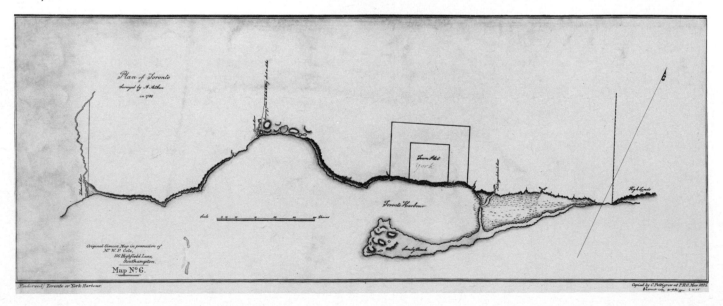

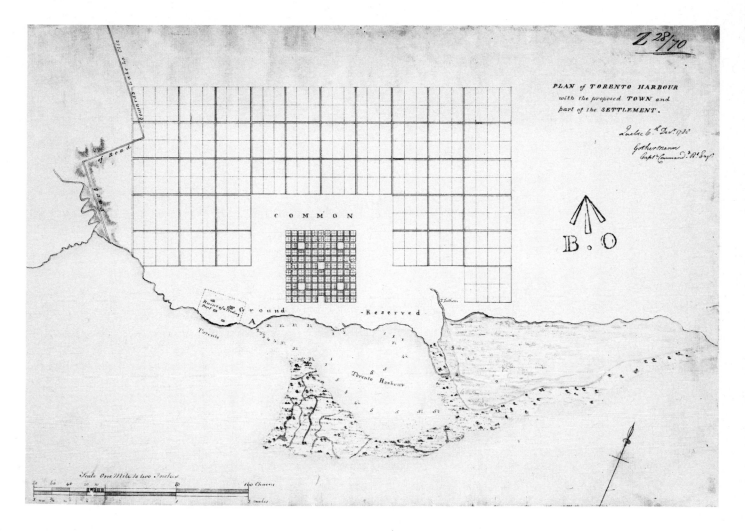

a 10-block grid bounded by George, Berkeley, Palace (now Front), and Duke (now part of Adelaide) streets. Yonge Street, Toronto's northern thoroughfare, which he also surveyed for Simcoe, was not connected to this grid, but rather came in independently to the west. South of the Old Town a strip along the harbour front was reserved for government use, and areas for military reserves were set aside. To the north of the actual town, Lot Street, or Queen Street as it was renamed in 1844, was surveyed as the base line from which the concessions of York Township stretched north, east, and west, at standard mile-and-a-quarter distances. Immediately to the north of Queen Street, long strip "park lots" of 100 acres each were laid out stretching north to what is now Bloor Street; these were to be gifts to the officials as partial compensation for moving to the new capital.

With Simcoe's proclamation, Aitken's survey, and the bush clearing and hut construction of the Queen's Rangers, York (Toronto) was reestablished with its new dignity as a colonial capital. The next task would be to make it into a viable town; but with its empty hinterland, remoteness from trade routes, and lack of settlers, the process was not to be an easy one.

Captain Gother Mann—twice in command of Canada's Royal Engineers—conceived the York townsite of 1788 in markedly 18th century terms. Here "Torento," harmony and order imposed on its undulating topography, is locked into a grid of 47 square blocks surrounded by a common and military reserve. PAC NMC 4434

CHAPTER III

AN IMPERIAL OUTPOST

1793-1812

Surveying the city was simple compared with persuading people to move there. Mrs. Simcoe may have liked the town, but she had little support in her opinion. The northwest end of the lake was virtually unoccupied; the lines of settlement were slowly moving along the Niagara Peninsula and into the Kingston area. There were as yet no York hinterland farms, and supplies in the growing town were expensive. Basically, at the capital as elsewhere in the province, land had to be given away to induce settlement. Grants were generous and free for genuine settlers; absentee landowners were not welcome, though impossible to eliminate.

When the Simcoes boarded the *Onondaga* and sailed away for the last time on July 21, 1796, leaving the government to Administrator Peter Russell, York's future was far from assured. Almost simultaneously, however, with cession of the Old Northwest the actual transfer of the government took place from Niagara-on-the-Lake to York. In 1797 the none-too-reliable minutes of the town meetings show a population of 241, which had grown to only 703 by 1812. In the surrounding townships of York, Scarborough, and Etobicoke, or today's Metro Toronto, there were 196 inhabitants in all in 1797 compared with 756 in York Township alone in 1812. This represented a much more rapid rate of increase. Many of the early settlers were technically Loyalist, but increasing numbers of "late Loyalist" Americans came for free land and soon formed the majority of the population. In addition, there were Maritimers and groups like William Berczy's Pennsylvania German settlers at Markham to the northeast by 1794 and a few French Loyalists at

the turn of the century. By 1812, when the war temporarily halted the advance of the frontier, York Town, Township, and County were at the edge of the settlement line.

It was during these years that the town's governmental and social institutions evolved and the land usage of today's downtown area began to take shape. Literally everything had to be done to cut a capital out of the wilderness; early York was basically a clearing in the forests. Defence was naturally the first consideration. Dorchester did not share Simcoe's ideas of extensive fortifications, and, as a result, defence funding was slow in coming. At the western Garrison Reserve, some round log huts and a blockhouse were erected. Storehouses rose across the Western Gap at today's Hanlan's Point and a second blockhouse at the Don River. The actual garrison was small and changing—even Simcoe's Queen's Rangers were temporarily disbanded in 1802—but still it provided some basis of defence.

In 1797 a New Town was laid out to the west, stretching to Peter Street and the Military Reserve. Between this New Town and the Old Town, lands were reserved for public purposes: hospital, church, school, gaol, and officials' residences. Despite the new survey, Yonge Street was still poorly connected. The result was the development of two rival communities, although the New Town was thinly populated for years. Some of the public buildings were not in the reserved space. Russell turned down the idea of relatively magnificent legislative buildings because of the cost, and a simple two-wing structure was built for the Legislature on Parliament Street. In 1797 the land on which St. James' Cathedral now stands was set aside for church purposes, and the first frame church was built in 1807. In 1798 came that equally important accoutrement of a growing urban community, a gaol: a log structure accommodating a keeper and three prisoners.

In 1799 Lieutenant-General Peter Hunter became lieutenant-governor. He attempted to improve the garrison, building his house there, and set aside five-and-a-half acres of land for a public market, now the St. Lawrence Market at King and New (now Jarvis) streets, in 1803. The market buildings came later, but from the first the temporary stalls presented a scene of lively activity, with their sales of produce and animals such as cattle, sheep, and poultry. In 1809 Toronto's oldest surviving official building, the Gibralter Point Lighthouse, was built of Queenston limestone. It forms the lower portion of today's Island Lighthouse.

With settlement growth commercial institutions appeared, and merchants quickly established themselves in the community. The general merchant was the great entrepreneur. Perhaps foremost was young William Allan, a Scottish emigrant who built a house and wharf on the water's edge and became postmaster and collector of customs. Another leader was Laurent Quetton St. George, a French Royalist refugee who turned his hand to commerce. Inns were quickly built providing lodgings and acting as social centres for meetings and dances. Beyond the town, wherever streams furnished the necessary water power, as on the Don

River at Todmorden, saw and grist mills were erected. Breweries and tanneries also had appeared by 1812. Toronto's industrial base was being established.

Interspersed with the new institutions and manufactories were the town's residences. The rich and officials like Administrator Russell quickly acquired town lots along the cool waterfront and began to develop farms on their rural 100-acre park lots north of Lot Street. The sudden transformation from the primitive to the elegant as quickly as conditions allow — one of the most remarkable characteristics of a pioneer town — was apparent in these dwellings. The original Government House may have been a tent; but as early as 1807 St. George erected the first dignified, Georgian brick mansion-cum-store at the corner of King and Frederick streets, the precursor of such surviving mansions as the Grange and the Sir William Campbell house. Fireplaces graced the better houses, and by 1797 stoves had appeared, although they were still scarce. Candles were used for illumination, and by their flickering light the local gentry attempted to ape the customs of the English country squires.

The other side of the story is hard to reconstruct, for slum dwellers do not leave letters and no one rushes in to preserve the historical hovel.

Much-trumpeted as Toronto's oldest surviving structure, the rude Scadding Cabin has been shifted from its original site near the Don River to become a permanent exhibit on the Canadian National Exhibition grounds, just a few feet west of the site of French Fort Rouillé. John Scadding (father of Toronto's first real historian, the Reverend Henry Scadding) lived in this building; previously he was manager of Lieutenant-Governor Simcoe's estate in Devonshire. AO S13368

35

The Scadding cabin in the exhibition grounds, which may date from this era, is misleading because it is the quite comfortable home of Simcoe's estates manager. Many dwellers of the lean-tos and huts spread along the Don and scattered around the city would have regarded it as something of a palace, as would the soldiers and their families crowded together at the garrison.

THE GOVERNMENT AND THE CITY

The growth of the capital was dependent on not one but three governments, for virtually from the first York/Toronto has been the centre of provincial, regional, and local administrations. In 1800 the regional administration was divided, the Niagara Peninsula was separated, and York also became the capital of a reduced Home District. These districts were the functional equivalent of the counties or regional municipalities of today, except that they were usually much larger in extent and were run by appointed magistrates (justices of the peace) sitting in Courts of Quarter (Quarterly) Sessions instead of elective councils. Again, most of the justices were leading merchants or provincial officials. Counties existed but basically as ridings.

From the mid-1790s York itself had a local town and township administration run by annually elected minor officials who operated under the close control of the justices of the peace. The elections were held at the annual town meetings, which often ended as drunken brawls. Most of the posts were unpopular: no one wanted to be a fence viewer telling his neighbours (who might be in his place next year) where their fences should go, or a pathmaster ordering people to dig stumps out of the road. Assessing and collecting taxes were other unpleasant duties. Although there is considerable truth to stories about the pioneer desire for democracy, the statutes establishing local government devote much space to penalties for refusing office and regulating the frequency with which an individual had to serve.

With such a limited system of government, lack of revenues, and thin population, there could be few services. Usually fire prevention was the first problem to require attention. Fire control ordinances regulated building construction and activities like cleaning chimneys, with heavy penalties for violation. Many other problems were classed as "nuisances," from garbage and offal thrown onto streets to stray pigs or other animals. Education was meager: there were various private schools but no particularly good system of public education; only small numbers attended, and children of widely different ages were mixed together. The government did set aside lands for sale to support education, and in 1807 opened grammar (high) schools at the main district towns. The York Grammar School, or the Blue School from its colour, was the remote ancestor of Jarvis Street Collegiate. The school was closely tied to the Church of England, with the rector of York as schoolmaster.

Welfare and charitable institutions were virtually nonexistent because of a lack of funds. Orphans could be apprenticed out and the mentally ill were kept in the district gaol at public expense, together with debtors and criminals. Public health was a constant problem, which grew with the city. Doctors were ill-trained, poorly paid, and few in number. There was no hospital. Agues blamed on swamp miasmas were common and epidemics were periodic, especially as there was little understanding of the causes of illness and a distrust of such measures as vaccination for smallpox.

Crime was handled promptly and severely. The administration of police in the Home District, which included York, fell on the sheriff. Assisting him were about a dozen constables appointed by the Quarter Sessions. Tavern keepers were constables for their own premises, although they often failed to eject the intoxicated as quickly as they might have.

In York's first recorded crime, two culprits were convicted of theft from a tavern; one was branded on the hand, probably in court, and the other received a public lashing. Like public hangings, such events constituted a major source of entertainment. Exposure of felons in the stocks provided the populace with a marvelous opportunity to dispose of over-age vegetables and eggs. When an enterprising woman, Elizabeth Ellis, and her husband, Stephen, were charged with operating Toronto's first recorded disorderly house, Mrs. Ellis was found guilty and sentenced to six months' imprisonment plus two two-hour sessions in the pillory, a standing stocks, and Stephen was acquitted! Other crimes received the ultimate punishment. In May 1800 Humphrey Sullivan, who passed a forged note for three shillings nine pence (about $10), was sentenced to death even though he was not the actual forger. Finding an executioner proved difficult. In the end a robber was released from gaol and paid to do the deed.

With this atmosphere of justice, one would expect immediate execution of all murderers; yet there were exceptions. One of York's first major crimes occurred in August 1796. An Ojibwa chief, Wabakinine, one of the parties in the Toronto purchase, came to York with his wife and sister to sell salmon. A soldier, Charles McCuen, solicited the chief's sister to provide certain favours. That night when McCuen arrived, Wabakinine, who had been drinking heavily, was awakened by his wife and told that the soldier was bothering his sister. A fight ensued in which McCuen hit Wabakinine over the head with a rock, causing fatal injuries. When brought to trial McCuen was discharged for want of evidence. There was a brief danger of Indian reprisals; however, Administrator Russell avoided any trouble by making some astute concessions to the Indians on land sales.

Similar failure to convict marked trials for the upper-class pastime of duelling. One of the most notorious cases occurred in 1800, when the clerk of the Executive Council, John Small, shot Attorney-General John White to defend his wife's honour. That Mrs. Small's honour was of a rather dubious quality was hardly a point of local dispute (though much gossip), nor was the fact that the attorney-general was apparently having an affair with her. The jury, at the same session that sentenced Sullivan to death, acquitted Small and the seconds under the code.

SOCIAL LIFE

The social life of the town was dominated by the handful of appointed, highly paid officials who had come to Upper Canada under Simcoe and quickly established themselves and their families in positions of power at the various levels of government. As always, the first to come obtained some of the finest land grants and most lucrative positions. In the years following, intermarriage became common, since the town was remote and there were only a limited number of marriage possibilities. This practice, along with the large size of families and hereditary tendencies in office holding, meant that gradually most of the ruling class came to be related in a sort of extended cousinship. This "Family Compact," as it came to be called, has been the source of attack by reformers down to this day. Yet while the system was inbred and undemocratic, it governed reasonably well in the early days, although it tenaciously retained power long after the province had grown and diversified.

Writing in 1893, J. Castell Hopkins, one of Canada's best early historians, stated that among the accomplishments of the group was the laying of "the foundation of the graceful social circles of modern Toronto." Whether graceful or not, they did attempt to carry on the ideas and customs of the English landed gentry in the New World, however inappropriate these might be to the society of a colonial garrison town on the frontier. Address was formal and titles were always used instead of Christian names or initials: "Doctor," "Colonel," "Honourable." Meals were extended and heavy, served with a wide variety of dishes, somewhat in Chinese style; wines and brandies appeared in profusion and the right of a gentleman to get dead drunk at supper was accepted. Social distinctions were insisted upon, hair powdered and fine dresses common, despite the levelling effect of the colonial mud. In fact, the elite, for all their apparent wealth, normally lived well beyond their means.

Below this gentry, so recently risen from obscurity, was a tiny middle class—the merchants, who were developing the commerce of the city and its hinterland, and, unlike the gentry, were saving money, not squandering it. There is all too little information about the greatest number of York's residents. The poor did not report on themselves, nor were they as yet the subject of voluminous government reports. Except for the church and court records, there is little to illustrate their life.

Thus the picture of colonial York, as well as of similar towns, is skewed, based as it is on life as it is seen through the eyes of the upper classes. The militia and their parades make frequent appearances in the records as do the officers of the garrison, but there is little of the problems of the ordinary soldier, burdened with poor accommodations, little money, and a Draconic military discipline. There were, of course, levels within the poorer portion of the population, varying from the clerks and skilled tradesmen, such as blacksmiths and tailors, to the very poor labourers. A large number of workers were needed for building and other trades; however, work was not regular. Generally, as through most of history, life was harsh, marriage young, families large, and death early.

Entertainment in little York was surprisingly varied. The upper classes visited each other, played whist, engaged in conversation, and read an increasingly wide number of books and newspapers; parties, dances, and subscription balls were regular pleasures. Sports were a varied source of recreation; hunting, fishing, horse races, and sleigh rides all figure in the letters. Fraternal societies developed early, the Freemasons providing a point of contact for many groups. Travelling players appeared toward the end of the first decade; a New York troupe performed Richard B. Sheridan's *School for Scandal* in February 1809. For the poor there were hunting and fishing, but such joys as the theatre would have been beyond their means. Basically their relaxation was to be found in the many taverns where one could escape the harshness of life.

Even though Toronto was to become known as the "City of Churches," there is little evidence that the people were particularly religious. There were very few churches and no accurate church attendance figures. The Church of England was an aristocratic faith that appealed to the masters rather than the masses, and official attempts to uphold its privileges were a constant and growing source of conflict. The first Anglican minister, the Reverend Thomas Raddish, remained only long enough to collect a goodly number of land grants. The second, the Reverend George Okill Stuart, was a gentle man, hardly suited to missionary work. When St. James' opened in 1807, members of other denominations attended, but the various sects were soon holding their own services whenever possible. Methodist circuit riders became the main religious support of most of the countryside. It was these religious groups who first applied pressure to control public houses and to prevent disorderly behaviour, particularly on the Sabbath.

THE RISE OF COMMERCE

While the earliest route to wealth in York was appointment to government office, as the province became established, the second was becoming a merchant. Settlements must be supplied, and as soon as the government transfer was announced, merchants were moving to York to provide for the capital's needs. This was a difficult task. The merchant had to operate a general store that sold everything from essential provisions to luxury goods. There were endless difficulties in transporting merchandise, with high expenses and constant losses, as well as continuous shortages of almost everything.

To obtain goods in an area that was not yet self-sufficient, it was necessary for each merchant to become an importer. At the same time, he used his outside connections with both the shippers and the wholesalers in major supply centres to export produce acquired from the local farmers, either by purchase or more frequently by barter in trade for supplies. These operations involved him in warehousing, milling, and distilling. To finance transactions in a barter-dominated economy where there was always a shortage of both metallic currency and paper money, the merchant began to supply credit. This led him into banking and acquiring mortgages on debtor's lands.

A merchant frequently became the town's collector of customs and postmaster, as well as holding various local appointments. Almost invariably he was a justice of the peace and a militia officer. The pioneer merchant was thus a sort of all-around Renaissance man of commerce: he bought, sold, imported, exported, and financed everything, speculated in land, and helped with legal matters. Although initially the establishment might not regard him as their social equal, many of them were soon in his debt, a factor that often helped him advance to higher office.

The fortunes made by these pioneer merchants are difficult to estimate, for they were carefully hidden. York's first great merchant, William

The financial kingpin of the Family Compact, William Allan had access to more local pies than he was able to put his fingers into. Allan was a general merchant, postmaster, collector of customs, militia officer, president of the Bank of Upper Canada, commissioner of the Canada Company, president of the British America Assurance Company, legislative and executive councillor and, not least, Canadian manager of the financial affairs of Edward Ellice, the prominent British financier and politician.
MTL T16678

Allan, came from Niagara at the very beginning of the town's history. He spent the next 60 years accumulating money and playing a leading role in every major provincial business venture. The activities of the "rich Mr. Allan" encompassed everything from the presidencies of the first bank, the first insurance company, the first Board of Trade, and the first railway, and the senior commissionership of the Canada Land Company, to speculating with the British consul at New York and managing estates of the Grey Eminence of English finance, Edward Ellice. Enemies saw him as the financial genius of the Family Compact. His sometime partner, Alexander Wood, prospered equally, as did Joseph Cawthra and French Royalist refugee Laurent Quetton St. George and his partners. Allan and Cawthra founded dynasties.

All faced great but decreasing difficulties in communication with the outside world. The postal service of the day was dismal but slowly improving, and transporting goods presented great problems, which were constantly being alleviated by successive breakthroughs in technology: the steamboat, canals, and, eventually, the telegraph and railways.

The dangers of lake transportation are well demonstrated by the wreck of the schooner *Speedy* off Presqu'ile Point in Toronto's first major disaster. In 1804 an Indian named Ogetonicut, a member of the Muskrat branch of the Chippewas, murdered a white man at Lake Scugog to the east of the city. His tribe brought him to York for trial; then it was discovered that the murder had taken place in the next district and the trial would have to be held there. Accordingly, on October 7 Ogetonicut was placed on board the *Speedy*, a regular caller at York, together with Justice Thomas Cochrane, who was to try the case, Solicitor-General Robert Gray, who was to prosecute, Angus McDonnell, a member of the House of Assembly who would defend, and the jury. Altogether there were some 20 passengers and the crew. The trip was stormy; finally on the evening of October 8, the *Speedy* was sighted off Presqu'ile. Then a shift in the wind prevented it from entering the harbour, and as darkness fell the schooner was beaten back into the lake. Huge signal fires were lighted to guide it in the darkness, but the *Speedy* was never seen again. The tragedy left nine widows and many orphans and wreaked havoc with the York and provincial legal establishment. It was all too typical of the lake hazards of the early days and pointed up the difficulties to which both shippers and passengers were subjected; yet both preferred the lake's moods to the roads' mire.

The last major problem of the early merchant was communication with the hinterland. To say that Upper Canada's roads were dreadful begs the case; they were often impassable, except under the snows of winter when they could be more or less ignored. Each little port town had its own network of roads connecting it with its local hinterland by the shortest routes possible. York, however, as the capital and the possessor of a broad, extensive hinterland that centred on Yonge Street, was able to develop a much larger hinterland than its rivals, and as the hinterland grew, so too did York's commercial opportunities.

CHAPTER IV

THE WAR OF 1812

As the second decade of the 19th century opened, Governor Simcoe's Imperial outpost was slowly becoming a settled town with 600 inhabitants. Yet peaceful growth was about to be shattered. Once again York was to be caught in the grip of an international conflict. The violence of the Revolutionary War had left a legacy of hatred between Britain and the United States, which was exacerbated by the many incidents involving trade and navigation that were a direct result of Britain's war with France. Further, Britain's blockade of the European continent disrupted America's European trade. Even more infuriating, American ships were periodically boarded and British deserters, or supposed deserters, taken off. On June 18, 1812, Congress, exasperated by what it called "insults to national honour," declared war. The remote villages on both sides of Lake Ontario were suddenly on the front line.

As the clouds of war darkened, two important personalities came to the fore at York: Major-General Isaac Brock and the Reverend John Strachan. In 1811 when Lieutenant-Governor Francis Gore went on leave to England, Brock as local commander-in-chief assumed the administration. When war broke out he provided the needed spark to activate his despairing colony. Strachan, a schoolmaster and Church of England rector, hardly seems a likely candidate for heroic leadership; but he was a man cast in the mould of the warrior prelate, not the country parson. In time he became first Anglican bishop, but for over a decade after the war he was Upper Canada's virtual prime minister.

Right: Francis Gore was lieutenant-governor of Upper Canada throughout the stormy years 1806 to 1817. However, from 1811 to 1815 while Gore was absent on leave from the province, his duties were performed by other administrators, Isaac Brock for one. Gore's absence, it might well be argued, was no great loss during a time of crisis, since he tended toward frequent bursts of rage and other exhibits of bad temper. One such incident occurred two years after his return in 1817, when he high-handedly prorogued the legislature, rife as it was with discontent concerning the state of the province at war's end. Within a month Gore took ship to England, never to return. PAC C6671

Previous page: Boston-born Roger Hale Sheaffe was knighted for his efforts at Queenston, the battle that had killed his friend and predecessor in command, Sir Isaac Brock. Sir Roger was to be criticized by locals for not defending York more effectively. In fact, his decision to withdraw was the only sensible military alternative, since preserving the British Regulars as a fighting force was paramount; time and effort defending indefensible little York were too valuable to waste. PAC C111307

Strategically the British power west of Montreal seemed doomed to quick extinction. The Americans had merely to cut the St. Lawrence trade route to capture the West, an action that did not present many difficulties. The British were engaged in Europe, the local supply lines were long, the geography difficult, and the people's loyalty dubious.

Fortunately for Upper Canada there were compensating factors. The Americans were overconfident; the efforts of their generals in the crucial opening months were blundering and ill-directed; the American army itself was much weaker than official records showed and had not fought a war for nearly 40 years; and, perhaps most important for Upper Canada, the Americans completely failed to understand that the many recent emigrants, content with their lot, might not give their support. At best they were neutral. In addition, there were positive factors on the British side. The regular troops in the colonies, though limited in number, were well trained and experienced. Further, Brock was a precipitous leader, and as the war opened precipitous action was needed to encourage a dispirited people.

News of the war reached York on June 27, 1812. Magistrate Eli Playter recorded that he "found all York in alarm; every one's countenance wore a mark of surprise." Yet there seems to have been no panic, although many officials faced loss of appointments and confiscation of lands in case of defeat. The merchants naturally saw the chance of making a fortune provisioning the garrison. A few Americans left hurriedly, selling their property for what they could get, sometimes to fellow immigrants who had taken the oath of allegiance.

Immediately the British regulars were withdrawn for frontier duty and the garrison taken over by the militia. York became a training post. Such dependence on the militia was dangerous. Militia training was limited to two or three muster parades each year, which often amounted to little more than farm boys escaping from their chores for a glorious drunk.

Militia commanders were usually the leading citizens of the colony: the higher their social or economic status, the higher their rank. The elite may have looked impressive on the parade ground, and they helped recruit militia regiments, but the ability of a senior civil servant or a prosperous merchant to lead troops into battle was problematical. At times both officers and men were reluctant to serve; individuals in the ranks frequently deserted. Yet many Upper Canadians, both farmers and scions of the Compact, trained and fought valiantly. When Brock called for volunteers at York, more enlisted than he could transport.

THE FIRST ENGAGEMENTS

The opening salvos of war greatly encouraged York. Initial defeatism was dispelled by Brock's capture of Michilimackinac at the head of Lake Superior in July and Detroit in August. Then on October 13 Brock died at the Battle of Queenston Heights. Reportedly, his last order urged on his "brave York volunteers," commanded by Major William Allan, who helped hold on until Roger Hale Sheaffe, Brock's successor, could take over. Brock's glorious death on the field of battle gave the colony a hero. His name, immediately made more illustrious by the news of a knighthood, became a rallying cry: "Sir Isaac Brock: The Saviour of Upper Canada!"

The war was a mixed blessing for the town of York. There were constant shortages as the military commissariat made heavy purchases and outside shipments were limited, although Sir James Yeo, the British lake commander, kept supply routes open. Salt, flour, and pork were all unavailable at times as York's hinterland was still too underdeveloped to provision the town. With the shortages went inflation; prices rocketed despite attempts to set maximums. Metallic currency, or specie, vanished, and the commissariat was forced to issue Army Bills, the beginning of Canada's paper money, which were not available in small denominations. The merchants, too, issued some bills—a few York paper notes survive—but inevitably barter became even more frequent.

But wartime economy had its good side, too. Before the war the merchants feared insolvency because of the depression; during the war virtually every citizen made money. In the winter of 1812-1813, a new dockyard for the Provincial Marine, located on the site of the present Union Station, employed 75 men. Merchants prospered greatly, particularly Laurent Quetton St. George, the largest merchant, Major William Allan, and Joseph Cawthra, a future Reform leader. In all, they received the phenomenal sum of £50,458 for supplying the garrison.

Charitable enterprises were quickly begun to aid the troops. The Reverend John Strachan raised £200 for the Niagara militia in November. He then organized the Loyal and Patriotic Society of Upper Canada to provide aid and relief and to grant medals for "courage and fidelity." By 1815 nearly £21,500 had been raised, the largest portion of which had come from Strachan's supporters outside the province. The medals were never struck, and the money was eventually used to build the first Toronto General Hospital.

THE FIRST CAPTURE OF YORK, APRIL 27, 1813

In 1813 American tactics on Lake Ontario changed with disastrous results for York. Major-General Henry Dearborn, the American army commander of the vast northeastern sector, decided to abandon his futile attempts to seize Upper Canada via Detroit and Niagara and instead cut the vital St. Lawrence lifeline. Conveying his troops on the Sackets Harbour fleet commanded by Isaac Chauncey, he planned a sweep from its base at the southeast corner of the lake to capture Kingston, York, and Niagara in quick succession.

As Kingston was the main British naval base and the key guardian of the St. Lawrence route and Niagara was the bastion of the frontier, Dearborn's even bothering with York seems surprising. Still, York was the capital, it was virtually undefended and indefensible, and its capture would open a route to the Northwest. Most important, the British were building the *Sir Isaac Brock,* a 30-gun frigate at York's dockyard. This would be the largest fighting ship on the lakes when completed. Also, the schooner *Prince Regent* was known to be wintering at York for repairs. Dearborn probably hoped to take the town, destroy or seize the ships, and sail away without great losses. He was to be badly mistaken.

As soon as the ice was off the lakes, the 14-vessel fleet sailed from Sackets Harbour led by Chauncey's flagship, the 24-gun *President Madison.* These carried 1,700 soldiers and an uncertain number of marines. Despite this strength, Dearborn did not follow through with his plan to attack Kingston, mistakenly believing the town was strongly defended. Instead, relinquishing the chance to sever the St. Lawrence communications, he made for York.

On the evening of April 26, an unknown person sighted the invading armada off Scarborough Bluffs to the east. Immediately all was activity. The signal gun at the garrison summoned the militia to battle. Major John Givins of the Indian Department organized assistance for the regulars. Donald McLean, clerk of the Legislative Assembly, hastened to remove the official papers. Chief Justice Thomas Scott and Justice William Dummer Powell rushed to the house of the dying Receiver-General Prideaux Selby to rescue more than £3,000 in provincial funds in his care.

Major-General Roger Hale Sheaffe, now knighted for Queenston Heights and adminstrator and commander of the province, was in town travelling to Niagara with some regulars. Although like Dearborn a man with long military experience, he still made the mistake of attempting to defend the town.

York's fortifications were completely inadequate. The unfinished fort, sprawled on both sides of the mouth of Garrison Creek, was little more than some wooden barrack huts, a powder magazine, the Governor's House, and some palisades and earthworks for defence. The batteries in front were not capable of holding off an attack. Beyond to the west was the Half-Moon Battery and beyond that the Western Battery, near today's CNE Princes' Gate, with two 18-pounder guns that could not be pivoted. In all, Sheaffe had some 700 men: two companies of regulars of the Eighth (King's) Regiment, some locally raised regulars of the Royal Newfoundland Regiment, and the Glengarry Light Infantry; a bombardier and 12 gunners of the Royal Artillery; possibly 100

Isaac Brock, English Canada's first hero-martyr through his spirited defence and personal sacrifice during the War of 1812, actually rather disliked Upper Canada and its seething political life. Brock's elevation to knighthood was unknown to him—he had been gazetted a KCB just three days before his death in battle at Queenston Heights on October 13, 1812. AO S1425

American Captain (later Commodore) Isaac Chauncey masterfully handled the American invasion fleet during York's capture. However, his statement "We may consider the upper province as conquered" was somewhat premature, considering his later, unsuccessful attempts to box in the British. PAC C10926

Mississauga and Chippewa Indians; and 300 York militiamen and dock-workers. One potential prize, the *Prince Regent,* had just sailed away to safety.

Tuesday, April 27, saw the Reverend John Strachan up at 4 a.m. ready for action. The American fleet moved more slowly. At dawn it sailed westward, following the outer shore of the peninsula, past Gibraltar Point (the Island) Lighthouse, and headed toward the ruins of Fort Rouillé a mile west of the harbour entrance (the modern Canadian National Exhibition grounds). By 8 a.m. the defenders saw small boats gathering around the *Madison* in preparation for the landing.

Sheaffe ordered the regulars to guard the ditch west of the fort and sent Givins' Indians and the Glengarry Light Infantry to ambush the Americans from the woods to prevent a landing. Meanwhile, the Americans, driven west of Fort Rouillé's site by the wind, landed at Sunnyside near the present western junction of King and Queen streets. There the green-clad riflemen established a beachhead with only the Indians opposing them from the bush, for the Glengarry Light Infantry had lost the way. Some grenadiers and local volunteers arrived, and there was a brief skirmish in which the British suffered several casualties, including Legislative Clerk McLean who was mortally wounded.

The defenders retreated to the Western Battery, halfway between Fort Rouillé and Fort York, which was being fired upon by the American fleet. Then a portable powder magazine blew up when someone forgot to close the lid, killing or wounding 35 grenadiers. Unable to defend themselves, the survivors retreated to the fort for medical aid. By then the Americans under the command of Brigadier-General Zebulon Pike had landed some 1,000 troops and were marching eastward to the Half-Moon Battery awaiting the surrender.

By noon the scene at the fort was approaching chaos. With the landing completed, Chauncey sailed into the bay and began bombarding the garrison itself. Soon the defenders were hiding under the fort's battery. They could do little, for their guns' range was too short to hit the American ships. Sheaffe now made the only sensible decision possible: to abandon York and retreat to Kingston leaving no prizes for the Americans. Strachan and others protested, but the situation was clearly hopeless. Unknown to militia leaders in the confusion, Sheaffe's final orders were to blow up the magazine and have the *Brock* torched.

As the regulars touched off the fuses to blow up the magazine, 600 feet to the west the victorious Americans had paused to reconnoitre. The explosion sent stones and debris hurtling down on them killing some 38, including Pike, and wounding 222. There were also casualties among the defending militia and the British regulars. Sheaffe, quite by accident, had delivered a crippling blow and turned Dearborn's easy victory into a major disaster. At the dockyards Sheaffe consulted with his officers and then retreated to Kingston, leaving Lieutenant-Colonel William Chewett and Major Allan of the militia to arrange the surrender. By 2 p.m. the Stars and Stripes flew over the fort and the battle was over.

Chewett and Allan, helped by Strachan and acting Attorney-General

John Beverley Robinson, now had the unpleasant task of negotiating the capitulation with an enemy that had received a shattering blow just as it grasped victory. In all, 300 Americans were killed and wounded. The victor's temper was not helped by Sheaffe's firing the *Brock* and the marine stores while the negotiations were taking place, thus destroying the only tangible fruits of the costly victory. The officers saw the burning of the ship as a dishonest act, but, fortunately, they did not blame the locals. At 4 p.m. the Americans marched into the town.

The conditions, which were subject to the ratification of Chauncey and Dearborn, were generous; Strachan successfully held out for proper treatment of the wounded and the prisoners and the protection of private property. There were four basic terms: regular militia and naval personnel, except surgeons, were prisoners of war; naval and military stores were to be surrendered; private property was to be guaranteed; and the civil government papers were to be retained by the provincial officials. The settlement was certainly fair, especially as the militia were not imprisoned but rather paroled, as there was no room for them on the American ships. Many defenders were never captured; pausing only for a quick drink at a local tavern, they fled north to freedom. Those who remained surrendered quietly while the Americans placed guards on the government stores.

From April 27 to May 2 the town was held in one of the gentlest occupations in history; as seven eminent citizens wrote, "we must acknowledge that they behaved much better than we expected." To a large extent, the "success" of the occupation was directly attributable to John Strachan. He harassed the American officers and acted as protector of the city, making sure that food was provided for the captive militia and treatment for the wounded. When the terms of the surrender were not ratified promptly, he claimed that the delays were planned to enable looting, and Dearborn and Chauncey signed the capitulation. Only £2,144 of the government funds was surrendered, mostly in uncashable British Army Bills.

The real problems were looting and destruction of government property. The capitulation gave the victors the government supplies, and the local farmers gladly accepted Yankee payment to haul commissariat stores to the ships. The fort buildings were burnt, including the Governor's House and two blockhouses. Official buildings elsewhere were looted and the public library was stolen, to Strachan's immense irritation, although Chauncey later returned what he could retrieve. The most contentious act was the American looting of the House of Assembly or Legislature on April 30 and its subsequent burning. Responsibility for the fire has never been definitely fixed. Was it done by Americans or by the locals? The answer remains uncertain.

Generally private houses were not looted if the occupants remained on the premises and had no government connection, but abandoned dwellings and stores were easy targets. There were 23 war-loss claims from the York neighbourhood: 13 homes entered and looted; 5 stores robbed; 2 cases of tools stolen at the dockyard; 2 incidents of livestock

Henry Dearborn, the American Revolutionary War hero, was not quite as successful in the War of 1812. Instead of launching an overwhelming attack at Canada's lifeline, the St. Lawrence River, Dearborn wasted time and manpower nipping at the western flanks— including, of course, the April 1813 attack on York. He had been told erroneously that Americans would be welcomed everywhere in Canada as liberators. PAC C10925

theft; and one private boat burned. There were no recorded rapes or murders. It has been asserted that there was no local looting, but this is doubtful. One report stated that "the enemy were joined by a number of Vagabonds who gave them every information."

Because of adverse winds, the Americans, who feared a British counterattack, did not embark until May 1 and 2 and only sailed away on May 8. They had little to show for their sortie except the uncashable Army Bills, some liquor, and some military supplies. Not long afterward both Sheaffe and Dearborn were removed from their commands. Indirectly the capture did have major repercussions, for the armament and equipment for Britain's Lake Erie squadron were captured at York. This contributed to the British defeat in the Battle of Lake Erie on September 10, which led to the forced retreat from Detroit that ended with the disastrous Battle of the River Thames and the fall of western Upper Canada to the Americans.

THE SECOND CAPTURE OF YORK, JULY 1813

The second capture of York was decidedly an anticlimax. A formidable American fleet sailed into the harbour on Saturday, July 31, apparently with intelligence on the location of government stores. The paroled militia could not fight, possibly to their relief. Many important inhabitants took to the woods. Bearing a flag of truce, the Reverend Mr. Strachan again marched forth to defend his flock. When the American troops landed at the burnt fort about 3:30 p.m., he cornered Chauncey and was assured that looting was not the objective.

The occupation that followed was extremely brief and hardly drastic. The Americans again let the prisoners out of gaol and removed from the hospital any of their men who had recovered sufficiently. There was some erratic looting, and a few cattle were slaughtered. At 11 p.m. the same night they sailed away. York breathed a sigh of relief.

Next morning some American schooners sailed back into the harbour, tipped off that two ammunition scows had been hidden up the Don River by dragoons. Warned in time, the dragoons and John Beverley Robinson, the future chief justice, who was hiding in the vicinity, concealed the arms and ammunition in the bushes, dumped the shot boxes in the river, and then sank the scows. When the Americans rowed up the Don, they found nothing and gave up. Frustrated, that evening they fired some buildings, including the storehouse at Gibraltar Point. At daylight on Monday, August 2, they sailed away for good.

THE CLOSE OF THE WAR AND ITS AFTERMATH

For the duration the town served as a base hospital for the Niagara frontier troops. During the summers of 1813 and 1814, there were an average of 370 to 420 injured quartered at York. There was something of a witch hunt for traitors in the summer and autumn of 1813, led by William Allan and members of the Executive Council. Then on February 15, 1815, news came that a peace treaty had been signed at far-away Ghent in the

Netherlands on Christmas Eve. The commissariat stopped buying supplies, prices fell, and York began to return to a peacetime basis.

Although its rhythm of development was interrupted by the war, York was extremely lucky. Niagara-on-the-Lake, occupied from May to December 1813, was burnt on one hour's notice as the Americans retreated. On capturing the American frontier shortly afterward, the British fired Lewiston and Buffalo. In 1814 came the famous British burning of Washington in reprisal for the destruction of York's Legislature. Had York's capture come but a little later, the outcome might well have been much more serious.

With war over, Old Fort York was constructed to replace the destroyed garrison. Seven buildings, including the two blockhouses that still stand, were erected within a triangular stockade and another blockhouse built on Garrison Creek, which protected the fort on the north and east. Fortunately its defensibility has never been tested. The fort building provided an economic boon with its job contracts. However, the general postwar slump was severe, largely because of the sudden depression of prices.

Much more frightening than price collapse was the sudden threat of the capital transfer, for after the war Britain decided to move the government from York to Kingston. The former, having been taken twice, was obviously vulnerable, while the latter, which had never been captured, was obviously defensible. The York officials and merchants, now so well settled in their "temporary" capital, had developed their businesses, mansions, and estates in the city and their farms around it. With York's hinterland developing rapidly after nearly two decades, they must have felt themselves secure as residents of the capital, even if Kingston remained the largest city. Now a repeat of the Niagara move was threatened.

Fortunately Lieutenant-Governor Francis Gore, returning after a comfortable four years' wartime residence in England, was persuaded that the proposal was a bad one. He managed to convince the government of Great Britain that it would be a mistake. On June 12, 1816, the official *Gazette* announced that York was confirmed as the seat of government. The Family Compact and its town breathed freely. The capital argument was to continue, but it came to nothing.

Equally important for the city and its rulers was the growth of the legend of heroic native defenders. For Upper Canadians/Ontarians, the War of 1812 is the only war fought on native soil; for a century it was the "Great War." Psychologically this provided an early boost for Canadian nationalism, especially since the War of 1812 was indecisive. Happily, all the contestants could go home feeling victorious, and there was no lost territory as an irritant. The Americans knew they had won, the French Canadians knew they had, and the British went home and forgot the whole sideshow to the Napoleonic Wars. But Upper Canadians knew the truth: they were the victors! In one way they were: the Americans had not overrun them. Now both sides gradually accepted the idea that there would be two domains.

CHAPTER V

"MUDDY YORK": A BURGEONING COLONIAL CAPITAL

1815-1828

The postwar years saw a prolonged attempt by the Upper Canadian government to stop the flow of immigrants from the United States; therefore the growth of the town of York, although steady, remained limited. In 1816 the minutes of the town meeting recorded a total population of 720. This figure grew by 520 to 1,240 in 1821 and by almost the same number to 1,719 in 1826. Then came a harbinger of the first great British wave of immigration, for another 500 arrived within only two years. In 1828 the town's population reached 2,235. Within the next decade the face of York was to be completely changed. Most of the immigrants were poor, but there were substantial numbers of farmers and artisans in their ranks, as well as some who belonged to the upper-middle class. Many were people who found themselves facing declining living conditions in postwar England and sought an improved future for their children in the New World.

The Home District was expanding at the same time as the town, for it was now on the frontier of settlement, as were the districts adjacent to it. In the pre-railway era this did not greatly help the trade of any single settlement, since the hinterland farmers dealt directly with the nearest port, and such centres as Oakville and Port Hope prospered along with the capital. York, however, was fortunate in possessing Yonge Street, which had been extended to the Military and Naval Establishment base at Penetanguishene by 1815 to improve wartime communications. As settlers moved into the district, side roads were run out from "the Street" as it was called, gradually broadening the town's hinterland base. Natural-

Previous page: James Cockburn, the best known of Canada's early garrison artists, was an inveterate traveller who passionately recorded all that he saw. He rendered York's courthouse and gaol on King Street in 1829. It should be noted that the space between these two buildings formed, for many years, Toronto's version of a civic square. PAC C12703

ly, as the hinterland filled up, York's trade in both importing supplies and in exporting staples expanded steadily.

GOVERNMENT AND POLITICS

In 1817 York, along with other Upper Canadian centres, was given extended powers, particularly for policing purposes. Generally services were very limited. In 1826 a volunteer York Fire Company was established. In 1831 a hook and ladder company was added, again on a volunteer basis. For both fire fighting and general use, one of the great problems was lack of water. Despite the fact that a town well was dug at the market in 1823 and the lake was next door, there was always a supply problem. Much of the water was undoubtedly contaminated, for the town grew increasingly filthy with the growth in population and garbage was frequently disposed of in the water.

A major positive development was the building of the first Toronto General Hospital in 1820 using the surplus of £4,000 collected by the Loyal and Patriotic Society to strike medals. The resulting structure was a brick building, which, disregarding the alignment of the streets, was carefully positioned exactly east-west to catch the supposedly salubrious breezes that flowed with the compass. Unfortunately so much money was spent on the building that there was nothing left for furnishings, and it stood vacant for four years until appropriated by the Legislature after their second building burned in 1824. Finally in 1829 a new governor, Sir John Colborne, found the funds for fittings and equipment and opened the hospital.

The most significant developments during the period were in the field of politics. Although there were no real parties before the 1840s, the factions that later evolved into parties were making their appearances with the 1820s marking an increased politicization and polarization of the province. With the increase of population, the development of a middle class with more free time, and the problems of accommodating increasingly divergent interests, factionalism was inevitable.

The Family Compact and the Reformers were the two main groups. The Compact saw itself as a meritocracy placed in office by virtue of its own ability. Like any political group it was loath to relinquish power, yet the growth of the province made it increasingly difficult to distribute patronage and appointments. The Compact liked to claim that it was merely upholding British institutions against its opponents' American ideas of radicalism. The Reformers were inevitably influenced by the American ideas of more democratic government. This contrasting pull of British and American examples and influences in politics, as in social development, was one of the main keys to the political wrangles of the period.

Although these squabbles make colourful reading in themselves, their historical significance is perhaps overshadowed by the work of the moderate Reformers who, with Britain, were responsible for the constructive developments that led to Responsible Government. The moderate leaders included many Torontonians, or Yorkers, such as the Reform

54

members of the powerful and wealthy Baldwin, Small, and Ridout families, all of which also contained Tories. The Reform group also had the support of medical doctors like John Rolph and Thomas D. Morrison and merchants and manufacturers like Jesse Ketchum and Joseph Cawthra. Most were British rather than American by background.

Still, the way was open for political radicals to seize the pages if not the command of history. They leaped onto the Toronto stage led by the fearless forces of journalism. For sheer irresponsibility, vicious infighting, and colourful expression, York newspapers of the 1820s and 1830s would be hard to beat. Both sides, Tory and Reform, were equally guilty of rabid journalism, and one of the dirtiest fighters was Tory Thomas Dalton of the *Patriot.* The Reformer who leaped to the forefront was, of course, William Lyon Mackenzie, most vocal of the Scottish emigrants, whose *Colonial Advocate* constantly baited the Tories. His rival for newspaper circulation, an Irishman who suffered worse persecution from the Family Compact than Mackenzie, and had worse things to say about Mackenzie himself than most Tories, was Francis Collins of the *Canadian Freeman.*

Neither Collins nor the Tories had the luck of Mackenzie, who immediately caught the public eye by his clever exploitation of Tory blunders. With his striking red wig, small stature, and unending attacks, he projected an image of a fearless little man fighting the giant Tory machine. He had begun his Upper Canadian journalistic career at Queenston, transferring his newspaper to York in 1824, just when the

ALEXANDER DRUMMOND,
[*Formerly of London & Liverpool,*]
SIGN, FANCY, & ORNAMEN-
TAL PAINTER,
King Street, next door to R. A.
Parker;

RESPECTFULLY informs the public, that he continues to carry on the painting business in all its branches; and will fulfil orders in his line, with the utmost punctuality and despatch.

Cabinet Furniture finished, in imitation of Wood and Stone; Oil Cloths and Floor Carpets, Steam Boat Cabins, Public Halls, &c., elegantly painted, to order.

Fancy and Windsor Chairs painted, bronzed, and gilt.— Fancy pieces, done on glass, silk, or velvet. Transparent Window Curtains; Labeling, and Enamelling. Imitations of Mahogany, Oak, Maple, Walnut, Marble, Freeston, &c.

On sale, an assortment of Fancy and Windsor Chairs.
Nov. 17.   87z.

Advertising a connection to England implied a craftsman's experience and expertise. Nevertheless, Alexander Drummond's name is not to be seen in the city directories of the 1830s. AO S16245

a) Second Market in York 1831, on site of present St. Lawrence Market. (Vol. 1. P. 64.) — Burned 1849. —

Toronto's second market, on the site of the present St. Lawrence Market, succeeded the first rough structure in 1831. It featured a wooden gallery above the butcher's stalls within. In 1834 during a packed political meeting the overcrowded gallery collapsed, hurling some of Toronto's most politically prominent individuals onto the meat hooks below. Damage effected by the Great Fire of 1849 led to the demolition of the entire building. MTL T11555

stage was ready for political enlivenment. There was a genuine need for government reform, but at the same time a very strong base of Tory support existed. North of York Town, York County had a large number of American emigrants and was one of the Reform strongholds of the province. On balance, York itself was probably Tory, and provincially the Tories managed to retain control of the Legislature in 11 of the 13 Upper Canadian elections prior to 1841.

Any action breeds reaction, and as Mackenzie and others organized the Reformers, so the Tories organized in response. They even had their shock troops in the newly established Orange Order, one of whose activities was cracking Reform skulls at political meetings, where they received just as many brickbats in return. Whatever else could be said about the York and Upper Canadian political activity that developed in the 1820s and remained rampant into the 1830s, it was not boring.

PHYSICAL DEVELOPMENT

With the population influx the town expanded rapidly; in 1829 Mary O'Brien, a settler on Yonge Street, said it was all suburb and "is so scattered that I hardly know where the centre may be." To further confuse the visitor, there was a complete intermixture of different land uses. Private residential, commercial, and industrial buildings were side by side mingling with the many taverns, boardinghouses, and vacant lots.

As the population continued to grow, some sorting out became apparent. Industry and warehousing began to concentrate near the harbour, and King Street East, with the market, became the shopping centre. The market was a focus of municipal life. After the War of 1812, a wooden building had been built, and new regulations were imposed by provincial statute to protect both buyer and seller. The justices of the peace, helped by an appointed clerk, oversaw its operations and drew up rules, which were posted at appropriate points. Under these, weights and measures were regulated, and all sales of meat, dairy products, fish, and vegetables in the town were prohibited outside the premises from 6 a.m. to 4 p.m., with fines for violation. These rules soon constituted a problem for many citizens, for, as York grew, walking to the only market from the western outskirts became a major expedition.

As today, almost across the street from the market stood St. James' Church, expanded in 1818 but soon overcrowded and hardly in keeping with the growing dignity of the city. In 1826, just west of St. James', the block from Church to Toronto streets was developed into a civic square with two balancing buildings, a gaol and a courthouse, possibly designed by Dr. William Baldwin, on its east and west sides.

The residential pattern also was evolving rapidly. Houses became more substantial with the increasing use of brick, although the walls of even the most elegant houses were often encased in wood for insulation. The mansions of the wealthy often stood on extensive grounds occupying a city block; in the poor areas clustering around the fringes of the city, both houses and their inhabitants were jammed together with increasing numbers residing in one structure.

The original area of wealth along the lake shore was now giving way to commerce in the Yonge Street area, although many large lakeside homes remained. At the west end the line of fine lake shore homes wound north to include the Elmsley mansion, on the site of the new Roy Thomson Hall. This property was taken over as the governor's residence after the War of 1812 and the new Legislature was erected next to it in 1829. To its north the entire block south of Lot (now Queen) Street between John and Graves (now Simcoe) streets was the estate of Attorney-General, later Chief Justice John Beverley Robinson. The original site of the town of York also contained some fine homes, such as the 1822 Sir William Campbell mansion, which has now been moved to the west of Osgoode Hall.

Many of the establishment preferred to live on their 100-acre park lots, which stretched north from Lot Street to what is now Bloor Street. To the east of Yonge these lots extended south of Queen to Hospital (now Richmond) Street and included the Jarvis property, through which Jarvis Street later ran, and the estate of William Allan, where he built his magnificent pillared mansion in 1830. To the west there were more estates, especially D'Arcy Boulton's Grange, a Georgian mansion built in 1818, now the nucleus of the Art Gallery of Ontario.

Even further north on the crest of the Lake Iroquois shoreline Dr. William Warren Baldwin, a leading Reformer, built Spadina just east of the site of Casa Loma. Baldwin's "commodious house in the country," as he described it, consisted of two large parlours, a hall, and a staircase on the first floor, four bedrooms plus a small library over them, three bedrooms in the attic, several closets on each storey, a kitchen, a dairy, root and wine cellars, a bedroom underground, and separate stables. The house was carefully furnished and had a good garden. All this was achieved at a cost of £1,500 (say $6,000). As Spadina was so remote, Baldwin also kept a substantial brick city mansion near the foot of Bay Street. Burnt in 1835, Spadina was replaced by a smaller house, which in turn gave way to the magnificent Victorian mansion of the Austin-Thompson family recently deeded over to the government.

THE SOCIETY OF THE TOWN

By the end of the war, the official elite was well established, but new men were moving into the government and seeking offices for themselves and their supporters, rivalling the second generation of the original appointees. As Strachan rose to dominance in provincial politics and became a target of the Reformers because of his control of patronage and his espousal of a state church, he sometimes chose associates who were not part of the old groupings, were frequently Scots, and could be—like William Allan—in business.

Many of the province's conflicts centred around the issue of freedom of religion. The Catholics and the dissenters always had the right to hold services, build churches, and vote in elections; initially they did not have the right to perform marriages or to share equally in the provincial largess. Their desire to mitigate the power of Strachan's Church of England led to a series of social and political clashes. St. James' Church was for the elite; its pews were largely rented by public auction and there was little place left for the poor. Methodism was initially slow to catch on because of American connections, but by 1818 it had its own chapel. A Presbyterian Secessionist (non-state) church followed in 1820. St. Paul's was the first Catholic church, built in 1824 partly as a response to the new Irish emigration. Social clubs, too, were beginning to appear; the Freemasons were refounded with St. Andrew's Lodge No. 1 in the early 1820s, and the Orange Order had its first parade in 1822.

Education was one of the main points of friction, again because of Church of England influence. The Common School Act of 1816, which had Strachan's full backing, brought in limited support for elementary schools set up by local boards to provide a basic education and a training ground for the already existing grammar schools. The town received its school in 1820: the Upper Canada Central School. However, many children continued to go to the private schools, which had appeared in large numbers.

Many other children never darkened a school door. Some had to work to support their families, some lacked the funds, others had parents who regarded school as unnecessary. Entrance to the skilled trades was through the apprentice system, as was training for the professions. Strachan obtained a university charter in 1827, the beginnings of the University of Toronto, but funding problems and general opposition to its Anglican control blocked any real development for years. The university did not open its doors until 1843.

THE COMMERCIAL STRUCTURE

Technology provided a major impetus for York's growth in the 1820s. New developments revolutionized the town's connections with the world at the same time as the growing number of immigrants revolutionized York's society. The first transportation change was the use of the steamship on the Great Lakes. The first steamer, the *Frontenac,* made its maiden voyage in 1817 and was soon plying a Kingston-York-Queenston route. Although supplemented by sails for decades, the new steamers made lake travel much easier, faster, and less subject to the whims of weather. By 1826 no fewer than five steamboats circled the lake on various regular schedules. Despite their expense, their reliability rapidly captured most of the passenger traffic. Although York was not a centre of boat building, many ship owners resided there. York's steamboat captains, such as Hugh Richardson, were well known on the lakes.

Steamers were soon followed by another major development: the canal-building boom of the postwar era. This began in New York State with the completion of the Erie Canal connecting New York City with Buffalo and the upper lakes in 1825. By 1829 the Erie was joined to the southeast end of Lake Ontario by the Oswego Feeder. At one sweep both the costs and the time of shipping to New York City were cut drastically, and a new world opened for the merchants of Upper Canada as well as those of upstate New York. The Upper Canadian and Imperial governments reacted with a series of disjointed attempts to establish a rival Canadian route, which was not adequate until 1848.

York, as well as the other port towns of Lake Ontario, benefitted greatly from this canal building and the quicker, cheaper, and more efficient New York connections that were now available to the English market. Simultaneously, the increasing size of the ships and the bulk of the goods being shipped meant that costly harbour improvements and new wharves were needed. This expansion was also necessary to bring in the increasingly wide variety of goods needed for the growing town. For a centre dependent on commerce, however, such construction was merely a sign of prosperity, and trade was still the nucleus of York's business.

At the same time, expanding demands, plus the high cost of shipments and the natural desire of the entrepreneur to keep profits at home, encouraged a rapid growth of manufacturing in both York and its hinterland, where industries like sawmills and tanneries could be more conveniently located. Soon the variety of industries in the town itself had increased considerably to include manufactories for furniture, waggons, soap processing, leather goods, and simple iron foundries. Older industries such as brewing and milling expanded along with the new ones.

York's commercial prosperity was such that several of the early merchants who had secured their fortunes were able to retire in great comfort. St. George returned to France after the peace with considerable wealth. He left his business affairs to two partners, John Spread Baldwin, the younger brother of Dr. William W. Baldwin, and Jules-Maurice Quesnel of Montreal, a former fur trader and explorer of the West Coast in whose honour Quesnel, B.C., is named. Equally astute and experienced

Brewer Joseph Bloor, looking in this snap rather unfairly like the victim of a bout with his own product, gave his name to the city's principal east-west thoroughfare. Before establishing his brewery at then-distant Yorkville in 1830, Bloor had been the proprietor of the Farmers' Arms Inn, not far from the old Toronto market.
MTL T13662

merchants, with an excellent commercial base, Baldwin and Quesnel, in turn, retired wealthy in 1832. They were not alone. In 1821 Alexander Wood, Allan's partner in the 1790s, now getting old and, like so many Scots, desirous of visiting his native land, wound up his business. William Allan turned his firm over to relatives in the same year, but the rich Mr. Allan was now moving on to a second career as a financier. In the place of these first entrepreneurs new merchants were arriving, setting up businesses, and expanding the growing middle class in the city.

The final stage of business is finance, and it was to finance that York business leaders now turned their attention to break away from the necessity of going outside the province for loans and to resolve some of the confusion that existed in the ordinary business activities of the town. Despite the growth of the provinces, the economic system was almost chaotic, with inflation, no real currency, and transactions in both pounds and dollars. There was never enough small change; no coinage was minted locally and there was a scarcity of English money. As a result, American money was used frequently, as well as French, Spanish, Portugese, or whatever other currency drifted to Canadian shores. These were supplemented by metal tokens, often of very poor quality. Paper money, issued only by individual banks, was in short supply, often lacked backing, and was easily forged. The result was that the barter system continued for a long time.

In essence, financial development means having a bank, and until Confederation, banks could be established in three ways in Upper Canada: by setting up a private partnership where the partners' personal funds were also at risk; through a special act of the provincial Legislature creating a limited liability company; and by a Royal charter granted in England. The first way was far too risky, so it was to the second that the Upper Canadian magnates addressed themselves, with both Kingston and York attempting to found a bank about the same time.

That the time was ripe for setting up banks in British North America was shown by the successful establishment, among others, of the Bank of Montreal in 1817. At York, Allan had been appointed local agent for the Bank of Montreal as early as 1818, a year after Kingston began its agitating for a bank charter. Using their influence in the government, Allan and other leading figures, including the presumably spiritual Strachan, quickly planned a countermove that by 1822 gave the charter to York, not Kingston. While tactically dishonest, it demonstrated the political clout of the York elite in advancing the interests of the capital. The victory marked a definite stage in the York-Kingston battle for the economic domination of the province.

Founding a bank proved to be more difficult than anticipated. In the end the government was forced to purchase a quarter of the stock and was given the appointment of 4 of the 15 directors. The directorate of the new Bank of Upper Canada was, of course, a division of the local oligarchy. It was soon accused of being the financial arm of the Family Compact, with considerable reason, although after a few years some prominent Reformers were to be found among its directors. For first

president the directors, not surprisingly, chose William Allan, soon to become the Honourable William Allan upon his elevation to the Legislative Council in 1825. He proved to be an excellent leader until he retired in 1835.

The bank carried on the usual functions of modern banking with some basic differences. It issued its own paper money, which was usual at the time, and greatly facilitated the commerce of the colony; and it did not pay interest on deposits until forced to do so by new rivals in the mid-1830s. The bank quickly established that characteristic of Canadian banking, a branch system. It also began to eliminate rivals. The Kingston effort soon collapsed and the Bank of Montreal and other out-of-the-province banks were eliminated by complex legislation. Until Kingston was finally able to establish the Commercial Bank of the Midland District in 1832, the Bank of Upper Canada ruled in Upper Canada without a rival. Yet, under Allan's guidance, it was an efficiently run organization; its stock was correctly thought to be as sound an investment as could be found. Allan's conservative style, with no concessions to reforms or acceptance of poor loan risks, gave the Reformers many points for attack, and the bank's monopoly position in York was assailed by other communities; but for York itself, not yet called Hogtown, the bank assured financial leadership in the province.

Royalist French officer Laurent Quetton tacked "St. George" to his name as a permanent memento of the saint's day in 1796 when he first arrived on English soil. He immigrated to Canada two years later, engaged profitably in the fur trade, and then opened a general store in Toronto which was immensely successful. In 1809 Quetton St. George moved into this commodious Georgian mansion. In later years the mansion served as the Canadian headquarters of the Canada Company, the large British land and colonization company. MTL B11-11a

61

CHAPTER VI

THE INCORPORATION ERA

1828-1837

The mid-1820s wave of British immigration almost instantly transformed York from a virtual village into a city. For more than 30 years it had been a colonial capital, essentially dependent on the government for its survival; now the town of York and its surrounding hinterland in York County became a viable economic unit. Although it would take a dozen years before the inhabitants discovered they were no longer dependent on the government for their prosperity, York itself had entered a new phase of evolution.

The population figures recorded by the town meetings tell the story succinctly:

1815—720	1831—3,969
1828—2,235	1832—5,505
1829—2,511	1833—6,094
1830—2,860	1834—9,252

The sheer numbers placed an impossible strain on institutions, regulations, and the whole system of town government. Appointed, part-time justices of the peace, working with almost no civil service, cannot govern a large population effectively, especially when faced with all the pressing problems of burgeoning urbanization. Further, York now needed to expand physically. However, it was bounded on the south by the lake; on the east by the eastern Military Reserve, the Don, and its surrounding swamps; on the north by the park lots; and on the west by the western Military Reserve. This last provided the first expansion point. In 1833 Lieutenant-Governor Sir John Colborne obtained permission to sell the

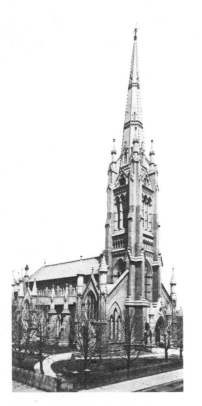

Above right and above: Designed by the prolific team of Frederic Cumberland and Thomas Ridout, St. James' Cathedral first opened in 1853; the spire was added circa 1873; and the clock came—a gift of public subscription—at Christmas of 1875. Visible in the foreground of the circa 1861 photograph of the church sans spire is the Cathedral School. The cathedral, in the popular international Gothic Revival style, is one of the city's masterpieces. MTL T10744, T10729

Previous page: H.W.J. Bonnycastle dedicated this 1834 map of Toronto—at the time of its incorporation as a city—to "his excellency Sir John Colborne." Courtesy, City of Toronto Archives (CTA), 9.2.4.G. 110

part of the western Military Reserve adjacent to the town for building lots and to use the funds obtained to improve the fortifications. The lots were sold off in 1833-1836 and road building and construction followed, providing jobs for many immigrants. Simultaneously, the development of the park lots to the west of Yonge Street was begun by their owners.

At the same time, larger public buildings were erected to provide services for increased population. In 1831-1832 the market shed was replaced by a new brick, courtyarded building designed by Dr. Baldwin and James G. Chewett. Its second storey contained offices, some of which were shortly to become the first home of the city government. Unfortunately, the estimated cost of £5,000 to £6,000 escalated to £9,240 ($36,960), and the payments became a heavy burden on the taxpayers. At the west end of the town, on the land between Government House and Front Street, a new three-building provincial Legislature, again designed by Chewett, was built in 1829-1832. North of Government House, beyond King Street West, the original buildings of Upper Canada College opened in 1831.

The town thus had developed two focal points: one for commerce and municipal government at the east and another for provincial administration to the west. Both survived till toward the turn of the century. St. James' Cathedral and the St. Lawrence Market still mark the focus at the east; the western governmental focus ran north from the CN Tower area with the 1875 St. Andrew's Presbyterian church standing to the east.

The social problems brought about by population growth were more difficult to deal with. The immigrants were largely poor. Generally they had no funds and few possessions, and many were in bad health. With their arrival the poor areas of the city expanded and miserable slums appeared, mainly in the downtown area. The section immediately east of Yonge Street was particularly bad: March (now Lombard) Street became a notorious centre of prostitution. Henrietta Street, on the site of the King Edward Hotel, was an alley lined with miserable hovels. Northwest of the intersection of Lot (now Queen) and Yonge streets, part of the Macaulay park lot grew into the slum suburb of Macaulay Town. The area was to remain blighted until it was razed, partly in the 1890s for the Old City Hall and partly in the 1950s for the New City Hall and Nathan Phillips Square.

Such conditions, combined with the filthy streets and an often contaminated water supply, opened the city to disease and epidemics. Then in 1832 the Asiatic cholera, which had been gradually spreading over Europe and had reached Britain in 1831, crossed the Atlantic in the immigrant ships. The whole area of the Great Lakes basin was particularly hard hit, with an estimated mortality rate of 10 percent. There was little that could be done. Medical knowledge of the disease was very limited; many blamed it on intemperance. No one understood the importance of the water supply.

As the epidemic advanced along the St. Lawrence, efforts were made to clean up the town. Sir John Colborne provided money for a cholera hospital and ordered the magistrates to appoint a board of health. Despite their efforts, the plague broke out on June 18, 1832, and was soon raging in areas like Henrietta Street, particularly affecting the recent immigrants. Many died because they refused to go to the hospital, which had some success with such drugs as opium in the early stages of the disease. The official mortality figures, which were probably underestimates, showed 565 cases and 217 deaths in York and Garrison. Strachan estimated that there were 90 widows, 60 orphans, and 400 fatherless children, for most of the deaths occurred among adults. The epidemic fueled the demand that something be done to improve the system of government.

St. Andrew's Presbyterian Church, built between 1830 and 1833 by John Ewart, was drawn by John G. Howard in 1840. The brick edifice, painted to simulate stone, was situated at the southwest corner of Church and Adelaide streets. St. Andrews was one of the first Presbyterian churches in Canada to employ instrumental music in the service.
MTL T10706

INCORPORATION, 1834

When the immigration wave began there was still no incorporated city in either Upper or Lower Canada. By 1834 Toronto alone in Upper Canada had sufficient population to receive city status, and the act of incorporation passed the Legislature on March 4, despite the objections of some of the inhabitants, including future first Mayor William Lyon Mackenzie. It received Royal Assent from Lieutenant-Governor Colborne on March 6.

One mystery in the process of incorporation remains unsolved. The bill to incorporate the "Town of York" was passed by the House of Assembly and sent to the upper house, the Legislative Council; it came back as the bill to incorporate the "City of Toronto." The reason for the reversion to the use of Toronto has never been clearly explained. The House of Assembly was taken by surprise. Sheriff William B. Jarvis, also the Tory member for the town, objected strongly. The Reform House leader,

Jesse Ketchum, pictured here in old age, amassed a fortune from his successful tannery. An enthusiastic supporter of political reform, he served in the Legislative Assembly from 1830 to 1834. Born in 1782 in Spencertown, New York, Ketchum retired to the United States in 1845 and died in Buffalo on September 7, 1867. Well known and much loved as a philanthropist, he was responsible for donating many large tracts of land for religious and civic use. MTL T13721

Marshall S. Bidwell, said that York was conveniently shorter. Others claimed that Toronto was the original name, could not be confused with American cities, and was "more musical." Possibly the clearest explanation was given by Speaker Archibald McLean, who rejoiced that the citizens would no longer reside in "dirty little York." Bidwell, however, produced the most magnificent dictum: "Toronto for poets—York for men of business." The unpoetic House upheld the amendment. Whatever the reasons, poetic, entrepreneurial, or otherwise, Toronto was once more Toronto.

With the inauguration of the new government, Toronto ceased to be part of the Home District, although it remained the seat of government for the district and later for York County, which assumed the district's administrative functions after 1849. The limits of the new city extended considerably beyond those of the former town: what is now Dufferin Street in the west; the Second Concession Road (Bloor Street) to the north; and the Don River to the east. Within this area there were two types of jurisdiction based on English precedents. The city proper, a central nucleus, extended between Crookshank's Lane (Bathurst Street) on the west, and Parliament Street to the east, and stretched north to a line drawn 400 yards beyond Lot Street. Beyond the city were the liberties, which encompassed all the outer territories and were, as yet, thinly settled.

The city was divided into five wards, appropriately named for the patron saints of the British Isles, St. Andrew, St. David, St. George, and St. Patrick, with St. Lawrence thrown in for Canadian flavour. Each ward annually elected two aldermen and two common councilmen, who then met and themselves elected the mayor from among the aldermen. That group required higher property qualifications to run than the common councilmen, and, sitting in a Mayor's Court, they replaced the justices of the peace of the Home District as the magistrates of the city.

The responsibilities of the City Council were an amplification of those of the magistrates: controlling the building, maintenance, and safety of the roads; surpervising fire protection and regulating fire hazards, the movement of animals, and the water supply; overseeing the market and produce sales; and regulating public morals. The mayor was a full-time official who was paid a salary of between £100 and £500 at the decision of the council. He was assisted by the city clerk and a full-time chamberlain or treasurer. Both these officers were themselves appointed by the council, as were the various minor officials, such as constables, assessors, and collectors of taxes. Naturally this opened the way to patronage on a spoils system along American lines.

The city's financial structure was one of the weakest points of the incorporation. Despite the additional problems and services of an incorporated area, the assessment remained based upon a province-wide schedule of charges designed for rural areas. Thus those who owned or rented the most land were the most heavily assessed and the large downtown stores got off lightly. Further, the rate of taxation itself was too low and the city was given inadequate powers of borrowing. Until the act was revised in 1837, city revenues were completely insufficient to pay for needed public works. To make matters worse, Home District taxes still had to be paid, as well as the debt for the market construction.

By the time Colborne signed the Act of Incorporation, factional strife between Tories and Reformers was at its height. The first elections were called for March 27 and both factions rushed to battle, seeing Toronto as a trial run for the coming provincial elections.

The city election was a Reform triumph, with the Tories defeated 12 to 8. The council, which promptly met to elect a mayor, included extremists and moderates in both groups. The favoured candidate for mayor was Dr. John Rolph, a prominent, if somewhat dubious, Reform politician who was acceptable to the Tory moderates. The Radical Reformers carried the day, however, and Mackenzie was elevated to the office in reward for his recent ejections from the provincial Legislative Assembly by the Tories.

The general situation the council faced was not auspicious; the problems of mushrooming growth were everywhere. The financial position was very bad, particularly as the Tory banks and merchants would not be too eager to make loans to a Reform council. Also, there were few precedents for the day-to-day operation of a city government, and the attendance record of many of the early councillors was abysmal. Meetings, unfortunately, were dominated by the extremists on both sides.

Until the Rebellion of 1837, municipal politics was a game of musical chairs. The Reform victory of 1834 was followed by disillusionment and a Tory council in 1835. They did not suit the voters either, and the Reformers returned, only to be again rejected by the electorate in 1837 in favour of the Tories, who under various designations, except for some short intervals, have tended to hold sway ever since.

There were some positive accomplishments under the 1834 council; municipal bylaws for the basic organization of the city were passed, and some work was done on sidewalks. There were also major disasters; the cholera struck for the second time, killing some 500, and part of the market gallery collapsed during a political meeting, causing several fatalities. Mackenzie's handling of the first was disorganized and Colborne and the doctors emerged as the heroes. Then in the fall Mackenzie ran for the Legislature, and once elected he neglected the city. By the year's end the council was virtually demoralized and the electorate recorded their opinion with a decisive defeat of Mackenzie personally and his supporters in general: Tories, 15; Reformers, 5.

The Tory council that succeeded in 1835, with lawyer Robert Baldwin Sullivan as mayor, could point to several accomplishments. However, taxation remained high, and public attention focused on Tory scandals being investigated by the new Reform Legislative Assembly. As a result the Reformers came back in Toronto: 12 to 8.

The third mayor, Dr. Thomas D. Morrison, like Sullivan an able man who attended to financial problems, further expanded public works, and began to develop the downtown city property. Yet Tory political winds blew in from the province, and when election time came the Tories won

17 to 3, and George Gurnett was elected mayor of Toronto. His mayoralty finally saw the revision of the Act of Incorporation to provide an improved basis of assessment and more flexible borrowing. The year 1837 also saw the city issuing its own paper money to alleviate the shortage of small change. In December came the Mackenzie Rebellion with its drastic effect on the Reform party; the city election that followed returned Tories to the entire 20 council seats. Toronto had entered a new era of politics.

THE EVOLUTION OF SERVICES

With such problems of finance and politics, the advance of municipal services was hardly a tale of triumph. However, definite strides were made, particularly from 1835 on. Aside from the fact that the services were basically more limited in the liberties, there was no uniform attempt to provide equal facilities to all areas at once. Public works were begun where most needed—the central business district on King Street to the east of Yonge Street—and gradually extended as growth of the city dictated and financial circumstances permitted. Then, as today, public works had difficulties in keeping up with the spread of the settled urban area. The councils were greatly helped by the fact that the population growth slowed up after 1834. In 1837 it had only risen by 1,619 to 10,871, and even by 1851 had only tripled to 30,775.

The City Council, even if it had not been strapped for funds, still had a very limited idea as to its duties. Many services that would be regarded as essential today, such as education or welfare, were left to either private charity or the none-too-generous care of the provincial government. Operating through several basic committees, the council concentrated on overseeing the market, the police, and the volunteer fire department, as well as major public works like road and sewer building.

The council did, however, find time to attend to the regulation of the city's morals, thus helping to establish Toronto's future reputation as "Toronto the Good." Legislation regulating morals in general and behaviour on the Sabbath in particular was not new, but with the broader powers of the new city and the puritanical outlook of some of the Reformers, attitudes became more rigid than they had been under the Tory, Church of England magistrates. Some changes were needed— drinking and prostitution were major problems; nevertheless, as time passed regulation became unduly stringent. For protection of the Sabbath, working and all sales of goods or merchandise were prohibited on Sunday, except for milk sales at specific hours. Ships were permitted to unload passengers but nothing else. Other prohibitions were included in the bylaw on "nuisances," which basically regulated such matters as the cleanliness of the streets, but was expanded to include, for example, the prohibition of swimming during most hours of the day, presumably because the swimmers did not wear bathing suits.

The nascent city departments, such as police and fire, were carryovers from the town administration. The fire department continued to be volunteer and was divided into two internally self-regulated sections: the

Fire Department itself, and the Hook and Ladder Company. As more equipment was added, these departments were internally subdivided. The firemen were young men from the good families who were exempted from other offices and militia duty. A small fire hall had been built in 1827, and one of the first projects of the City Council in 1834 was the construction of a bell tower.

Water was a constant problem. There were no hydrants, and the carters who supplied the town with water in large barrels or puncheons were required to attend fires where they were paid per puncheon. Special payments were made to those who arrived first, with the inevitable result that there was a good deal of unfriendly rivalry among the carters, much slopped water, and a few fights as they rushed to the blaze. Despite the problems, the firemen were reasonably successful in their efforts.

The policing of the city presented a variety of problems, many related to the lack of funding. There was a high bailiff who was usually assisted by four constables plus supernumeraries when needed. Because of the changing politics of the City Council and the spoils system, there was a constant turnover in the early years. The stipend was another problem. The high bailiff received £125 ($500) per annum, but the constables' pay see-sawed with each administration, varying from £25 to £80. It was not a situation that encouraged satisfactory applicants, but applicants did appear in large numbers.

The Home District gaol, erected in 1824-1827, was increasingly unable to accommodate the growing number of malefactors of the town, aside from the lunatics and the debtors, who were frequently respectable citizens. Although the grand juries regularly pointed out the gaol's inadequacies, it was some years before a new building was erected. The lunatics were housed in the gaol until 1850 and imprisonment for debt was not abolished until 1859.

The new market, which was inherited from the Home District along with its debt, was another problem. Opened at the beginning of 1833, it soon proved deficient in many respects, and there were constant expenses for repairs and remodelling. Although provision had been made for butchers and dairymen, there was no space in the market for the fishermen, whose catches were purchased by hucksters who then sold them at a profit. As a result, in 1835 a fish market was built on the lake shore directly across Front Street from the meat market at a cost of £100. Its successor on the same site forms the southern part of the present St. Lawrence Market, and the sloping land on which it stands marks the lake shore of that day.

With the expansion of the city, the inhabitants of the northwest quarter found it difficult to get to the market, the only place where produce was sold during most hours. In 1837 the problem was solved when D'Arcy Boulton, Jr., of the Grange gave part of his land along the north side of Lot (Queen) Street, south of today's Art Gallery of Ontario, for a second market. The construction costs were borne by three citizens who agreed to be reimbursed out of revenues. The structure came to be known as the St. Patrick's Market, from its ward, to distinguish it from the original market, which gradually became known as the St. Lawrence Market. Both retain their names despite the fact that named wards have been abolished for nearly a century.

Sewers accounted for the first major public works expense of the early councils. In 1835 Mayor Sullivan and his council approved the construction of a large brick sewer along King Street with branches up York, Bay, and Yonge streets to Lot and up Church Street to Newgate (Richmond) Street. This was used for both storm and sanitary purposes, the citizens being charged to make a connection with their homes. Financing it was the first major expenditure: £5,000 was spent on the initial construction and costs continued over the years as the system was expanded. One problem discounted by the early councils was harbour pollution. The sewer flowed into the harbour and, as the years passed, seriously endangered the water supply.

Roads were another problem, for the dirt surfaces of the city were notorious for their mud wallows. Macadamization, surfacing roads with pounded gravel, had just been developed in England and was adopted by the council because of the favourable initial costs. In 1836 King Street was macadamized through the central business district from Beverley to York streets and up Yonge Street to Lot at a cost of £4,900; gradually macadamization was expanded throughout the city. Bridge building over the creeks involved more costs. However, in 1835 the major bridges over the Don River, which connected with the Island and points east, had been rebuilt as toll bridges by the provincial government. Sidewalk construction began in 1834, pre-dating macadamization. These were plank sidewalks, generally only two feet wide, except on King Street where they were double, and were again extended throughout the city as funds permitted. Later King Street was flagstoned and crossings for pedestrians at intersections were provided by the use of squared logs or the placing of stepping stones in the streets.

The inevitable nuisances were first dealt with in an 1834 bylaw that attempted to regulate wandering animals, particularly cows and pigs, which found the mud wallows in the streets very attractive. Rubbish removal was a further difficulty, the town inhabitants tossing garbage, offal, and debris of all sorts on the streets and on the ice in the harbour, where it was hoped the spring melt would clear everything away. In 1835 the city established rubbish dumps at the foot of York and Church streets for the dual purpose of waste disposal and filling in sections of the street at the harbour. A public dung heap was also set up, and the manure collected was sold at auction. Some attention was paid to dangerous holes and impediments on the streets, such as projecting signs, posts, bay windows, porches, and other encroachments, but the battle was an unending one and successive councils regularly had to reenact and expand the legislation.

THE CHANGING SOCIETY

By the mid-1830s the social structure of Toronto had assumed a fully developed form. The Family Compact, now gradually losing their political power, still held their social position. Many intermarried and formed business connections with the rising commercial elite. Below these groups a solid middle class was developing and below that a growing working class and ever larger numbers of poor. The population was highly mobile, as befitted an immigration centre, yet there was a growing core of settled, sometimes long-established, Torontonians.

With population growth the ethnic picture was becoming more complex. Added to the English, Scottish, and Anglo-Irish settlers were some Welsh and Germans and the Catholic Irish, who now formed one of the largest groups of immigrants. Driven out of their homeland by poverty, they found work on the Canadian canal projects and later on railway construction. With their arrival the Catholic Church expanded rapidly and Irish radicalism appeared, adding a new dimension to society. Another refugee group were the Negroes fleeing slavery in the States. They, of course, formed only a portion of the many American settlers of all ethnic backgrounds who were arriving in the city.

The larger population meant the firm establishment of religious denominations, and the church building of the 1820s continued. St. James' itself was reconstructed in brick and stone in 1833 and became a cathedral in 1839. The Kirk of Scotland Presbyterians, who supported the church-state connections, erected their own St. Andrew's, at Hospital (Adelaide) and Church streets in 1830, ancestor of the later St. Andrew's churches on King and on Jarvis streets. The Methodists put up a good-sized brick church in 1833, and smaller groups founded meeting houses that later developed into parish churches.

In education Strachan's university remained immersed in political squabbles, but Sir John Colborne took logical action in another direction. Pointing out that it was madness to have a university when there was "no tolerable seminary in the Province to prepare Boys for it," Colborne founded Upper Canada College, which took over the buildings and students of the Home District Blue School until its own quarters near the Legislature were ready. Government funded, but not a part of the regular system, UCC rapidly became the elite preserve it has remained to this day. The Home District School was revived in 1836 to eventually become Jarvis Collegiate. Legal education was basically by apprenticeship, but teaching began at Osgoode Hall as early as 1831. The next year Dr. Thomas Rolph opened his private medical school, the first in the city.

The churches aided in welfare, which the council did not regard as part of its responsibility, but the increase in the numbers of poor made it impossible for the churches or private charity to provide the needed aid. With the depression of 1837 a House of Industry, or workhouse, as it was popularly known, was established with the clearly stated objective of aiding "the industrious and distressed poor." However, funding by both city and province was marginal and grudging, and the house existed in a state of crisis.

Social clubs began to flourish, and a touch of culture was added to the city when the York Mechanics Institute, ancestor of the Toronto Public Libraries, was opened in 1830. It was modelled on the Scottish idea of uplifting the workers, and provided lectures as well as books. By 1834 the city had a Society for Artists led by men like architect John G. Howard, the owner of High Park. In 1832 the businessmen, led by future Mayor George Monro, formed the Commercial News Room, which subscribed to a wide variety of periodicals, and in 1834 the first Board of Trade began meeting with William Allan as president. In 1835, in the euphoria of an economic boom, the city's establishment even opened what is now the Toronto Club, the first gentleman's retreat.

Recreation was thus being supplemented by some loftier diversions than those provided by the 80-odd taverns and hotels in and around the city, although these institutions remained the social centre for most of the population. Plays sometimes had been produced in the taverns; now several theatres opened in mid-decade. There was even a Roman-style attraction: James Cull's Floating Baths on the lake, in which were available either warm or cold baths, a promenade deck, a drawing room, a reading room, and a refreshment room.

BUSINESS AND THE NEW CITY

The business boom of the mid-1830s coincided with incorporation, and the population burst provided another impetus to growth. These events helped alleviate the lack of development capital, as did the growing interest of Montreal and British firms in the city. The greatest difficulty faced by expanding Toronto business was the continuing lack of an adequate transportation network. The Great Lakes were the arteries of the city's commerce, but the canal system was still far from satisfactory.

Land transportation outside Toronto remained dismal. Yonge Street and the other trunk roads were gradually macadamized, but this took years. Travellers frequently had to get out of their carts or stagecoaches and trudge through the mud at every hill or bad spot. But there was promise for the future: watching British and American development, business leaders were planning to connect Toronto and its hinterland by a railway stretching to Lake Huron. Just to be safe, when they applied for a charter in 1836, they made sure they were given plenty of leeway by obtaining authority to build a "Rail, Planked, or Macadamized or Blocked Road." William Allan was to become the company president.

Commerce was distinguished by increasing specialization. Some merchants were moving into the wholesale trade, and other specialized businesses were gradually supplementing the general stores. With them more lively advertising made its appearance. Thomas Thompson, a Yorkshire schoolmaster who emigrated to Toronto in 1833 and founded a retail boot-and-shoe store, became a mid-19th-century "Honest Ed." "Cheap Thomas Thompson's Shoe Warehouse" was one of the first stores to market goods on the basis of a large stock, high volume, low markup, and advertising that frequently verged on the spectacular.

Although Toronto did not really become an industrial centre until the railway era, the volume of manufacturing in the 1830s increased significantly. From an early period the Todmorden area on the Don River had been a mill centre; it was there that some of the first paper in Upper

Canada was manufactured. Another hub of industry formed along the waterfront, where one can see Peter Freeland's soap factory at the foot of Yonge in many early engravings. In 1832 William Gooderman and James Worts set up their flour mill somewhat to the east, and when an over-supply of grain developed, they quickly diversified into distilling. The largest firm was probably the foundry operated by Sheldon, Dutcher & Company, which employed some 80 workers. John Jacques of the famous furniture manufacturing company had also opened his business by that date. In October 1836 the printers of the city struck unsuccessfully for higher wages; they were quickly followed by an equally abortive tailors' strike.

The same era saw a broadening and diversification of financial institutions. In banking, the partnership bank of Truscott, Green & Company appeared in Toronto in 1834 and immediately caused a furor both by financing the Mackenzie council when no one else would and by paying interest on deposits, a practice unheard of in the province. Then the Reformers set up their own Bank of the People, with Dr. John Rolph as president and James Lesslie as cashier (general manager). A flurry of applications for bank charters followed, which were duly passed by the Legislature, but turned down by British authorities—probably fortunately for Toronto considering the looming depression. One other entry to the financial scene was the British-chartered Bank of British North America (now merged with the Bank of Montreal), which opened a Toronto branch in 1836.

Fire insurance had presented a problem in Toronto for some time; although there were various agents of British and American companies in the city, it was often difficult to obtain an adequate amount of insurance. In 1833 a 52-member group of both Tory and Reform leaders incorporated the British American Assurance Company (now the Royal Insurance Company) to do business in the city. William Allan shortly gave up the presidency of the Bank of Upper Canada and became the company's governor or president. Its successful operation set the pattern for others, including the Home District Mutual Fire Insurance Company established by the Reformers with Dr. W.W. Baldwin as president. No stock market had as yet appeared to crown Toronto financial business, but stocks of the local companies were advertised for sale in the papers.

The boom era that accompanied incorporation came to a sudden end in the spring panic of 1837, brought on partly by American banking policies. Suddenly Toronto found itself in one of the worst depressions of the 19th century. The Truscott, Green & Company partnership failed, and other enterprises, such as the railway plans, went into abeyance; but Toronto had a sound economic base, and most of its institutions rode out the storm without great difficulty. The city was to be swept up in the political unrest that accompanied the depression, and rebellion was to break out in the province. Nevertheless, although the city and its people did not yet realize it, Toronto by 1837 had come of age. It could weather economic troubles on its own, and the presence of the government was no longer necessary for survival.

CHAPTER VII

THE REBELLION OF 1837

The Upper Canadian Rebellion of 1837, often called the Mackenzie Rebellion, is the most colourful episode in the history of Toronto and Ontario. In a nation lacking glorious military exploits, the incident has made a hero of Mackenzie, even though he lost. Yet the rebellion did not open the way to our obtaining self-government; in fact, it was a setback. Further, although fortunately only a few were killed, many were exiled and the lives of a great number of innocent people disrupted.

The most amazing thing about the rebellion is that it happened at all. Upper Canada, despite the effects of the depression, faced no insuperable political problems and had an increasingly conservative population. Probably the very stability of the colony created a false sense of security, making it difficult to credit evidence that plans for an insurrection were underway.

Considering the circumstances in 1837, setting off a rebellion required a conjunction of ineptitude on both sides. Only a Reform leader with little sense of reality would have attempted to seize the province; only a lieutenant-governor so self-assured that he refused to accept the clearest evidence of a plot could have failed to crush the rebellion before it broke out. That the result was closer to a comic opera than to a catastrophe was extraordinary luck.

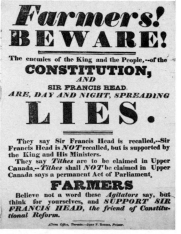

SETTING THE STAGE

The immediate circumstances behind the rebellion can be traced to the autumn of 1835, when Mackenzie, who had been chairing a committee of the Reform Assembly to report on ills in the province, brought in a document entitled the *Seventh Report of Grievances*. This catalogued many serious problems as well as trivial ones; it caused the replacement of Tory Lieutenant-Governor Colborne by Sir Francis Bond Head of the Royal Engineers, who was chosen to implement more liberal Colonial Office policies. He was given the *Seventh Report,* ordered to appoint and listen to liberal advisors, and sent posthaste to Toronto.

Trouble began immediately. Head was probably at least as Tory as his military predecessors. He instantly took a dislike to the Reform leaders, particularly Mackenzie, whom he called "a tiny creature," although they were the same size. Quarreling with Reform advisors, Head soon began fighting with the Reform Legislative Assembly, which responded by cutting off his salary. Head, in turn, refused to sign any money bills, bringing the provincial economy to a halt; he then dissolved the Assembly and called an election on the issue of loyalty. In the contest that followed, Head, a natural campaigner, managed to blame the Reformers for all the economic woes, added a touch of gerrymandering,

and captured the imagination of the province. The final results were Tory, 43 and Reform, 17, with Mackenzie and all the most "obnoxious" Reform leaders defeated.

Winning an election is one thing; governing a province, another. The new Tory majority were soon faced with the panic and depression of 1837 and an economic situation that was beyond anyone's control. The defeated Reformers felt maltreated, with good cause; Mackenzie particularly was disillusioned with the Upper Canadian democratic process. Lord Glenelg, the colonial secretary, attempted to make some amends but found himself frustrated by Head, whose resignation he accepted in late 1837, too late for the news to reach Toronto before the political situation exploded.

THE GATHERING FORCES

Mackenzie had already founded a new paper, the *Constitution*, which started on July 4, 1836, to show his sympathies. After the election, frustrated by his defeat, he became even more radical. By the spring of 1837, with the depression deepening, he was hinting at violence. In July he arranged a military drill of his supporters in the townships north of Toronto as a show of strength and also held a series of meetings in the

breweries owned by some of his wealthier supporters to discuss a new constitution.

By October, with harvesting, threshing, and autumn chores completed, Mackenzie decided that a rebellion would never take place unless it was engineered and he could present the Reformers with a *fait accompli.* Taking advantage of the poor communications and his own mobility, he developed the idea that the Reformers in the city and its hinterland could be given two very different stories. Those in the city were to be told the countryside was about to rise and they had better be ready to lead it for their own protection. The farmers were told the opposite: the city would rise and unless they came in to back the movement they might find their lands confiscated. They were also given the idea that all that would be needed was a demonstration. At the beginning of November, Mackenzie began to hold a series of demonstrations for his supporters in the York, Vaughan, and Markham Township areas. The largest, which met in the Sheppard and Yonge area, brought out about 400 to 500 people; others seem to have run about 50 to 150.

In November he selected December 7 for the rebellion, coordinated it with Louis-Joseph Papineau, the Reform leader in Lower Canada, and appointed Colonel Anthony van Egmond of Huron County, one of Napoleon's soldiers, as his commander-in-chief. Van Egmond promised to arrive at Toronto on the set day. Mackenzie then sold the inevitability of hinterland rebellion to his sometime rival, Dr. John Rolph, and ex-Mayor Dr. Thomas D. Morrison in Toronto. Rolph was to be provisional president of the new republic of Upper Canada. The mustering place chosen was the tavern of a good Reformer, John Montgomery, on Yonge Street just north of what is now Eglinton Avenue, four miles beyond the city.

Despite all these discussions there was hardly a well-conceived master plan for action. Some 1,000 men were expected to gather at Montgomery's Inn, march to the city, seize 5,000 guns and the ammunition that were stored in the City Hall, and capture the governor and his advisors. Then, joined by the local radicals, they would "spontaneously" call on Rolph to head up a provisional government. The crucial question of what they would do about the Tories and the British army went unanswered.

All this activity could hardly be kept secret, and Mackenzie was incapable of keeping a secret anyway. He quickly made the plan even more obvious on November 15 by publishing a draft constitution for an independent government, based on that of the United States, with some radical English ideas thrown in.

In Toronto some Tories had already become more than a little concerned, but the majority could not take Mackenzie seriously and thought a rebellion was impossible in the province. Colonel James FitzGibbon, a War of 1812 hero who now commanded the local militia, thought otherwise. He had no illusions about the limits to which Mackenzie would go and tried to warn Head that trouble was brewing, but Head pooh-poohed his fears.

Unlike Head, Colborne, now appointed commander-in-chief at Quebec, was preparing for trouble in Lower Canada and asked Sir Francis to send him any Upper Canadian troops he could spare. Head responded by ordering every British regular to Lower Canada. The troops marched out of the garrisons at Kingston, Toronto, and Niagara, leaving the province undefended except for the militia, who were forbidden by the lieutenant-governor to prepare for trouble. The arms in the City Hall were turned over to Mayor Gurnett and the City Council for protection, then left unguarded. The capital was ripe for a "coup d'etat."

James Hogg, a Reformer turned Tory, learned the details of the rebellion plan from Mackenzie himself and rushed to Toronto to warn the government. But Hogg and others found it impossible to convince the lieutenant-governor of danger. The governor's friend Chief Justice John Beverley Robinson backed his stand, asserting that the Reformers were not "so desperate and daring as to rise in open rebellion." FitzGibbon and other Tories now gave up on the governor and began planning the defence of the city behind his back. It was agreed that the militia should organize instantly at the news of potential trouble and rush to the City Hall to protect the guns. To spread the alarm in the east, Mayor George Gurnett would ring the bells of St. James' and the boys at Upper Canada College would ring their bell to warn the western part of the city.

The comic opera side of the drama now attained new heights when President-designate Rolph panicked after hearing largely untrue news of Tory preparations. Without waiting for Mackenzie to return from the north, where he was organizing his followers, Rolph moved the date for the rebellion forward from Thursday, December 7, to Monday, December 4. Rolph completely overlooked the fact that, except for supporters in the nearby townships, it would be impossible to advise most of the rebel forces of the change.

On December 3 Mackenzie heard of the change of date and sent out other messengers in an effort to reverse it to the 7th. The result could only be chaos, but even without changes the rebels were bound to be straggling in both before and after any set date. To make matters even more complex, it was only at this juncture that Mackenzie contacted Montgomery to arrange for billeting and provisioning the forces. Unfortunately, though Montgomery was a true Reformer, he had just rented his tavern to a man called John Linfoot. Linfoot did not object to having the tavern used as a mustering centre, but he put payment of bills for room and board ahead of political principle. Even had Mackenzie had money, of course, it would have been impossible to gather the necessary supplies.

The overture was ending and the curtain rising, yet the stage was certainly not set.

REBELLION

December 1837 was unusually warm for the Toronto region, so the would-be revolutionaries had no trouble making their way to the city. By the evening of the 4th about 100 were gathered at Montgomery's Inn.

Above: A proper Victorian hero, Colonel James FitzGibbon, "Saviour of the City of Toronto," kept his head when all those around him were in a state of panic during the rebellion. MTL T30753

Opposite page, top: Lawyer, physician, and legislator John Rolph, seen here late in his long life, was trusted by both sides in the rebellion fracas and contributed to the chaos of both. Slated to head the provisional government if the rebellion were successful, Rolph slipped off to temporary exile in the United States when the rebellion failed, returning to Upper Canada in 1843 to resume his work in medicine. MTL T15092

Opposite page, bottom: George Gurnett devoted much of his energy to the betterment of Toronto. Gurnett served as a journalist, politician, mayor (in 1837 and again from 1848 to 1850), and eventually police magistrate. MTL T15028

Immediately there were troubles. Aside from arguments over tavern bills and a lack of clear plans for taking the city that lay undefended before them, there was no leader with real military experience. Van Egmond was not due to arrive till the 7th and Anthony Anderson, a Reformer with some military experience, was appointed to lead in his place. Then there was the argument over what to do next: to march or not to march.

The rebels' increasing numbers and the lack of secrecy settled the question for them, and Mackenzie had circulated a poster calling for rebellion; the uprising could no longer be started at their convenience. Lieutenant-Colonel Robert Moodie, a Tory from the north, attempted to ride down Yonge Street through their ranks to warn Toronto and was shot and fatally injured. Next, Alderman John Powell, a grandson of a former chief justice, was captured. Although out reconnoitering for FitzGibbon, when cross-examined he assured his captors that he was merely taking the evening air. He also assured them he was not armed and, almost unbelievably, he was not searched. Instead Mackenzie turned him over to Anderson to take away and lock up. Anderson foolishly let him trail behind, and as soon as they were out of sight Powell pulled out his gun, killed his captor with a shot in the back, and rode to warn the city.

The rebels now had no military leader; they either took Toronto immediately or the advantage of surprise would be lost. Mackenzie quickly appointed himself generalissimo of the forces, but he was in no state to make a decision; he was already distraught, and the complexities of planning a proper rebellion were beyond him. The march on the open city was not made, and the guns were not captured. Meanwhile, in the townships to the north, with the rebels departed for Montgomery's Inn, the Tories began organizing their forces. Fortunately, leaders on both sides were reluctant to shoot opponents they had known all their lives.

In Toronto, however, all was total confusion. Powell, instead of warning FitzGibbon and having the bells rung, rode straight to Government House to arouse the governor. After great difficulty he got in and awakened Head, who ran around in his nightcap crying treason. With the gallantry that characterized the Royal Engineers, Head quickly ordered Lady Head to flee to the solicitor-general's home, which presumably was not an immediate target. Otherwise, his activities were more of a nuisance than an asset.

The other defenders hardly needed him to create confusion. By this time there were several warnings of the gathering to the north, but as with Mackenzie's mustering, everything went wrong in the city. When the boys at Upper Canada College began to ring the bell, they were stopped by one of the masters and told to go back to sleep. For St. James', Gurnett could not be found. The key to the bell tower could not be found either. Fortunately, just before FitzGibbon broke down the door with an ax, a key arrived and the bells duly rang out to warn the city, which was thoroughly aroused already, with 200 to 250 people rushing to guard the City Hall. The curtain descended on act one with the rebels arguing at Montgomery's Inn and the citizens milling around in the streets.

THE ADVANCE ON TORONTO

Monday, December 4, had to be the day of the great rebel march on the city with or without a general. At Montgomery's Inn 300 to 500 men had gathered by dawn, but there was no food and even those rebels with money could not get breakfast. They had to march with a growling stomach. Most were not armed properly, and very few had real military experience. Mackenzie was in no shape to lead them. As one observer said, "All day Tuesday Mackenzie went on like a lunatic. Once or twice I thought he was going to have a fit." At dawn he started to march his army southward across what now is Eglinton Avenue, riding a small horse and wearing so many coats as bullet stoppers that he looked "stuffed."

The march south took all day with Mackenzie's digressions and was interrupted twice by negotiators sent by Head under flag of truce to ascertain what the rebels wanted. Head's choices were Robert Baldwin and, to complete the comedy, would-be President Rolph. The latter asked Baldwin to withdraw so he could talk with more ease, then told Mackenzie to rush ahead to Toronto while success was still possible. Fortunately, rushing was beyond Mackenzie, and what could well have been a bloody battle in the heart of the city was avoided.

With all the marching and countermarching it was about 4:30 p.m., dusk at that season, when the army reached McGill Street at Yonge just north of Gerrard Street. Many had already wandered back to Montgomery's Inn. FitzGibbon, against Head's orders, had placed a small group of men under Sheriff William B. Jarvis at that point, and they fired on the advancing troops from the shelter of the bush (around the edge of the present Ryerson Polytechnic campus). Several casualties were inflicted and the rebel forces, already starved and dispirited, promptly broke up and fled northward. Jarvis and his men fled south. The scene of the skirmish was deserted. Many of the more intelligent rebels departed homeward under cover of darkness.

While the rebels marched south there was complete confusion in the city. However, about 9 p.m., a small body of armed volunteers arrived from the eastern part of York County, a harbinger of coming support, and then a steamer from Hamilton with Allan MacNab, Speaker of the Legislative Assembly, and more than 60 militiamen of the neighbouring Gore District. As John Charles Dent, the great 19th-century historian of the rebellion, noted, this "filled the Lieutenant-Governor with transports of delight, insomuch that for a moment he became well-nigh hysterical."

THE TORY VICTORY

Tuesday, December 5, was a day of waiting at the rebel camp and a gathering of forces for the Tories. Mackenzie led an expedition to reconnoiter to the west. At the Peacock Inn on Dundas Street near Keele they robbed first the tavern and then the mail stage, ostensibly to get information, but actually to obtain money, part of which went to tavern keeper Linfoot. In the city spirits were boosted by the arrival of the steamer *Traveller* carrying men from Niagara, Ancaster, Dundas, and Oakville, all dressed in their working clothes and bearing muskets ready to fight the rebels. Smaller groups were beginning to arrive from northern townships, such as Markham, having bypassed the rebels on the way. Rolph, pretending to go to see a patient, fled to the States. Morrison was arrested.

Thursday, December 7, saw the final act of the fracas played out. Van Egmond arrived promptly at the inn and prevented Mackenzie from taking the impossible course of attacking the city with the troops at hand, a course he saw as "stark madness." When he insisted upon waiting for hoped-for reinforcements, Mackenzie wanted to shoot him. Agreement was finally reached to await reinforcements, but then news arrived of the Tories gathering to advance on the tavern. The only action taken was to send Peter Matthews and 60 men east to burn the Don Bridge as a diversion to draw off the loyalist forces. Government troops guarding the bridge had been withdrawn shortly before Matthews arrived, and he fired the bridge itself and some surrounding buildings. Then, after a skirmish in which one bystander was killed and another injured, Matthews fled with his men.

While the rebels were disagreeing over strategy at Montgomery's Inn, the Tories were lining up on the Esplanade along Toronto's waterfront and preparing for the march northward, under FitzGibbon's command. Believing there were 1,500 well-armed rebels instead of 400-odd poorly armed ones at the inn, FitzGibbon organized his troops into a central column of about 700 men, which would proceed directly up Yonge Street, and two flanking bodies of 150 to 200 men each, which would head northward on roads and trails to the east and west. All the leading citizens had turned out, as well as many future luminaries, including a young law student named John A. Macdonald. About 10 to 11 a.m., the procession set off to the cheers of the populace and the music of two bands. Sir Francis was naturally conspicuous "in his every-day suit with one double-barrelled gun in his hand, another leaning against his breast, and a brace of pistols in his leather belt."

At Gallow's Hill (St. Clair Avenue) Mackenzie concealed some rebels in the woods to ambush the advancing party, but they quickly retreated to Montgomery's when fired upon. By then those rebels without arms were in flight. With the arrival of the artillery a shot was fired at the tavern and the rest quickly poured out both doors and windows. In 20 minutes the battle was over. Sir Francis, who had been riding up and down the lines waving a little flag, rushed forward to supervise the burning of the rebel headquarters. Meanwhile, since the flanking columns had made poor progress due to the bad roads, the insurgents were able to flee across the fields and through the hedges toward safety with the victors racing after them in equally tangled pursuit. As FitzGibbon described it, "The attacking force broke ranks and pursued in such disorder that it was little more than one crowd running after another."

The confusion was compounded by the incompetence of many of those involved. Judge Jonas Jones rode too far ahead of his men during the assault on the tavern, was mistaken for a rebel by MacNab, and was ordered shot. Only the troops' poor aim saved his life. FitzGibbon was temporarily removed from command when his horse was shot out from under him by the rifle of an "experienced" military pensioner who was dragging it along the ground by the barrel. Sir Francis was at his most magnificent. When the troops rounded up a batch of men, including some pro-government noncombatants, he gave them a lecture on loyalty and then magnanimously let them go.

The victors now turned to indiscriminately plundering everything in the area; the roads were strewn with loot, and waggons were stolen and loaded with goods and furniture. Other parties chased rebels around the countryside for days, sometimes with success. Mackenzie himself, with his money from the stagecoach robbery, mounted a carefully placed horse and rode off to the United States, having many adventures along the way. In what Dent has described as one of the most blameworthy of his indiscretions, he left behind a large carpetbag containing incriminating correspondence and an almost complete set of "rolls of revolt" with the names of everyone who had joined the political meetings during the summer. This material enabled the government "to arrest and prosecute scores of persons against whom they had previously entertained no suspicion." In fact, the misleading title meant some were arrested who had played no part in the revolt itself.

THE AFTERMATH

The total mortality of the rebellion was fortunately light: no loyal troops were killed, two rebels died in battle, and six died in hospital. Van Egmond, a pathetic victim of what he had been led to believe was a just cause, died as a result of age and imprisonment. Including Moodie and the man killed at the Don Bridge, at most some dozen lives were sacrificed. Also, fortunately not too many were wounded. In 1838 Peter Matthews and another chief lieutenant, Samuel Lount, were hanged for their part in the rebellion. The horror over their execution points up the fact that so many other rebels escaped with prison terms or exile. Matthews had been responsible for killing a bystander, but he and Lount were, in part, victims of the furor raised by Mackenzie and others who had escaped to the United States. When Mackenzie was pardoned and his property reinstated in 1849, he took up a collection for a fine tombstone in Lount and Matthews' memory.

The real winner in the rebellion, if there was one, was Toronto. That nothing happened to the city, despite Sir Francis obstinately ignoring facts and Mackenzie's desire to pursue his personal brand of liberation regardless of consequences, was a virtual miracle. In early December 1837 the city was probably in more danger than during the American captures in the War of 1812; it could easily have been taken, sacked, and burnt by the rebels. Also, if captured, the city could have been subjected to a second battle as the British troops, victorious in Quebec, returned to the pacification of the upper province with the support of a very large number of its inhabitants. Instead, Toronto, merely a little shaken, continued to grow unimpeded by disaster.

CHAPTER VIII

PARLIAMENT LOST AND THE RAILWAYS GAINED

1838-1867

The aftermath of the rebellion completely shook up provincial politics, and the situation remained in turmoil for a year. Immediate action by Britain was necessary. Sir Francis Bond Head was fired; Sir George Arthur, the last lieutenant-governor of Upper Canada, was sent out in his place; and Lord Durham was appointed overall governor to make recommendations for the complete overhaul of all the colonial governments. Durham, a leading Whig politician, reported that the Canadas should be united into one province and that it should receive Responsible Government, that is, the right to govern itself as it pleased in internal matters. The British government accepted the union recommendation immediately but not the recommendation for Responsible Government. A new governor, Charles Poulet Thompson, soon created Lord Sydenham, was sent out to implement the union.

Many Upper Canadians wanted no part of union or connection with the French of Lower Canada. In the end, to get union through, Thompson had to use all of his considerable tact, promises of financial aid, threats of reprisals for opponents, and lots of liquor at many banquets. Even then there was a large and vocal anti-union minority. Upper Canada prepared with little grace for the new political picture, even though it was given as many members of the new Legislature as the much more populous lower province.

A united province meant the selection of a new capital, Toronto being too far west of the new centre. Kingston was the choice. But Kingston suited no one, and after three years, just as proper accommoda-

Above: Built in 1844-1845 from a design by Henry Bower Lane, Toronto's second City Hall was well integrated into the city of its time. When the city government relocated in 1898, the old hall was merged into an extended market building. Today it remains a central part of the recently renovated St. Lawrence Market, with the upper floors restored to serve as The Market Gallery, a showplace for urban exhibits arranged by the City Archives. MTL T11786

Previous page: The first locomotive to be manufactured in Canada West—in May 1853 at James Good's locomotive works—proudly bore the name the Toronto. *MTL T13602*

tions were nearing completion, the government moved eastward to Montreal, in 1844. But then the Montreal Tories opposing Responsible Government burned Parliament in 1849. Next a joint system was adopted in which the capital migrated back and forth: Toronto, 1849-1851; Quebec, 1851-1855; Toronto, 1855-1859; Quebec, 1859-1865. Finally, at Parliament's request, Queen Victoria made the choice and government moved to her selection, Ottawa, in 1865.

TORONTO PULLS THROUGH

When Sir George Arthur called the last session of the Upper Canadian Legislative Assembly to proclaim the union of the Canadas on February 10, 1841, most of his Toronto audience were suffering from both shock and despair. The Tory *Patriot*, Reform *Examiner*, and Catholic *Mirror* all made forecasts of doom, depreciation of property, flight of business, and grass growing in the streets. The city did have problems; the large municipal debt and much of the construction undertaken had assumed its continuance as capital. Many of the leading figures had invested heavily in land and feared great losses. Some, such as William Stennett, a leading jeweller, even decided to transfer to Kingston with the capital.

Nevertheless, despite the forecasts Toronto continued to boom. One of Kingston's leading merchants wrote home to his wife, "You would be surprised to see how buildings continue to be run up in Toronto notwithstanding the certainty that it will lose the benefit of a large government expenditure—I really cannot understand it." The city of 1841 was not the same frightened little town that fought for its tenure of government in 1815. Toronto had not yet realized this, but by 1841 it no longer needed the government base, having become a viable centre on its own. By the time Parliament left Kingston in 1844 Stennett and the others were sneaking back sheepishly, the depression of 1837 was ending, and Toronto was planning its railway network. Toronto's confidence was perhaps best shown by the erection of a new City Hall in 1844. (Part of the building is now encased in the south part of the St. Lawrence Market and has recently become the municipal Art Gallery.) The Board of Trade, which had been a victim of the depression, was reestablished in 1844-1845.

The continuing prosperity had two roots: institutional retention and hinterland growth and control. The actual government departure meant little direct loss to the city. It was more important to Toronto that, because of the dual legal system of the new United Province, which incorporated both English and French civil law, the two halves (now sometimes known as Canada West and Canada East) retained their own courts at Toronto and Quebec. The Law Society of Upper Canada, too, remained in Toronto, as did the Medical Board for Upper Canada. The city was also the seat of the Anglican and Catholic bishops and the synods of other denominations.

Other institutions were developed during the decade. In 1841 a new barracks, later the Stanley Barracks, the surviving building of which is now the Marine Museum, was opened at a cost of £60,000. The university finally opened in 1843, and included a faculty of medicine. The new Provincial Asylum, designed by architect John George Howard, long known as 999 Queen Street West, was occupied in 1850 and became Toronto's most impressive building in the eyes of many.

Hinterland control was well established before 1841, but a British grant made vast public works possible. Most important was the rebuilding and completion of the canal system by 1848, greatly expediting the commerce of the lake towns. Toronto's ships could now sail to Halifax or

One of the most outrageous demolitions of historic Toronto occurred between 1975 and 1976 when the provincial government thoughtlessly tore down John Howard's most successful architectural monument, the Provincial Lunatic Asylum at 999 Queen Street West. The enormous building—which owed a great deal in its design to William Wilkin's 1846 National Gallery in London— dominated the city's western extremity for many years. An 1846 lithograph shows the asylum with massive east and west wings, as originally projected by Howard, running south from the central block. The site is now occupied by a parking lot. MTL T10261

Liverpool with its hinterland's products. Inland, the road system of Upper Canada was greatly improved and extended with British money, and the talk of a railway was revived. In December 1846 new communication possibilities opened with the first telegraph message from the mayor of Toronto to the mayor of Hamilton. The telegraph lines quickly spread further, and as soon as a European boat docked at New York, Toronto knew of the events and commercial quotations of that continent.

With the 1840s came a new flow of immigrants. Toronto grew from 14,249 in 1841 to 19,706 in 1845 and then to 25,166 in 1850. With the Irish potato famine, the flow became a flood: 40,000 Irish refugees passed through Toronto in 1847 alone. By 1851 more than a third of the population was Irish. Also, by that time the good agricultural land to the north was pretty well settled, and the Home District, which became York County in 1850, was nearly filled up.

The city these emigrants saw was described by Charles Dickens in 1842, in perhaps too glowing terms: "The town itself is full of life and motion, bustle, business, and improvement. The streets are well paved and lighted with gas; the houses are large and good; the shops excellent." Along these streets brick was replacing less substantial materials. King Street was still the shopping and business centre during the decade. A well-developed west end now spread out beyond Yonge Street, and to the north Queen Street was filling up, although in 1845 Michael Power, the first Catholic bishop, was thought mad to begin constructing St.

The Royal Mail steam packet Princess Royal *was one of a number of steamboats plying Lake Ontario by the 1840s. It is pictured here as it appeared in 1844. Many took it between Toronto and Kingston; one, lawyer Larratt Smith, recorded in his diary embarking at 2 p.m. on a Friday, and after a cold journey where "there was no wind of any consequence on the lake & very few passengers," docking at Kingston at 8:30 on a "very snowy Saturday morning...." MTL T10253*

Michael's Cathedral on its present site just north of Queen, which had just had its name changed from Lot in a sweeping revision. In the far north beyond Bloor, the village of Yorkville was taking shape, and the first St. Paul's Anglican Church was built in 1842.

New businesses opened. Copp, Clark & Company, manufacturing stationers, appeared in 1842, and in 1844 came the founding of Canada's national newspaper when Peter and George Brown began printing the *Globe*. The Browns were Reformers, but not of the Mackenzie breed; rather, they belonged to what could be called the Toronto establishment Liberals, whom it was and is often difficult to tell from the establishment Tories. George Brown was a leading figure in many Toronto corporate ventures, landowner in southwestern Ontario, and eventually a senator of Canada. His newspaper became the standard bearer for those demanding Canadian, and hence Torontonian, expansion over the Hudson's Bay Company lands in the West.

The new technology of the era could also lead to labour problems. When Walker & Hutchinson acquired Toronto's first sewing machine in 1847 their employees promptly walked off the job. Fortunately for labour accord the device proved to be of little use. The workers were called back and given it to carry along King Street in triumph and ship back to New York City, before joining their employers in a banquet—a much happier ending than has marked most labour disputes, even if technology was only in temporary retreat.

George Brown, pictured here in the 1870s, established The Globe *in 1844. The newspaper—as* The Globe and Mail *—remains Toronto's and perhaps Canada's most influential journal. Liberal Brown, however, might worry about the paper's present political stance. MTL T13668*

TORYISM TRIUMPHANT: TORONTO POLITICS, 1838-1850

Toronto may have begun as a Tory settlement founded by a Tory governor, fairly consistently voted Tory, been confirmed in its Toryism with the War of 1812, and grown even more Tory with the British emigration; but it was the Rebellion of 1837 that really confirmed what some might claim was its destiny. The radical Reformers disappeared and the new Reformers/Grits/Liberals such as Brown followed in the moderate traditions of the Baldwins rather than the radicalism of Mackenzie.

Municipally, Mackenzie's Rebellion wiped out the Reformers on the City Council for over a decade, and the political party basis of council has never returned. The council began to enjoy an unusual continuity of membership. Of the ten aldermen elected in 1837, eight were still in office in 1841, as were six of the ten common councilmen elected that year. George Walton, a Tory journalist who prepared the first city directory in 1833 and first numbered Toronto's streets, lasted from 1836 to 1845. Councilman John Craig, a stained-glass painter, lasted from 1834 to 1849. Survivor of them all was George Gurnett, the mainstay of the 1840s councils, who sat on all the key committees and the Board of Works. There he directed both the city's business and the distribution of patronage; in addition, he attended as a magistrate at the police court. In 1848 he was appropriately returned to the mayor's chair where he efficiently ran the Board of Health during the 1849 cholera epidemic.

The 1840s also saw the consolidation of political power by an organization which often provided the shock troops for the Tory party:

This squat but attractive building stood, a monument to the efforts of Egerton Ryerson in fashioning the province's education system, in the splendid isolation of St. James' Square, a seven-and-a-half acre park. Erected by Cumberland and Ridout in 1851-1852, the Normal School functioned both as a training school for teachers and a model school for students. After the Second World War the site was swallowed up by Ryerson Polytechnic, which erected an ugly quadrangle of drab brick and left in the centre as a sad relic the front facade of the old middle section.
MTL 30149

the Orange Order. Orange-Catholic riots on Orangeman's Day, the anniversary of the defeat of Catholic King James II by Protestant King William of Orange on July 12, were practically becoming an Upper Canadian tradition. Although the order had few members on the council in the early days, by the 1840s it was a very powerful group. Probably the first leading Orange on the council was Lodge Master John Armstrong, an alderman from 1834 to 1848 except for two years, who is said to have supplied the property qualification for George Gurnett to sit. At a lower level, Inspector of Streets William Davis was a specialist in organizing an Orange mob when required.

The main development in city services was the beginning of the water and gas system when the council gave a charter to a Montreal group incorporated as the City of Toronto Gas-Light and Water Company. By the end of 1841, the first gas lamps were illuminating the streets, but there was less success with the water supply. This was pumped from an intake at the foot of John Street through wooden pipes to a reservoir north of the city. The result was far from satisfactory; there were constant complaints about both the quantity and quality of the supply. Finally in 1848 the city took over the water system, and a private corporation, the Consumers' Gas Company, was established to supply gas, as it still does today.

In 1840 a new, three-wing gaol and courthouse designed by John Howard was built, and at the end of the decade proper local courts were set up under a recorder and a police magistrate, Gurnett receiving the latter post. Education was extended with the division of the city into 15 primary school districts in 1844. Separate schools appeared following an 1843 act. Gurnett attempted to establish free education, but the majority of the council were for "self-reliance" and opposed to "pauper education" and extra taxation for schooling. The large number of primary school-age loiterers on the streets of the city demonstrated the continuing problem, but despite this, with the increase in city costs for Irish emigrant relief, the schools were closed for six months in 1848 and 1849.

By 1845 the city had a single, amplified fire code regulating a wide variety of hazards, such as smoking in stables or carpenter shops, the disposal of hot ashes, and the inspection of chimneys. A chief engineer was appointed over the four fire companies and two hook and ladder companies, all still staffed by volunteers. Yet the water supply was anything but adequate, and many of the regulations were unenforceable. Also, even with the growing number of brick buildings, the city, like any other developing centre of the period, was full of hazards with its many stables and intermixture of more solid structures with frame or shingle-clad buildings, often roofed with wood shingles. The wonder was less the total number of fires than it was the number the fire department managed to get under control. Yet, almost every city or town has had its great fire or fires, and Toronto was to be no exception.

THE FIRST GREAT FIRE, 1849

The First Great Fire of Toronto started in the heart of the congested business district of the city, just to the northeast of the intersection of King Street East and Nelson, earlier called New and now Jarvis Street, about 1:30 a.m., on April 17, 1849. The frame stables and outbuildings in the centre of that block ignited rapidly and began burning in all directions. To the east the blaze destroyed the Home District Savings Bank along with some frame houses and a tavern. Simultaneously it attacked the large brick stores and offices to the south on King Street, burning out the plant of the *Patriot* and killing George Watson, a leading Toronto publisher who was trying to rescue the type. It also destroyed the *Mirror's* premises. By that stage a wind had come up and the flames jumped Nelson and raced westward through the area now covered by the park east of St. James' Cathedral, which at that time consisted of a line of substantial stores on King with a tangle of smaller streets to their rear.

By now the flames were visible in St. Catharines, and the wind was hurling blazing shingles and brands as much as two miles to the west. One of these blowing across the cemetery that surrounded St. James' lodged in the latticework of the tower. The firemen, frustrated by a lack of water as only one hydrant had worked in the crucial first stages, seemed to have been busy elsewhere. The spectators, instead of taking action, discussed whether the tower would catch, and the cathedral burned from the top down. Next the wind changed direction, blowing from the north, and swept the fire south of King, burning out the northern portion of the St. Lawrence Market and damaging the fronts of the mercantile buildings across from the church. The firemen scored one of their few successes in saving the other three sides of the market and the new City Hall to the south.

About 3 to 4 a.m., the city was rescued by a combination of circumstances. There was a sudden rain shower that wet down wood shingle roofs, the wind-driven wall of flames was blocked by the cemetery around St. James', and, as was customary in large fires, troops from the garrison arrived to aid the exhausted firemen. By 6 a.m. the flames were virtually out.

The newspapers calculated the insurance loss at £59,500, but this could only have represented a portion of the total, which was variously estimated at £100,000 to £300,000. The loss was enormous, but so were Toronto's recuperative powers. Before the year was out substantial buildings were rising over the six blocks that had been damaged or obliterated by the fire. The large, rather derelict four-storey business block still standing on the northeast corner of King and Jarvis is a good example of store architecture of the period. But while such plain structures dominated, Toronto had now passed beyond the era of pure functionalism. The St. Lawrence Market and present St. James' Cathedral were to rise as mementos of the fire and symbols of the mid-century prosperity of Toronto. The capital may have departed, the colony may have still not completely pulled out of the depression, but the city was prosperous and well on its way to becoming Upper Canada's metropolitan centre.

THE RAILWAY AGE ERUPTS

Although Toronto became the capital of the United Province of Canada on an alternating basis in 1849, the real theme of the years that followed was not government changes, but economic swings: first rising prosperity and then overexpansion to 1857; then a panic and depression that lasted until 1861; and finally another period of prosperity. Coupled with the first of these cycles was the railway building boom that was either to make or break the cities of North America. Those that became hubs of railway networks consolidated their hold over their hinterland and prospered; those that failed to do so declined.

For Toronto, although the completion of the canal system had improved its lake communications, access to its hinterland was still difficult. With a railway it could establish year-round communications, reduce the cost of moving out staple products, and capture the inland hinterlands of the rival towns along the lake shore. Torontonians, like the inhabitants of most lake cities, dreamed of wider prospects and saw their city as the key point on a route stretching from the Atlantic and the St. Lawrence to the American Midwest and even the Pacific. By the mid-

1840s, with the revival of good times underway, William Allan and other entrepreneurs were dusting off the railway charters they had acquired earlier and reviving their grand schemes.

In the end three routes came together at Toronto. Lady Elgin, wife of the governor, turned the first sod for Toronto's Northern Railway, the city's own scheme to consolidate its northern hinterland. The line reached Aurora in May 1853, just in time for William Allan to witness the success of his last enterprise before he died at age 83. The trains ran to Barrie in October and Collingwood on Georgian Bay in January 1855. Later extensions were run to Penetanguishene, Orilla, and Gravehurst.

Simultaneously Hamilton opened its Great Western Railway from Niagara to Hamilton to London in 1853 and on to Windsor in January 1854. Spurlines were then built northward to Galt and Guelph and a branch run to Sarnia by 1858. Meanwhile in 1855 Hamilton joined its line to Toronto, hooking the southwestern peninsula to the larger metropolis, which had already stretched its road communications westward. Toronto was inadvertently given a line to both New York City and the American Midwest, and Hamilton and its hinterland were on the way to absorption into the territory of the larger metropolis.

In 1856, only a year after the Great Western connection, Montreal's Grand Trunk Railway reached Toronto and went on to Guelph, Stratford, and Sarnia. Toronto was thus joined to the Canadian metropolis' network. However, with its rich hinterland, greater distance, and excellent harbour, coupled with the cheaper cost of water shipment and the alternative New York route, Toronto escaped domination by the larger city.

Railway development was immediately followed by further expansion of the harbour facilities. Although there were lumber shipments from Toronto, wheat, flour, and other grains were the major export items. To handle these, large grain elevators were necessary and the first, with a capacity of 200,000 bushels, was built in 1863; others soon followed. The harbour also acquired its Eastern Gap when a series of storms opened a permanent channel by 1858. This was marked by buoys and within a year was being used in shipping.

THE CONSOLIDATION OF BUSINESS

The boom times that accompanied the railroad construction, which were spurred on by the Crimean War from 1853 to 1856, further consolidated Toronto's control of Upper Canadian business. Although the city's exports did not yet dominate in the province, the merchants were turning to wholesaling and rapidly expanding their areas of activity. John Macdonald founded his great dry-goods firm in 1849 and soon moved to extensive premises on Wellington Street East. In 1859 another important dry-goods business, Gordon, Mackay & Company, was established. It built its impressive warehouse at Front and Bay in 1871.

Following the railway, larger hotels made their appearance. Two were outstanding. The 252-room, gas-lighted, steam-heated Rossin House, later the Prince George, was erected at King and York streets in 1857. On Front Street several buildings were joined together to form the

Queen's Hotel in 1862. This was the most elite of Toronto's hostelries until it was replaced by the Royal York in 1927.

Newspaper publishing expanded, too, with George Brown's *Globe* taking over the earlier *Examiner* in 1865. Leather merchant James Beaty founded the Tory *Leader* in 1852 and purchased the old Conservative organs, the *British Colonist* and the *Patriot*. General publishing was also expanding into large-scale operations. Hunter, Rose & Company, founded in the mid-1850s, produced both general literature and vast numbers of school books.

Most important, the railways provided the basis for Toronto's growth into a major manufacturing centre. The city already had a large number of manufactories. For some of them, such as Jacques & Hay's furniture factory, the railways opened new markets. By the 1860s that firm was employing 400 hands, had its own sawmills, and was making a wide variety of furniture for homes, schools, and offices. In addition, many new manufacturing businesses were established, some of which lasted for many years. The growth potential of the city attracted firms and individuals from outside in the sort of magnet effect that characterizes successful urban centres. Charles Boeckh moved to Toronto from New York City about 1850, as he correctly saw it as an ideal location for a brush factory. Most transfers, however, were made from the more immediate southern Upper Canada area.

The new manufacturing concentrated on transportation supply. Ships' engines and boilers had been made in the city for some time, some of considerable size. The Hayes Brothers' white oak, 1,070-ton *City of*

A retouched photo, thought to be from the firm of Armstrong, Beere & Hime, shows the wreck of the two-month-old paddle steamer Monarch, *which foundered on the narrow neck of (what was then) the harbour peninsula just west of (what is now) the Eastern Gap. The photo was taken December 30, 1856, more than a month after the wreck and shows the salvage work moving rather slowly. (In fact, the boiler remained on the spot for some 40 years—a menace to navigation.) The Eastern Gap itself was punched through the peninsula in a savage April storm 18 months after the wreck, fashioning what are now called the Toronto Islands. MTL T13290*

Toronto was, in 1855, the first Toronto-built ship to cross the Atlantic. James Good made locomotives for the Northern Railway, as well as threshing machines, engines, and boilers. James Beaty's Toronto Locomotive Works turned out its first engine, named *Toronto,* in 1853. The Toronto Car Wheel Works was established as a branch of a Buffalo firm. Finally there was the Toronto Rolling Mills, headed by David L. Macpherson and C.S. Gzowski, both of whom made fortunes in the railway business and were knighted by the Queen.

Beyond railway equipment manufacturing, the list of new businesses in the 1850s and 1860s was extensive and included many well-known Canadian names. William Christie founded his biscuit firm in 1852; J.&J. Taylor established their safe-making firm the next year; and Eugene O'Keefe got his brewery underway in the early 1860s. Not all the manufacturers were natives of Canada or the British Isles; Theodore A. Heintzman, a Jewish immigrant who came from Berlin by way of the United States, started his piano manufacturing business in his house in 1861.

Successful manufacturing and commerce encouraged financial expansion. In 1856 James G. Chewett, son of the surveyor general who had commanded the militia at the capture of York in 1813, left the Bank of Upper Canada to become president of the Bank of Toronto, which was backed by the well-established Gooderham & Worts distillery. Toronto's

The Swords Hotel—later the Queen's—stood on the site of the present Royal York. Proximity to Parliament made the Swords-cum-Queen's the logical home away from home for legislators, although the peripatetic nature of the government's presence in Toronto could hardly guarantee success—at least until Confederation. In 1862 the place was modified, extended, and given a cupola. Dignitaries and visitors often stayed there, including the future King George V, a few Russian archdukes, and sundry United States presidents. MTL T11052

95

growth was also confirmed by the opening of branches of Molson's Bank and the Quebec Bank.

The Western Assurance Company (now in the Royal Insurance Company) was established in 1851, with Isaac Gilmour, one of the wholesale dry-goods merchants, as its first president. It soon had agents at such centres as London, Woodstock, and Montreal. The building societies, the mortgage and trust companies of today, had begun in the 1840s as terminating or limited-term companies. In the 1850s they assumed permanent form. Canada Permanent Mortgage Company was established in 1855 with Chewett as chairman and another Family Compact descendant, J.D. Ridout, as president. The Toronto Stock Exchange traces its origins to 1852, when a group of businessmen began to meet at each other's offices for a half-hour each morning to trade securities. For all these entrepreneurs, and the citizenry generally, the 1857 adoption of the decimal system with the dollar replacing the pound came as a blessing, reducing costs of business operation and simplifying daily transactions.

But boom is followed by bust, and in the post-Crimean War reaction the world was shaken by the panic and depression of 1857, a repetition of

Nothing suggests the dark, satanic quality of Victorian working conditions better than this 1864 pastel drawing of the Toronto Rolling Mills by William Armstrong. The work was hot, dangerous, and ill-paid, a crucible for working-class consciousness and a vigorous industrial proletariat.
MTL T10914

the economic collapse of 20 years earlier. In Toronto many firms failed to survive. Mayor John Hutchinson himself was forced to declare bankruptcy and send his resignation to the council, which gallantly asked him to complete his term. Worst of all was the beginning of the collapse of the earliest Upper Canadian banks led by that grand dowager, the Bank of Upper Canada. All of them had overexpanded in the land speculation of the 1850s, loaned money on dubious collateral, often at the behest of the government, and all were badly overextended when the panic struck. Recovery began with the American Civil War, when Upper Canadians prospered by supplying the North. Soon new financial institutions, run on a sounder basis, took the place of the old.

A NEW CITY ARISES

The railway boom was coupled with another population explosion. In the years 1851-1856 Toronto grew from 30,775 to 41,761 people. The ensuing depression slowed the increase and growth became more gradual, reaching 49,016 by 1867. Expansion took place largely within the liberties, though there was considerable building on Yonge Street beyond Bloor. The new city was substantial; the centre section was constructed entirely of brick and even the new areas had far fewer frame buildings. It was also a more differentiated city with developing areas of concentration. Warehousing and wholesaling located at the foot of Yonge Street and along the lake shore, and the retail district began moving up Yonge Street from King; the first stores appeared in the Queen Street area.

Physically Toronto was still grubby, despite periodic attempts to keep the streets watered; but the sidewalks were sufficiently good that visitors like Anthony Trollope could compare them favourably to Montreal and Quebec. The hogs and cows had almost disappeared from the central areas but flourished in the slums, which were still located in such areas as that around modern Lombard Street. The newly created St. John's Ward covering Macaulay Town plus the sector northwest of Queen and Yonge streets was the poorest in the city.

With prosperity came elegance. Many of Toronto's finest buildings date from the railway era. Fortunately when funds became available to build these major structures, Toronto could boast several architects of great ability. William Thomas designed St. Michael's Cathedral and St. Lawrence Hall in the 1840s, and Frederic William Cumberland's legacy from the 1850s includes St. James' Cathedral, University College, and the central section of Osgoode Hall.

Like the public buildings, Toronto residences were displaying considerable improvements. Piped water, indoor plumbing, more efficient stoves, central heating, and gas lighting were all available, although few houses as yet had all these amenities. In the mid-1850s only one house in nine was attached to the water mains. The solid brick row houses of the period are still to be seen in many areas, and a few of the mansions built by the growing numbers of the wealthy survive. John Macdonald chose Venetian Revival for his warehouse, and Oaklands, his country mansion on the crest of the escarpment overlooking the city (now De La Salle-

Because Britain recognized the South as the belligerent in the American Civil War, fears that the U.S. would retaliate by conquering Canada were rife. Many thought an "unofficial" incident might provoke an invasion, and the group most likely to foment it was the Fenian brotherhood, a group of Irish patriots and exiles organized in New York in 1857 whose goal was Irish revolution. Arguing that Canada was Britain's soft underbelly, Fenian agitators launched a series of raids across the border, the most serious in June 1866, when almost 1,000 men crossed the Niagara River and captured Fort Erie. British regulars eventually drove them off. Pictured are four members of Number Nine University Company of Toronto's Queen's Own Rifles who were themselves involved in the fracas. MTL T13746

Oaklands), is a magnificent example of Gothic Revival. A little to its west, James Austin, wholesale grocer and banker, purchased Spadina and built the large Mansard mansion, which was recently transferred to the government. Most magnificent of all was William Cawthra's 1852 city residence at the northeast corner of King and Bay streets (the site of the Bank of Nova Scotia), which considerably exceeded many of the mansions rising on New York's Fifth Avenue in the splendour of its classical design and cut stone decoration.

Toronto was also acquiring parks. The extensive university grounds were as yet little built on, but in 1853 the Legislature expropriated part of them for the Queen's Park oval, which still surrounds Ontario's Legislature. The most important development was the first Exhibition Park. From 1846 the Provincial Agricultural Association held annual fairs at different sites in Ontario. In 1848, and again in 1852 and 1858, it chose Toronto. These gatherings were a key factor in the rescue of a part of the ordnance lands for the Exhibition Park in 1856. Two years later Toronto built its own iron and glass, cross-shaped Crystal Palace, a structure 256 by 96 feet. In 1857 old William's son, George William Allan, who was to become known as the "Squire of Toronto," gave five acres of the family park lot to the city, the Allan Gardens and Conservatory of today.

MUNICIPAL POLITICS AND SERVICES

The municipal franchise remained limited, but after 1857, except for the years 1867-1874, the mayor was elected directly by the people. Generally the mayors continued to represent the same gentlemanly classes as before, although there were exceptions. Irish emigrant John George Bowes, reportedly a good man in a brawl, was ousted in 1853 after three years in office over an unholy railway financing deal with Reformer Francis Hincks, the premier of the province. Ten years later Bowes was returned for three more terms. The old guard was represented by George William Allan in 1855, John Beverley Robinson, Jr., in 1856, and William Henry Boulton of the Grange a year later. Present, too, were some of the up and coming leaders of the future. Ontario's most enduring and possibly greatest political figure, Liberal Premier Sir Oliver Mowat, found his first elective post as an alderman for St. Lawrence Ward in 1857.

In the boom-bust economy, the development of services to parallel the growth of the city presented a great problem; both the police force and the fire department suffered from drastic changes in organization and funding, and public school financing remained limited. The greatest advances were made in the city's internal communications. In 1849 H.B. Williams, a cabinetmaker, began an omnibus service that ran west from the St. Lawrence Market along King Street and up Yonge to the Red Lion Hotel in Yorkville beyond Bloor Street. His six-pence fare proved very popular. A dozen years later, in 1861, Alexander Easton received a 30-year franchise for the Toronto Street Railway, which ran horse-drawn cars or sleighs along Yonge, King, and Queen street routes. This was the beginning of today's Toronto Transit Commission. The cars operated 14 hours a day in winter and 16 in summer, were not to exceed the speed of

Opposite page, top left: Photographed in the 1860s, Frederic William Cumberland was one of Toronto's most energetic and able citizens. Much of his legacy as an architect remains in the prominent shapes of St. James' Cathedral, University College, and other buildings—including the centre section of Osgoode Hall. He found time also to be an engineer, railway baron, Member of the Legislative Assembly, and Member of Parliament. MTL T13682

Opposite page, top right: Historically, the St. Lawrence Hall is arguably Toronto's most significant secular building, although many would give that honour to Osgoode Hall. Since its erection in 1850, the hall has greeted royalty, glittered with dozens of formal balls, echoed to the sounds of Jenny Lind, and—less elegantly—served as a Depression flophouse. The hall is pictured here about 1873. MTL T12102

Opposite page, bottom: Osgoode Hall is Toronto's worthy equivalent of London's Inns of Court. The first part erected was the east wing, built in 1829, and a centre section and west wing were added in 1844. But much of the magnificence that the building now exudes is the product of the extensive remodelling by architects Cumberland and Storm in 1857; to them Toronto owes the present facade and the building's chief ornament, the Great Library. Osgoode Hall is shown here with its elaborate iron fence in a William Notman photo of 1868. MTL T12016

Right: Members of a family garden party pose on the grounds of the commodious Cayley house at 152 Beverley Street. The family seen here is not the Honourable William Cayley's, but rather that of his tenant, a Mr. Leslie, who took over the house in the mid-1860s. Whoever they are, they will have more success at taking tea than at playing croquet on Cayley's unkempt grass. AO S2824

Below: Government House's vice-regal tenants are shown frolicking on the grounds, the central figure sans parasol thought to be Lady Head, wife of the Governor-General Sir Edmund Head. MTL T11871

One of the most stunning achievements of 19th-century architecture was Sir Joseph Paxton's Crystal Palace, erected in London for the Great Exhibition of 1851. Toronto built its own version in 1858 (in 90 days), although rather more iron was used than glass. Called the Palace of Indusry, the forerunner of the Canadian National Exhibition was located on King near today's Shaw Street. The future of the building was often in doubt, principally because the annual exhibition, then sponsored by the Provincial Agricultural Association, was a travelling one. Occasionally schemes would be put forward for the building's use, including the rather droll idea of converting the place into cavalry barracks. In 1878 the Palace of Industry was dismantled, carted to a new site near the Stanley Barracks, and re-erected. The building then acquired another floor below and a large, peculiarly poised cupola on top, shown at left. It was put out of its misery by fire in 1906. MTL JRR552, MTL E4 95a

Right: The fire hall at the corner of Duke and Berkeley streets was built in 1859. A tower was added in 1871 from which one could spot fires and hang hoses to dry. One of Toronto's precious few steam-driven water pumps (probably a Silsby) is shown, suggesting that the photograph was taken in the late 1860s. AO S14180

Opposite page: The Toronto Home for Incurables stood on Dunn Avenue in Parkdale. An eccentric building, it was substantially the gift of Alexander Manning, businessman and mayor. Among the many properties that Manning had a hand in developing were the Manning Arcade on King Street, the old Normal School, the Grand Opera House, and Ottawa's impressive, Neo-Gothic Parliamentary Library. AO S1299

six miles per hour, and included such luxuries as straw to warm the feet in winter. The fare was five cents and there were no transfers. Almost immediately Easton had 2,000 passengers per day. The postal service also improved after Canada took it over in 1851. In 1859 Toronto became the first Canadian city to have street letter boxes.

Private funds played a leading part in the operation and expansion of health and welfare services, although the government could point to the building of a new Toronto General Hospital on Gerrard Street in the mid-1850s. Various dispensaries also appeared, as did societies for aiding orphans and the poor. Often these operated on a denominational base, such as the huge Catholic House of Providence that opened in 1856.

SOCIETY IN MID-CENTURY

Toronto in the mid-19th century was a typical Upper Canadian city of the period. Its pioneer days were over, and, although it was a gateway for immigration, it had developed a large stable population core and a powerful middle class. Ethnically the population still derived predominantly from the British Isles. The Negro population continued to increase; their Baptist and Methodist churches were located in the poor emigrant area northwest of Queen and Yonge. The first Jews also made their appearance. In 1851 there were about 50 Jewish residents, largely engaged in the clothing, jewellery, and tobacco businesses. Some achieved prominence, such as Marcus and Samuel Rossin, who built the hotel that bore their name, and Abraham and Samuel Nordheimer, who, like the already mentioned Heintzmans, were prominent in the musical supply business.

In recreation the traditional sports retained their popularity and a

new one, baseball, made its appearance. The Toronto Rowing Club was organizing formal races for both keel boats and single sculls by the late 1840s, and the Canadian Yacht Club (the Royal came later) was established in 1852. Organized horse-racing had been popular since the 1840s, and in June 1860 four thousand spectators gathered at remote Dundas Street West near modern Keele Street to see the first Queen's Plate race. Don Juan won the 50-guinea prize. The next year, 1861, saw the Civil Holiday in August celebrated for the first time.

Cultural and political events centred at the St. Lawrence Hall. Sir John A. Macdonald and George Brown spoke there, as did Horace Greeley and Lieutenant Alexander R. Dunn of the 11th Hussars, Toronto's first VC, who returned in triumph from the Charge of the Light Brigade to be feted by his native city in 1856. The next year Toronto's first performance of Handel's *Messiah* was held in the hall, and the world's greatest sopranos, Jenny Lind and Adelina Patti, sang there on their North American tours. Lind's selections included "Comin' Through the Rye" and "Home Sweet Home," which brought the house down.

Literature and science were flourishing. The Toronto Atheneum was founded as a library, museum, and lecture society in 1848, with Canon Henry Scadding, Toronto's great 19th-century historian, as president. The Canadian Institute followed the next year, presenting lectures on a wide variety of subjects, particularly scientific topics. Theatre was especially popular. The overwhelming majority of the performances were presented by American troupes on circuit. Their fare varied from Shakespeare to the ephemera of the day and often mixed both together in the same bill. P.T. Barnum's "Grand Colossal Museum and Menagerie" arrived in Toronto with 10 elephants pulling a huge car juggernaut and a baby elephant carrying midget Major Tom Thumb, who was a great hit in the city. There were also choral and fraternal societies and even a municipal art contest in 1850 for the best view of Toronto. The £25 prize was won by William Armstrong. Still, for most, the taverns with their whiskey at 25 cents a gallon remained the major attraction.

The great social event of the era, however, was the first royal visit in 1860, when 18-year-old Edward, Prince of Wales, later Edward VII, came to survey his future domains. The royal tour, like the rebellion, had an air of comic opera as the Prince and his minister attendant, Colonial Secretary the Duke of Newcastle, found that the Orange Order, which was not recognized in Britain, took delight in erecting arches festooned with Orange symbols under which they hoped the royal visitor would have to pass. However, Edward was a great hit, and Newcastle returned to England so thoroughly impressed with Canadian loyalty, even that of Orangemen, that he became one of the greatest supporters of Canadian Confederation.

The Prince of Wales made his triumphant tour of Canada in 1860. This scene of the event, from the Illustrated London News, *shows Albert Edward's disembarkation and entrance into the city. The* News *reporter gushed, "At every step during his progress the Prince was welcomed with genuine British cheers; but at Toronto at least a hundred thousand British American throats gave out the loyal cry." PAC C10912*

Mechanics Institutes, middle-class efforts to help the lower classes help themselves, were originally established as a form of adult education centre in Britain in the 1820s. By 1835 a branch was established in Toronto and—as in Britain— soon became less a working-class affair than a middle-class reading room and meeting place for literary and scientific discussion. The old Mechanics building, erected in 1850, eventually became the core of the Toronto library system. The reading room was photographed in 1890. MTL T12006

CHAPTER IX

THE QUEEN CITY OF ONTARIO

1867-1884

On July 1, 1867, Canadian Confederation came into effect, and the new province of Ontario was born with Toronto as its capital. The newspapers proclaimed the dawn of the new era, the newly installed bells of the rebuilt St. James' rang out the birth of the Dominion, the Union Jack was hoisted to the sound of 21 guns, bands played, an ox was roasted for the poor, and there was a military parade, dancing, and fireworks. Three years later, with the new Dominion taking over its own defence, the last British troops left the city.

By the Confederation era Toronto stretched from the Provincial Lunatic Asylum at Ossington Avenue in the west to across the Don River in the east. To the north Yorkville was a separate municipality but physically already part of the city. With an almost undue lack of modesty, the Board of Trade recorded that "the streets wore the stirring crowded appearance of a busy American city, but its buildings in the solidity of their style and architecture, and the beauty of the grounds surrounding the private houses, partook more of the grace and wealth of a large English town."

The long-favoured residential district around Duke and Duchess streets (now Adelaide and Richmond streets east), which were just east of the business district, had now lost its popularity, and Jarvis Street, which stretched north from this area, was becoming the favoured abode of the wealthy. To the west other prominent families located near the Legislature again situated in the old Upper Canadian Parliament buildings; in 1869 a new Government House was constructed north of these struc-

Above: Erected in 1874, Knox College has served as Presbyterian Theological College (its intended use) and as a hospital, armoury, and medical laboratory—its present guise. The development of both penicillin and insulin was furthered here. AO Acc. 14313-6

Previous page: The carte-de-visite of Toronto businessman and lawyer Larratt W. Smith shows a prominent Torontonian of the Confederation era. What distinguishes Smith from so many of his commercial friends and acquaintances was that he was a committed and able diarist. His recently published diaries (Young Mr. Smith in Upper Canada, 1980) form a rivetting portrait of privileged life in an energetic yet provincial city from the 1830s through the late 1850s. MTL T13790

tures. The result was a pleasant residential enclave, but one that could hardly last because of the spread of the business area westward and the fact that the government buildings were inadequate for the growing civil service. Unfortunately the slums spread at an even more rapid pace. Surveying these sections of the city, the *Globe* found large areas of poverty, dirt, and dilapidation and many uninhabitable houses. With the slums went the usual problems of child labour, prostitution, and alcoholism. In 1864 and 1878 federal temperance acts were passed on a local option basis. These were never brought into force throughout the entire city, and conditions remained deplorable.

Alexander Manning, a builder-architect-mortgage holder, may be taken as an example of the new type of entrepreneur who was now appearing. Born in Dublin in 1819, he emigrated to Canada in the mid-1830s and made a fortune in contracting in Toronto, in the construction of the Parliamentary Library in Ottawa, and in railway work. He reinvested his profits in various financial and land operations, and his property holdings became so extensive that he was reported to be "the largest individual taxpayer in Toronto" at the end of the century. A Tory, Manning was an alderman and the mayor in 1873 and 1885. He was president of a wide variety of organizations: the St. Patrick's Society, the Irish Protestant Benevolent Society, the National Club, and the Trader's Bank. He died in 1903 in one of the mansions that were rising around the new Legislature on Queen's Park Crescent and was buried in a massive, stone, hillside vault in the newer establishment row at St. James' Cemetery. His career stands as a late-19th-century success story.

Adequate and properly staffed police and fire departments were finally making their appearance. In 1866 the provincial government forced the establishment of a well-organized police department under an independent police commission. A professional fire department had been organized in 1855, then changed to a combination professional-voluntary system in the 1860s; the organization of a fully professional department came in 1874. In 1869 the Board of Health was given sweeping powers to investigate and regulate nuisances and clean up the city and harbour, but the duties were far beyond the control of the staff available. The water supply was gradually improved, although there were continual difficulties over obtaining an adequate flow for fires. The city finally took over the water company in 1874 and built a proper waterworks. The quality of water during this period may be judged by the fact that on one occasion there was an infestation of polliwogs flowing joyously out of the taps; at the same time the firemen were complaining of catfish blocking the hydrants.

The institutional situation, to a great extent privately funded, was much more promising. Under Alexander Manning's aegis, the Home for Incurables (now the Queen Elizabeth Hospital) opened in 1874. It moved to its present Dunn Avenue location four years later. In 1875 the Sick Children's Hospital was organized by Mrs. F.S. McMaster. Backed by the funds and energy of John Ross Robertson, the forceful editor of the *Evening Telegram*, the hospital progressed rapidly and moved to more extensive quarters. The YWCA began to look after the well-being of self-supporting young women. It soon expanded to add a home for women just released from gaol after petty crime conviction. Later the YWCA opened an Industrial Institute, which served hot meals and offered both basic education and work-training classes. In 1883 the free public library system was founded and took over the Mechanics Institute's books.

BUSINESS IN A NEW POLITICAL ARENA

Confederation meant that Toronto now had a potentially broader market right across Canada and an immediate hinterland in Ontario, where it could take steps to protect its interests from Quebec and Montreal influence by legislation. To capture the Canadian market it was obvious that Toronto business leaders would have to be active in the development of any Western railways system. By 1873 Toronto and Montreal rivalled each other for the charter for a Canadian Pacific Railway. Another phenomenon that played a role in the development of all the larger cities, but that benefitted Toronto in particular, was the ongoing transfer of businesses from the smaller towns of the province, a process that was accelerated by the better railway communications.

Communications developed in other ways than by railway. In 1875 the post office began to use letter carriers to deliver mail. Then in 1879 Toronto received its first telephone exchange, which had 40 subscribers. Nevertheless, business was not solely in an upward trend; there were the usual cycles of depression and expansion. In 1869 many commercial houses collapsed, and in 1873 a long depression set in, which lasted with

Alexander Jacques is seen in the foreman's uniform of the Volunteer Fire Department about 1858. A book and job printer and a life-long Toronto resident, Jacques was active in amateur theatricals in the 1830s and 1840s and was a tireless fireman through to the 1870s. As late as the 1890s Jacques, an Eastern correspondent for certain Western newspapers, was writing under the pseudonym—by then appropriate—"The Old Man." MTL T13317

varying intensity until nearly the end of the century. But in spite of the depression, Toronto continued to grow.

Financial reorganization was one of the most important aspects of this growth. Under the British North American Act, only the federal government could charter banks. With the loss of the Bank of Upper Canada in 1866 and with the other old Upper Canadian banks obviously failing, the city's entrepreneurs took steps to counteract the Bank of Montreal's attempts to gain control of Canadian finance. They did so both by founding new institutions themselves to supplement the surviving Toronto banks, such as the Bank of Toronto, and by fighting at the federal level to make sure that the first Banking Act of 1871 did not favour Montreal interests. Both battles were waged successfully. In Ottawa, Montreal's domination was prevented, and some of Canada's major banks were founded in Toronto. The first was the Canadian Bank of Commerce, with William McMaster, an Irish Baptist emigrant who also founded McMaster University, as president. The Commerce soon absorbed the failing Gore Bank of Hamilton and the Niagara District Bank, helping consolidate finance at Toronto. The Dominion Bank was founded in 1869 when one of McMaster's associates, James Austin, disagreed with the Commerce's policies. The Imperial Bank followed in 1873.

Insurance also expanded. The Confederation Life Assurance Company was founded in 1871. The established general insurance companies were extending their territories into new regions at the same time. The British America Assurance, of which George William Allan was a director, was establishing agencies throughout the United States, as was the Western Assurance. Both were in the forefront of the Canadian business advance into the Caribbean. Commercial unification was becoming frequent. In 1883 the various fire insurance companies came together to develop a rating and inspection organization, the Toronto Underwriters, which later developed into the Canadian Underwriters' Association. In 1866 merchants organized the Toronto Corn (Grain) Exchange for produce dealing; it later amalgamated with the Board of Trade. Finally the Stock Exchange was taking form; incorporated in 1878, in 1881 it located in quarters on King Street East.

In manufacturing the same trend was apparent; the Canadian Manufacturers' Association was founded in Toronto in 1871 to represent factory owners' interests, including tariff protection for Canadian firms. The phenomenon of outside firms opening branches in Toronto, or transferring their operations to the city, was especially visible in manufacturing. The Gurney Foundry Company of Hamilton, long one of Canada's greatest stove manufacturers, opened a Toronto branch in the late 1860s. In 1879 the Massey-Harris firm came, bringing the city its outstanding family of philanthropists. Robert Laidlaw transferred his lumber business from Barrie and Elias Rogers his coal company from Newmarket. The latter was soon advertised as the largest coal firm in Canada, having 10 branch offices in the city alone.

As a major manufacturing city, Toronto was a growth centre for the

This circa 1880 view of King Street East includes the Notman & Fraser photography studio (second from the left) and Robert Walker and Thomas Hutchinson's dry-goods store, The Golden Lion (to the right of Notman & Fraser). The use of cast iron as a building material had recently become increasingly popular, allowing merchants to design shop fronts with large plate-glass display windows like those of the Golden Lion and the shop visible at the far left. PAC PA 121530

Canadian labour movement, especially as the *laissez-faire* outlook of most manufacturers frequently led to low wages and poor working conditions in the expanding plants. There were several unions in the city by the 1860s and a Toronto Trades Assembly was established in 1871. In 1872 there was a printers' strike. The Toronto Typographical Union demanded a shorter, nine-hour day and higher wages. Most papers were opposed; Senator George Brown was particularly forceful in calling the strike an unlawful combination in restraint of trade, although James Beaty, Jr., MP and editor of the Tory *Leader*, was supportive of the strike. Fourteen strikers were arrested for striking and the case against them won under the existing legislation. Public reaction then led the federal government to adopt the British legislation that made trade unions legal, although at the same time legislation was passed that made it decidedly dangerous to strike. The effect was to undermine the case against the 14 Toronto strikers; a compromise settlement resulted. Nevertheless, factory conditions in Toronto were little improved.

The depression that began in 1873 slowed union development, but with the return of prosperity in 1881, the Trades and Labour Council of Toronto was founded under the sponsorship of the International Typographical Union. The governments, too, began to take some action. The federal government appointed a commission to look into "the Working of Mills and Factories," which reported in 1882 that it lacked the cooperation of many of the captains of industry, particularly those who were the main offenders. The list of problems was lengthy, including long hours, child labour, and safety, health, and sanitary deficiencies. In 1884 Mowat's Ontario Factories Act addressed some of these issues, yet, while it was a step forward, proper enforcement was difficult.

The shopping patterns of the city were also changing in mid-century. The long retreat of the pioneer general store before specialist shops was reversed with the appearance of the department store, really the old general store updated, which provided a great variety of goods under one roof. Fixed prices, cash payments, and bargain sales were among their methods. The first great retail merchant prince, Thomas Thompson, with

Taken from the acclaimed late 19th century publication Picturesque Canada, *this 1882 scene is of a sculling match in Toronto harbour. In the engraving Toronto's eager fans take to the water themselves to get a better view. PAC C83032*

his Mammoth House, had developed many of these business strategies, such as the bargain sale, but his heirs were not as forceful and the store remained on King Street while the business district began to move north.

The development of the Queen Street car line as the best connection to the growing districts to the east and west created a traffic conjunction at Queen and Yonge streets parallel to the one that the subway has created at Bloor and Yonge streets today. Timothy Eaton and Robert Simpson were the two merchants who were canny enough, or lucky enough, to locate there in 1869 and 1872 and adopt the new commercial practices. They were quickly on their way to making their fortunes and becoming Canadian household names.

Publishing and journalism were also undergoing a rapid expansion. In 1872 the Conservatives, not satisfied with the *Leader,* founded the *Mail.* In 1876 Professor Goldwin Smith, an English Liberal literary figure who had married the widow of the last Boulton and become squire of the Grange, provided much of the funding for John Ross Robertson to found the *Evening Telegram.* That journal quickly became quite conservative in its outlook and quite lively in editorial content. As one writer expressed it, the *Telegram* "has had great financial success, but the personalities which its columns often contained are not admired by a large class of citizens, though undoubtedly clever in composition and expression." The *Evening News,* founded five years later, acquired an even more notorious reputation. Specialized papers like the Methodist *Christian Guardian* and the *Canada Temperance Advocate* continued to flourish, and magazines like *Grip* and the Orange *Sentinel* were established. Robert Carswell founded his law book firm in 1870, and also printed the *Canadian Law Times* and a

112

wide variety of school books. The city was well on its way to becoming Canada's publishing capital.

Toronto also gained Canada's largest fair when the Provincial Agricultural Association decided that the annual agricultural exhibition should locate permanently at the capital and gained the support of the Mechanics Institute, such newly formed organizations as the Ontario Society of Artists and the Manufacturers' Association, and other local and business groups. In 1879 they obtained a charter for the Industrial Exhibition of Toronto, now the Canadian National Exhibition. The old fair site west of Strachan Avenue was too small, so a lease was taken on part of the Dominion lands on the lake shore and the Crystal Palace was moved to the new location. In September Governor-General the Marquis of Lorne and his wife, Princess Louise, daughter of Queen Victoria, arrived to open the 23-building show. The approximately 100,000 visitors that year augured a successful future. The exhibition immediately became a combined agricultural, educational, artistic, and entertainment show, with special attractions like the electrical illumination of the grounds in 1882, which made night opening possible, and in 1883 the first electric train in the city, which carried people from the Queen Street streetcar to the grounds.

Other recreational areas were also opening. In 1873 John G. Howard deeded High Park to the city in return for a life pension for himself and his wife. This brought Toronto 120 acres, plus another 45 acres and Colborne Lodge when they died. The city added 170 acres to the park in 1877, which gradually expanded to 408 acres. High Park quickly became a popular sport centre. Public ice and roller skating rinks were also developed. In 1876 the Toronto Golf Club was founded, the third golf club in North America. With the railway network expanding, Torontonians now were able to move farther for their holidays, not only to Niagara by boat but also north to Muskoka by rail.

Toronto's name entered the international sports field with the most famous sporting figure of the era, oarsman Ned Hanlan, who in quick succession became Ontario champion, American champion, and in 1880 World's Rowing Champion when he defeated an Australian contender on the Thames in England. Hanlan did the 440-yard course in 26 minutes and 12 seconds and beat this speed by 21.5 seconds shortly after when he won the English championship and a purse of $5,000. At the same time another Toronto figure, Sir Sandford Fleming, was achieving international fame in a very different field with his 1879 invention of standard time, which was adopted by the nations meeting at the Washington Conference in 1883. When it came into effect on November 18, Torontonians advanced their clocks by 17 minutes.

For those less athletically inclined, or those who preferred the contest of the board room to that of the sports field, the club picture in Toronto was becoming more diverse. In 1864 the Toronto Club had to move to more commodious quarters on York Street. The National Club was founded in 1874 with a Liberal accent, and in 1882 the Albany Club appeared with its definitely Conservative focus.

Canadians were particularly enthusiastic about sculling, Toronto's Ned Hanlan having become world champion in 1880. Hanlan is pictured in the 1870s. MTL T13699

CHAPTER X

"TORONTO THE GOOD: THE CITY OF CHURCHES"

1884-1901

In 1884 Toronto celebrated its semicentennial as the Canadian Pacific Railway linking east and west neared completion and the city began to annex new areas to accommodate its growing population. Semicentennial Week was celebrated from June 30 to July 5 with a new spectacle every day. First were fireworks and a parade of floats that depicted Toronto as the "Centre of Agriculture" and the "Queen City," as it now proudly called itself. Then came a military review and a "Trades and Industrial Procession," which was nearly two miles long. Rain unfortunately intervened the next day, but the end of the week saw performances of two oratorios, *The Creation* and *The Redemption*.

As the century drew to a close, High Victorian Toronto was given ample opportunity to demonstrate its loyalty to Queen and Empire. In 1885, when the Northwest Rebellion broke out, the Queen's Royal Rangers, the Royal Grenadiers, and "C" Company of Infantry (later the Governor-General's Body Guard) joined Major General Frederick Middleton in his expedition westward to put down the uprising, using the new railway on much of their route. Their departure was virtually a holiday celebration and their victorious return on July 23 was greeted with wild enthusiasm.

Toronto, however, was not only known for its imperialist zeal but also for its bigotry and its excessive and eventually outmoded puritanism; what is often overlooked is that the city was not unique in these attitudes. The Lord's Day Alliance was founded in Hamilton in 1888 for the protection of Sunday with the backing of 117 congregations. That

TORONTO, LOOKING EAST 1884

SEMI-CENTENNIAL CELEBRATION TORONTO, JUNE 16th to 21st

INDUSTRY, INTELLIGENCE, INTEGRITY.

Toronto 1834 Looking West

organization soon became headquartered in Toronto and had both Dominion and provincial divisions to enforce laws that were already on the statute books and demand still others to cover any loopholes. Other Canadian legislation to prevent working and sporting activities on Sundays had been passed as early as 1845, but it was only in 1906 that the alliance was able to secure an overall federal statute that imposed its strictest values across the nation.

By that time there were definite signs that such observances were no longer too popular. Prohibition of gambling, lewd books, and immoral plays was publicly accepted; prohibiting the operation of Sunday streetcars was a major inconvenience that resulted in a long battle in many cities. Also the Lord's Day legislation could result in ridiculous court cases; small boys were arrested for playing in the streets. Yet when the Toronto Golf Club appealed a conviction for operating on Sundays in 1895, they won their case on the grounds that golf was not a similar game to those prohibited by statute. In the minds of many it must have confirmed that there was one law for the rich and another for the poor. Conversely, the dominant middle and upper-middle classes were long content with the legislation, and for all Toronto's "dullness," it still typified the outlook of Ontario and much of English-speaking Canada.

That Toronto was neither too dull nor too obscure a place is shown by the fact that it was already becoming something of a convention centre. Improved rail and steamship connections allowed the late Victorians to travel with relative ease, and by the 1880s Toronto was hosting frequent gatherings with great success. The American Association for the

Advancement of Science came in August 1889, and two years later the National Convention of American Teachers arrived in Toronto. Their 20,000 delegates from across the continent must have strained all varieties of accommodations. The high point was probably the selection of the city for the 1897 meeting of the British Association for the Advancement of Science.

THE FACE OF THE HIGH VICTORIAN CITY

The face of the Victorian city was rapidly changing in the 1880s as buildings gained in bulk and reached skyward in a new style of architecture. Richardsonian Romanesque, which was later popularized by Boston architect Henry H. Richardson, can be seen in Toronto in such buildings as Cumberland's 1856 University College. It was the perfect style for North America in the late 19th century—the flamboyant expression of a continent that had gained maturity, wished to flaunt its wealth and stability through conspicuous consumption, and loved massiveness, height, excessive ornamentation, and spaciousness. The pacesetters of this style were the public buildings. In Toronto one of the first was the new Ontario Legislature built in 1886-1892. But the pride of Torontonians was the new (now the old) City Hall, designed by local architect E.J. Lennox, whose elaborate design won out over 50 other contest entries.

Toronto's need for a new City Hall had been obvious for some years before the necessary land was expropriated in the slum area of Macaulay Town in 1884. In late 1891 the foundation stone was laid by Mayor Edward F. Clarke. No expense was spared, and many local materials were incorporated—the stone, for instance, came from a quarry at the forks of the Credit River. The cost was estimated at $1.77 million, but the construction took eight years and the final figure escalated to $2.5 million. Yet Torontonians got good value for their money in the City Hall's wealth of carved stone, imported Italian marble, door knobs emblazoned with the municipal arms, and the fine clock in the high tower, which replaced St. James' Cathedral as the lookout over the city. In September 1899 Mayor John Shaw and the City Council rode up from the older City Hall in a procession of two streetcars, each drawn by 12 horses, and opened the new door with a gold key. The city government had a home with which it could be proud. The City Hall became a symbol of Toronto for decades, and after a 1960s threat to its survival, it is a symbol once again.

With these buildings the pace was set, and all over Toronto elegant structures began to appear. Often these were Romanesque, such as the recently refurbished 1890 Confederation Life Building at Richmond and Yonge streets or the now-demolished Board of Trade. Other offices, like the former Bank of Montreal at the corner of Yonge and Front streets, were classical in style. Not to be outdone by business institutions, the Orange Order laid the cornerstone of its new national headquarters, Victoria Hall on Queen Street, on Dominion Day, 1885. Tallest of all these buildings was the 10-storey, cast-iron-frame Temple Building, the highest in the British Empire, built by the Independent Order of Foresters in 1895 and demolished in 1970.

Opposite page: The cover of the official programme for Toronto's semicentennial appropriately contrasts the sprawling city of 1884 with a sedate and tranquil scene from half a century before and (in the lower left) an Indian village of 1793. The choice of the term "semicentennial" was curious—why not "Golden Jubilee"? Doubtless, Torontonians of the period would argue in proper 19th century fashion that they were looking ahead. MTL BDS 1884 Programme

Previous page: Stonemasons pause from their work on the College Street Baptist Church, College at Palmerston, circa 1889. The working-class congregation had previously occupied cramped quarters at College and Lippincott, but the parishioners' frugality and generosity enabled them to build a new and commodious building at the then-considerable cost of $57,000. By the time this photograph was taken, probably in early spring, the rough stonework was largely accomplished; these men were working on the fine finishing. AO S15086

A classic 19th century portrait of the "City of Churches" by F.W. Micklethwaite shows Bond Street looking north from Queen. To the right is the first Metropolitan Methodist Church, erected in 1873 by Henry Langley. Further down the street is William Thomas' St. Michael's Cathedral. The tower of Bond Street Congregational is visible in the distance as is the cupola (at the head of the street) of the Provincial Normal School. AO Acc. 14313-34

Our Lady of Lourdes Roman Catholic Church on Sherbourne Street was photographed circa 1885. Italian Renaissance style influenced the architecture of both Our Lady of Lourdes and St. Paul's on Power Street; the two churches are a refreshing change from the city's preoccupation with Neo-Gothic architecture. AO Acc. 13222-64

New churches were also rising throughout the rapidly growing suburbs, and the rich were displaying their affluence in the size of their mansions just as they had demonstrated their wealth through their opulent business premises. These mansions now spread north up Jarvis and St. George streets, and then joined along Bloor Street in a "Golden Horseshoe." Soon there was no further room on these thoroughfares, and the rich began to advance into Rosedale. A group of residences were also springing up on Queen's Park Crescent surrounding the new Legislature.

A few of the most magnificent of these houses have survived and give something of a flavour of the era: George Gooderham's mansion (now the York Club) at Bloor and St. George streets, the Sir Joseph Flavelle house on Queen's Park (now the University of Toronto Law Faculty), and the Massey mansions on the east side of Jarvis Street just north of Wellesley Street East. While designing the family manor and business office the architect sometimes also received the commission for the family mausoleum. St. James' and Mount Pleasant cemeteries both have some fine examples, especially the latter. It contains the Massey family Richardsonian Romanesque mausoleum with its superimposed angel, which must be one of the highest private tombs on the continent, and the Eaton family Greek temple with its guardian lions, which must be one of the most elegant and dominates a sort of "Royal Crescent" of tombs.

The immigrant slums lurked in many parts of the city, some under the very shadow of the new City Hall. The surviving mansions give us an idea of the age of elegance that they highlighted, but only photography gives us some idea of immigrant living conditions in the last half of the 19th and early 20th centuries. The congestion, filth, and smells of many

Thought by architectural historian Eric Arthur to be Toronto's "most-photographed piece of architecture," University College, eclectic, ambitious, and expensive, was erected by Frederic Cumberland in 1856 in spite of the "assistance" rendered by Governor General Sir Edmund Head. The building was photographed circa 1875. MTL T13086

119

Above: In Toronto of Old, *the Reverend Dr. Scadding wrote: "A depression in the dry sand just beyond the fence which bounds the cemetery of St. James, northward, shews to this day the exact site of Castle Frank. . . . The pedestrian from the town, by a half-hour's easy walk can here place himself in the midst of a forest solitude; and from what he sees he can form an idea of the whole surrounding region, as it was when York was first laid out." In the photograph Dr. Scadding, bearded and bespectacled, locates the leafy retreat. MTL T11506*

Right: For more than 125 years the Denison family's history was—effectively—the history of Toronto. Active for generations in political, social, judicial, intellectual, and military life, they embodied the conservatism that exemplified Old Ontario and its stuffy capital. For the colourful, Imperialistic, and individualistic Denisons, society's solidity was its virtue, not its vice. MTL T10120

of the homes of the unemployed, unskilled, and non-unionized workers are impossible to reconstruct. No wonder Toronto was happy to accept a $45,000 gift from Erastus Wiman of New York, a former Torontonian, to be used for the building of public baths. For all its wealth, social conditions in Toronto had improved very little.

The upper classes by the end of the century were an amalgam of the evolving aristocracy of the city over the past 100 years. Family Compact clans were still to be found—John Beverley Robinson, Jr., was lieutenant-governor of Ontario from 1880 to 1887—but the new groups intermixed and intermarried with the earlier ones, and men like Alexander Manning often possessed greater wealth. The rich entertained themselves in their clubs, with their travels, and through the endless banquets and receptions so characteristic of Victorian life.

On a more cultural level, the city was developing a variety of places of entertainment. The Grand Opera House was visited by most of the greatest actors and actresses, the Toronto Conservatory of Music (now the Royal Conservatory of Music) was founded in 1887 and the Mendelssohn Choir in 1894. In 1892 Vincent Massey, young scion of that wealthy family and much later the first Canadian governor-general and founder of the Canada Council, laid the cornerstone for Massey Hall, one of his family's many benefactions. This replaced the St. Lawrence Hall as the centre of the city's cultural life.

Late Victorian entertainment was often on an amateur level. There were many performances of carefully selected plays and music at the churches, the social centres for many citizens, and there were also literary salons and quiet entertainments at home. The variety of material to read

Allan Gardens and its centrepiece, the Horticultural Pavilion, were given to the city by George William Allan, one-time mayor and longtime president of the city's energetic Horticultural Society. This circa 1880 photograph was taken by James Esson. AO ST108

increased: *Saturday Night* made its appearance in 1887 and *Maclaine's Magazine* in 1896, and other long-term publications, such as the *Canadian Annual Review*, began.

A restructuring of higher education took place with the affiliation of some of the theological colleges with the University of Toronto in 1884 and the development of university federation in 1887. Women began to achieve greater access to education, as well as limited political representation. Victoria College, which soon moved from Cobourg to Toronto and built one of the most magnificent Romanesque structures, was the first college to federate. Higher education for women had already been advanced by Victoria when in 1883 it gave Augusta Greenwood the first degree awarded to a woman in Ontario. The University of Toronto opened its doors to nine women undergraduates in 1884, despite fears that a duenna would be required. The president, the somewhat eccentric but very scholarly Sir Daniel Wilson, expressed his unhappiness that the

Right: William George Storm collaborated with Frederic Cumberland in the design of several Toronto buildings, but the design of Victoria College was entirely Storm's own. The biblical message over the main entrance—"The truth shall make you free"—is given even greater authority by the solid arch and pilasters. The Methodist college became federated with the University of Toronto in 1887 but did not shift from Cobourg into this new building until 1892. AO Acc. 13222-59

Opposite page: Recent commotion about the permitted length of a policeman's moustache would have been considered absurd a century ago. In this 1888 photo the furred outnumbered the clean-shaven six to one. The principal regulation governing facial hair was that a beard should not obscure a police constable's identification number, which was affixed to his collar. The "Britishness" of the officers' bobby-like headgear is lessened by home-grown maple leaf badges. PAC PA42356

governors had done this in haste without consulting him properly. Now he was forced to make provision for two sets of washrooms in the building without warning!

In March 1884 the Ontario government gave women the right to vote in municipal elections, provided they were property owners and were single or widows, thus lacking a man to take on the task for them. In Toronto some 2,000 women were enfranchised. Whether this was a victory for women's rights or for the sanctity of property rights regardless of who owned the property is a moot question.

URBAN GOVERNMENT

The period from 1883 to 1891 witnessed the first expansion of the city's boundaries. By 1880 Toronto had literally burst its bounds and was becoming the centre of a collection of villages. It was difficult to provide services for these areas, many of whose inhabitants came into the city to work but did not contribute to the tax base. The result was a series of annexations totalling 5,231.8 acres; this was a little more than half the original size of the city and liberties combined. The population of Toronto rose from 81,372 in 1882 to 181,215 in 1891.

The new wards created were also given saints' names so that Toronto now had 13 wards named after saints. This was too much for even the "City of Churches." Most of the names were confusing as they had no relevance to the longstanding area designations—such as Yorkville, High Park, or Parkdale. To resolve the problem, the entire system was revamped in 1891 by provincial statute and the named wards were replaced by six numbered ones. These were all carefully designed as strips running from the lake to the northern boundary to ensure that the poorer voters in the older lakeside areas would be outvoted by the more conservative areas to the north. Under the new setup each of the six wards had four aldermen, a total of 24 compared to 39 under the earlier system. The Board of Control was set up as an executive committee in 1897 and became elective in 1904.

The whole reorganization made little difference in municipal politics, nor did municipal services greatly improve. The council was kept more than busy with just the day-to-day management of the progressively more complex city. Some new private institutions appeared, such as the Humane Society, which was founded in 1887 for both children and animals, and the Children's Aid Society, which separated from it in 1891. Grace Hospital, run by the Salavation Army, opened in 1888 as a dispensary for the poor and operated for an hour a day. Soon it was accepting resident patients. Health inspection improved in 1890 when a city bylaw provided for the appointment of as many sanitary inspectors as were needed. Electricity became available in 1884 through the Toronto Electric Light Company, but it took years to change the street lighting from gas to electricity.

The water supply presented a major problem as the harbour became ever more dangerous and contaminated with sewage. The water pipes, which were still made of wood, ran through the harbour to the cleaner water beyond the Island. After much searching for a better method, the city ran a five-inch steel pipe out to the lake, but it tended to rise to the surface and develop leaks. Not surprisingly there were serious typhoid epidemics, in 1891 and 1895. Finally the council adopted the suggestion of its city engineer and ran a tunnel under the harbour and Island into the lake. It also set up better pumps and reservoirs. But the water still was

Right: Patients at Toronto's Hospital for Sick Children were taken to the Lakeside Home for Little Children on Toronto Island during the summer. The Lakeside Home was built in 1883 and enlarged in 1891, entirely through the generosity of John Ross Robertson, publisher and proprietor of The Evening Telegram. *Resting on one of the breezy verandas are two look-alikes with what appear to be two look-alike broken legs. PAC C90992*

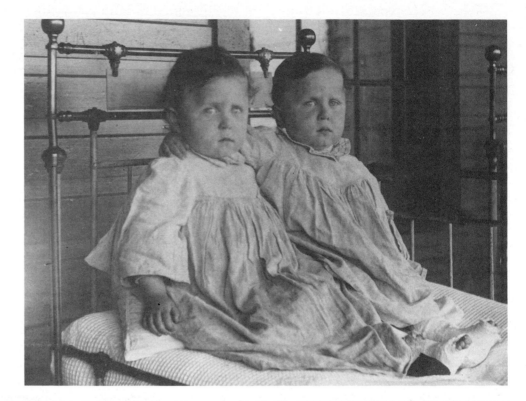

SPRING VALLEY,
ON THE BELT LINE RAILWAY.

Left: The idea of the Belt Line Railway grew out of the inefficient and ineffective nature of street railways in 1880s Toronto. A steam railway was promoted to run up the Don River Valley, turn west north of Mount Pleasant Cemetery, proceed through Forest Hill, and loop south down the Humber River Valley to the lakeshore, where it would link up with the main line Grand Trunk Railway. After much haggling and a great deal of property speculation, the line was finally opened under the auspices of the Grand Trunk in 1892. It proved a collosal failure and was abandoned two years later. This idyllic drawing is from a promotional booklet advertising the railway. AO Acc. 14578-la

not really pure, and bottled spring water remained popular. Chlorination finally began in 1910.

Transportation was a controversial matter. When the 30-year franchise of the street railway company expired in 1891, the city took over the services for about $1.5 million, only to find that the public was opposed to the payment. After four months a new 30-year franchise was granted to the Toronto Railway Company headed by William (later Sir William) Mackenzie and his partners, who bought out the city at the same price and agreed to make an annual payment of $800,000. Almost immediately several improvements took place: transfers came into use, stoves were installed in the cars, and night runs were permitted. In 1892-1894 the horses were replaced by electrification. The problem of no Sunday service remained; the prohibition was upheld by a plebiscite in 1892 but finally was defeated in 1897, much to the horror of the Sabbatarian lobby. The new charter of the street railway unfortunately prevented the company from operating streetcars outside the 1891 city limits, and, as a result, a bewildering maze of suburban lines grew up over the next 30 years. Still, the overall service was a great improvement.

THE ECONOMIC PICTURE

The economic situation in Toronto was largely dominated by the long depression, which only lifted in 1896 but did not limit Toronto's expansion into new markets. There was an increasing interest in the possibilities of Ontario's new territory to the north and northwest, and in the early 1880s Manitoba became the scene of one of the greatest land booms of the century, with Toronto speculators and speculative com-

Opposite page, bottom: The Model School was attached to the Normal School on what is now the Ryerson site. In this carefully posed photograph, mothers (seated), student teachers (standing), and Queen Victoria (on the wall) observe learning through play. The severe, no-nonsense quality of the photo is relieved by the occasional smirk and the fantastic toy castle on the table to the left. AO S17889

Above: Young men had been employed in the running of early telephone exchanges, but by 1888 Bell decided to hire young ladies instead. Women, the company argued, worked harder and longer and—unlike the men—did not "talk back" to irate or frustrated customers. This photograph shows Bell's main office in 1907. Note that the supervisors are women as well. CTA William James Collection (James) 138

Opposite page: Torontonians were photographed while they—in a burst of British pride—celebrated the fall of Pretoria on June 5, 1900. AO S1244

panies in the fore. As is usual, the boom came to a sharp end and many Toronto fortunes were considerably diminished.

The completion of the Intercolonial Railway to the Maritimes in 1876 and the Canadian Pacific Railway to Vancouver in 1885 opened up the prospect of ocean-to-ocean expansion for Toronto commerce. One of the most successful in this expansion was Timothy Eaton, whose mail-order catalogs were soon to be found across the nation. Some Torontonians went west to make their wealth and often to represent Ontario firms. Two Toronto-born youths who left for Winnipeg are excellent examples. Sir Augustus Nanton started in the brokerage business, became one of Canada's leading financiers, and shortly before his death in 1925 returned home as president of the Dominion Bank. George William Allan the younger, grandson of William, became a Winnipeg lawyer who, before his death in 1940, was chairman of the Canadian Committee of the Hudson's Bay Company, president of the Great-West Life Assurance Company, and director of almost countless corporations. "Go west, young man, but keep your Toronto ties," could be sound advice.

In Toronto itself the depression hurt the banking system, causing some mergers and forcing at least one bank to wind up its affairs with no loss to depositors and one spectacular failure. However, the majority of banks continued their expansion, and the Canadian Bankers' Association of today dates back to an 1887 committee of the Toronto Board of Trade. In 1900 the Bank of Nova Scotia decided to move its executive offices westward, bypassed Montreal, and opened in Toronto.

In the insurance field the Western group, under the firm leadership of Senator George A. Cox, expanded its operations to Europe, the Far East, India, and, after the turn of the century, to South Africa and Australia. Toronto's corporations were moving into the world stage. In life insurance new companies were being formed. The Conservatives founded the Manufacturers' Life Insurance Company in 1887, which elected as its first president a reliable gentleman of sound Tory principles: Sir John A. Macdonald. Not to be outdone, the Liberals under the leadership of Cox founded their own company, the Imperial Life Assurance Company, in 1897 and elected former Ontario Liberal Premier Sir Oliver Mowat as its first president. A Temperance and General Life Assurance Company also was established. Other branches of business also prospered. Eaton's and Simpson's continued their expansion, and one of Toronto's greatest publishing firms appeared in 1899 when the striking printers of the *News* united with Joseph E. Atkinson to found the *Star*.

Labour had a difficult course with the depression and inflation problems. The Canadian Labour Congress was founded in Toronto in 1883, and in 1886 the Royal Commission on Labour was appointed. Its subsequent report demonstrated poor working conditions and other problems that workers faced. Exacerbating these difficulties was, ironically, the return of good times, for inflation began creeping up. Although the price of coal at $4.50 a ton may appear ridiculously low, labourers earned only

$8 to $10 per week and semi-skilled workers about $12, so comparatively the price was high. Renting a house cost about $15 per month. Not surprisingly, there were some bad strikes.

The century ended with another rally to the colours as Toronto's troops marched off to the not-so-quickly settled Boer War, happily singing "The Girl I Left Behind Me" as they embarked. The war took more lives than had been anticipated. The citation for Victoria Cross recipient Lieutenant Hampden Z. Churchill of Toronto noted that he had held off the Boers to save some guns and went on to state that "to do so he had to sacrifice himself and all his party, all of whom were killed, wounded or taken prisoners, he himself being slightly wounded." Imperial victories were becoming very costly for all concerned.

CHAPTER XI

EDWARDIAN TIMES AND MODERN TECHNOLOGY

1901-1914

The Toronto seen by the troops returning from the Boer War, or by the Duke and Duchess of York, the future King George V and Queen Mary, who visited in October 1901, was a booming centre. The little settlement in the wilderness of a century before had grown to a city of 208,040, not far behind the 267,730 population of Montreal. Under the impact of technology, Toronto's prosperity was soon to undergo further development. Central heating systems and hot water for houses had long been known but were now common, as was indoor plumbing. The automobile had made its debut, but really began to gain in popularity during the first decade of the new century. Electricity, already used for transportation and street lighting, began to improve living standards with such devices as electric clothes washers, sewing machines, and vacuum cleaners. High-rise development changed the face of the city, and strict regulations governing building standards were enacted after the Second Great Fire.

New community leaders were emerging. A second generation of Toronto's old families was dying out, and the immigrant generation who had joined them in the middle and late century were also passing away. George William Allan and Alexander Manning both died in 1901. But new entrepreneurs had been making their way forward and moving into dominant places in Toronto's affairs. The most colourful was certainly Sir Henry Pellatt, who in his castle and stables has left Toronto one of its most exotic legacies. Son of an English immigrant baker and stockbroker, he was born in Toronto in 1859 and followed his father's careers, as well as becoming extremely active in the militia. Pellatt took an immediate

interest in electricity and was one of the founders of the Toronto Electric Light Company, which planned the development of an Ontario power monopoly.

He soon became noted for the flamboyancy of his personal life and the shadiness of some of his financial deals. In 1902 he took the bugle band of the Queen's Own Rifles to England at his own expense for Edward VII's coronation. Later he took the entire 620-man regiment to attend manoeuvres at Aldershot in 1910. Around the same time, Pellat was building the stables of Casa Loma, the house on the hill that stands just to the west of Spadina, the old Baldwin residence. In the stables with their fantastic towers and gables, Pellatt's horses were better housed than most of the poor in Toronto.

Meanwhile, Pellatt's financial operations were not doing well. The idea of a Toronto-based hydro monopoly fell victim to Ontario Hydro's low rates, Casa Loma proved an unmanageable expense, and the Home Bank, with which Pellatt was closely associated, went bankrupt under suspicious circumstances. In the early 1920s Sir Henry was forced to leave his castle and declare bankruptcy; he died in relative obscurity in 1939. The castle, one of Toronto's greatest tourist attractions, is his memorial and one of the most remarkable extravaganzas of the wealthy built in North America.

Previous page: Bill and Joe, sons of photographer William James and photography enthusiasts themselves, are pictured in 1912 off on a picture-taking foray. CTA James 3501

130

Sir Edmund Walker (1848-1924) pursued a much less spectacular, but infinitely more successful, career. Born in southwestern Ontario, he joined the Bank of Commerce, working up to general manager in 1886 and president from 1907 to his death, as well as becoming a widely published authority on banking and finance. He was also a man of wide scientific and cultural interests. The list of institutions of which he was a founder, organizer, or benefactor is very long and includes the National Art Gallery in Ottawa, the Champlain Society, and such Toronto institutions as the University of Toronto, the Royal Ontario Museum, and the Gallery of Ontario. Walker lacks a personal memorial: Longarth, his fine residence on St. George Street, was demolished by the University of Toronto for a parking lot; but the central court of the Art Gallery of Ontario was named in his honour.

ECONOMIC DEVELOPMENT
In the period from the turn of the century to the beginning of World War I, Toronto achieved complete connections with both its remote markets across Canada and its more immediate hinterland. The rapid development of the west spurred the development of new railways, and Toronto made sure that these lines were joined with its system. The first of the two new ventures, the Grand Trunk Pacific, was a Montreal enterprise built between 1903 and 1915 to extend the Grand Trunk across northern Ontario to the prairies and Prince Rupert, British Columbia. The second new transcontinental line, the Canadian Northern, was a cross-continent railway in which Toronto, for the first time, had major financial and administrative interests. A third railway was the

Opposite page: The 1901 Toronto visit of their Royal Highnesses, the Duke and Duchess of Cornwall and York, epitomized the British link— with all its pomp and splendour. The Duke, second son of Edward VII (and within 10 years his successor), stands at the right with his wife, the future Queen Mary. Properly plumed on the left is the Earl of Minto, later governor-general, and in the centre of the photo on the top step sits the bespectacled Sir Oliver Mowat, former Premier of Ontario and federal cabinet minister, and at the time of the visit lieutenant-governor of the loyal province of Ontario. MTL T13215

Below: In 1911 the city still depended upon the horse for its myriad duties associated with public works. CTA DPW 55-17

Flamboyant Sir Henry Pellatt was dressed simultaneously in the uniforms of Colonel of the Queen's Own Rifles and Chief Tawyaunansara of the Mohawks when he was photographed in 1910. Sir Henry's building of turreted Casa Loma did not do him in financially, although it helped. Rather, a series of sticky and shady deals—especially involving the Home Bank— secured his collapse. In 1939 Pellatt died almost penniless in Mimico, far from his castle on the hill. CTA James 4012

Temiskaming & Northern Ontario, now the Ontario Northland, built by the Ontario government to open its northern hinterland and make connections with both the new transcontinental railways and the opening mining areas of northern Ontario and Quebec. Completed to Cochrane in 1907 and Rouyen, Quebec, in 1911, it was extended to James Bay in 1932. It played a great role in capturing northern Ontario and the mining industry for Toronto.

Hinterland connections in Toronto's immediate area were greatly facilitated by the intercity electric railways, or radials as they were popularly called, which were really long-distance streetcar lines. They provided an efficient means of communication, but fell victim to the motor car's convenience before many years were out. In a way they were the ancestors of the GO Trains of today. Most important for Toronto was the extension of the line up Yonge Street to Richmond Hill in 1896 and then gradually beyond to Lake Simcoe in 1907. There was also a Guelph line to the northwest by 1917. Finally Toronto's recreation facilities were expanded by the building of Niagara Peninsula lines that connected with the Toronto boats and ran from St. Catharines through to Niagara Falls and Lake Erie.

The mining boom in silver and gold, the long-term evolution of the copper-nickel industry, and the development of the forest products industry all opened new prospects for Toronto and the Toronto stock market. The popularity of less-conservative penny stocks had led to rival exchanges which merged as the Standard Stock and Mining Exchange in 1899; but the Toronto Stock Exchange itself was rapidly becoming more influential. By 1907 its quotations were cabled to London, England, the centre of world finance, and published regularly in that city. The Toronto Stock Exchange also moved to more spacious quarters on Bay Street in 1912.

The opening of the century saw outside corporations take over some Toronto banks, but at the same time the major Toronto banks themselves were taking over several long-established Canadian institutions based in other provinces. Between 1900 and 1912 Sir Edmund Walker's Bank of Commerce absorbed the Bank of British Columbia, the Halifax Banking Company, the Merchant's Bank of Prince Edward Island, and the Eastern Townships Bank in Quebec. These had all been established between 1825 and 1871 and had a long history of successful development as well as important branch systems.

EDWARDIAN REDIRECTIONS

By 1900 Toronto was again ready to burst its boundaries, mainly because of a large immigration from the British Isles. The years 1905 to 1914 saw a second wave of annexations as a result of the population increase, which expanded the city from 17 to 35 square miles, virtually the same limits as the city proper of today. Many of the new additions, such as North Rosedale, Deer Park, and Moore Park, had developed as the result of northward growth, but there were also annexations in other directions, such as West Toronto and Dovercourt. By far the largest area taken over

Toronto's old Union Station—the train shed and Victorian cupolas visible to the left—was erected in 1871-1873 by Grand Trunk Chief Engineer E.P. Hannaford on the south side of Station Street west of York. The building, which was expanded in the 1890s, was crammed to capacity by the turn of the century. After the Great Fire of 1904 plans were made for a new station, which eventually opened in 1927. Two years later the old monument came down. CTA James 99

One-and-a-half million immigrants poured into Canada between 1901 and 1911. Much of the flow was from Southern and Eastern Europe, but Britons still flocked to the colonies, many intending to take up land in the Canadian West. Many got no further than Toronto and Montreal. William James photographed the newly arrived Kentish railwayman George Cane and his sons Herbert, Sydney, Frank, and Arthur near Union Station. CTA 107

was North Toronto in 1912. These extensions resulted in the creation of three more wards in the city.

The structure of the city was also changed, but in a very different manner, by the Second Great Fire in 1904. It was perhaps inevitable that another major conflagration would occur. Toronto's building code was inadequate for the new larger buildings and industrial hazards. Also, the city had not remotely kept up to date with the adoption of new fire-fighting devices, such as automatic sprinklers or a high-pressure water system. Despite three major fires in 1895, all of which involved several buildings, no new precautions were taken.

The actual outbreak of the fire came on April 19 in a neckware manufactory in the heart of the warehousing district on Wellington Street West. The building, of the type that has correctly been called a "conflagration breeder," was entirely ablaze from cellar to roof very quickly. Then everything went wrong: there was inadequate water pressure; there were not enough hydrants where the fire began; and the fire chief was injured while escaping from a building he never should have entered. Soon the flames were completely out of control, spreading from warehouse to warehouse, and a general alarm was sounded. The mayor telegraphed the neighbouring cities for aid, and the rail lines quickly cleared the way for special trains bearing fire fighters and equipment from Buffalo, Hamilton, London, Niagara Falls, and Peterborough.

*Opposite page: The Great
Toronto Fire of 1904 began in
the Currie building on the north
side of Wellington Street West;
by the time it was extinguished
it had wreaked more than $10
million worth of damage on the
city. Although 6,000 people
were left jobless in its wake,
miraculously the fire killed no
one. Through the ruins of
buildings pictured on the north
side of Front Street West one can
see the water towers atop the
Kilgour Brothers building,
whose sprinklers worked
effectively during the
conflagration. MTL T13278*

*Left: North of Wellington on the
southeast corner of Bay and
Melinda stood the Evening
Telegram building, left. The
burnt-out structure to its right is
the Office Specialty Company.
The Telegram, in a tradition of
"on the spot" news coverage,
posted this sign: "The Evening
Telegram is carrying on
Business as Usual. Read Special
Fire Edition." MTL T13263*

In the end the fire was stopped by a combination of the outside help, some fortunate fire breaks, partly thanks to the few sprinklered buildings in the downtown area, and the wind blowing the flames toward the lake. The blaze destroyed between 98 and 104 buildings covering 19.7 acres and containing 220 firms that employed 5,000 to 6,000 people. The loss was estimated at $10.35 million, of which about $8.3 million was covered by insurance. Much of the heart of the business district had been wiped out, but fortunately no dwellings or major public buildings had been destroyed.

Toronto was lucky that the fire occurred at a time of prosperity; there was a rush to rebuild. The Toronto Board of Fire Underwriters took immediate action to make sure the city was not rebuilt without proper building codes. The basic fire rate per $100 insurance was increased by one dollar in the downtown area. Even the City Council acted quickly, setting up a special committee to amend the building bylaw, with the result that new legislation was on the statute books by June. Further, a high-pressure system went into operation in 1909. By that time a great deal of the destroyed district was rebuilt. Like the First Great Fire in 1849 the Second Great Fire in 1904 gave the city a fine legacy: virtually the last structures to be rebuilt were the present Union Station in 1915-1927 and the new Customs House of 1930, which stands just to the east of it. They form one of the most impressive combinations in the downtown city.

Opposite page, top: There were 44 new car dealers in Toronto in 1913. Used car dealers would soon proliferate as would—as this photo suggests—repair shops and wrecking yards. CTA James 61

Opposite page, bottom and far right: Any sort of transportation could be difficult on the muddy Toronto streets of around 1909. It is little wonder that home delivery disappeared under these circumstances. CTA James 31, 21B

Toronto now was growing rapidly skyward using the newly available building technology. The Richardsonian Romanesque style had developed a more massive building, but it was the use of structural steel, coupled with the development of reasonably high-speed elevators, that made real high-rise construction possible.

While the Wellington-Front Street area was rising again after the fire, a group of four 13-to-20-storey buildings, which still stand thanks to a shift of the financial district westward, was erected at the intersection of King and Yonge streets using the new structural steel frame method: the Dominion Bank, the Royal Bank, the Trader's Bank, and the Canadian Pacific Railway offices. The significance of the buildings was more than technological or stylistic. As in other growing North American cities, new problems of density, adequate services, and even a lack of sunlight on the streets faced the city administration.

Another problem appeared with increased use of the automobile. At first cars were a sign of wealth, beyond most budgets. Even as inexpensive a car as the 1907 Ford, which could be purchased for $750, represented an outlay that few could afford. But soon the number of cars grew, and the old traffic laws had to be extended to include motor-driven vehicles. In 1912 a federal statute set the maximum speed limit at 15 miles an hour. Earlier, auto agents like the Hyslop brothers were advertising makes like Oldsmobile and Cadillac in the papers.

A wide variety of local car manufactories appeared in most municipalities as many bicycle and carriage factories began to manufacture autos. In 1907 the Canada Cycle and Motor Company at Toronto Junction was producing the Russell for sale. Their cars ranged from 18 to 40 horsepower and cost from $1,000 to $3,750, the latter for the seven-passenger special. It was soon apparent that road surfaces adequate for horses and

Although the automobile was slowly replacing the horse, in this photo the substitution seems rather unsuccessful. Pictured is an "autopolo" match at the CNE grandstand. CTA James 212

Right: Illuminating Toronto required much man- and horsepower. Here over 20 linemen labour to sink one of the 60-foot power poles on Mutual Street in July 1910. AO S17362

Right: Illuminating Toronto required much man- and horsepower. Here over 20 linemen labour to sink one of the 60-foot power poles on Mutual Street in July 1910. AO S17362

Opposite page: The staff at the City Works Department head office posed in 1898. By the turn of the century some women had obtained white-collar positions as clerks in various city departments. The proportion pictured is representative: one woman to six men. CTA 9.2.3G 669

carts were not satisfactory for cars. Asphalt was used more frequently for street paving, but there were still many macadamized roads and slippery cedar-block pavements.

PROBLEMS AND SERVICES

With city growth in the late 19th century came an increasing demand that action be taken to improve the quality of life in urban areas through "beautification." The result was the City Beautiful movement, which in Toronto led to the formation of the Guild of Civic Art in 1897 whose objective was to improve the city both functionally and ornamentally. By 1909 this 400-member group had put out a report that pinpointed some of the problems and made suggestions for planning. However, in spite of city involvement with the issues, improvements were haphazard until the 1940s.

One suggestion that was quickly taken up by Horatio C. Hocken, who became mayor in 1912, was the construction of a subway system. Hocken was a Conservative (the party later made him a senator), Methodist, and the proprietor of the Orange *Sentinel*. The *Canadian Courier* uncharitably described him as "one of the most pugnaciously aggressive men that ever lived." Even he gave up, however, when the voters turned the idea down twice because of the costs. But the attempt left its legacy, for, when the Prince Edward Viaduct was built linking Bloor Street East to the Danforth, the engineers provided for a subway deck under the road level. Nearly half a century later this saved the taxpayers considerable expense.

138

The harbour was a major problem during this era because of the increased volume and size of shipping. By 1901 there were 39 wharves, but these were none too adequate. In 1911 the Board of Harbour Commissioners was incorporated to make recommendations and oversee development, and new plans were drawn up for improved waterways, additional land reclamation, industrial expansion, and the setting aside of some 900 acres of the harbour shores for parks and recreation. Most of this land was to be on the Islands.

Housing was a continuing problem given the number of poor immigrants and the chronic shortage of units. Since landlords could get tenants without cleaning up their properties, wretched conditions existed, and an increasing number of houses were being bought up by speculators while a decreasing number were occupied by owners.

Crowding, unsanitary conditions, rats, and wells for water were all too familiar. Some of the worst streets were to be found just north of Osgoode Hall and east of it almost in the shadow of the City Hall. Shantytowns consisting of shacks covered with tar and paper were built in several outlying areas of the city, much like the slums that rise around some Latin American cities today. One of the largest stretched west from Poplar Plains Road between Davenport Road and St. Clair Avenue West. To clean these up, the Toronto Housing Authority was created in 1913 with the objective of building and operating cottage flats for the poor at reasonable rents.

The prosperity of the early years of the century had its effect on the cultural and entertainment life of the city. The fair was reconstituted as the Canadian National Exhibition in 1904, and three years later a new,

A photograph of the Toronto skyline from just before the outbreak of the First World War shows that the Edwardian period was scarcely a golden age as far as pollution was concerned. The fetid air was complemented by brackish water. CTA James 592

Right: Toronto summers could be stiflingly hot, especially in the cramped quarters of "the ward." Here, about 1910, a family literally takes to the streets to escape the heat. CTA James 1033

Below: This child welfare clinic, held in September 1914 at St. Christopher's House, was one of many such educational sessions developed to combat Toronto's high rates of infant mortality. Women put on their "Sunday Best" for these visits with physicians and public health nurses. CTA DPW 32-334

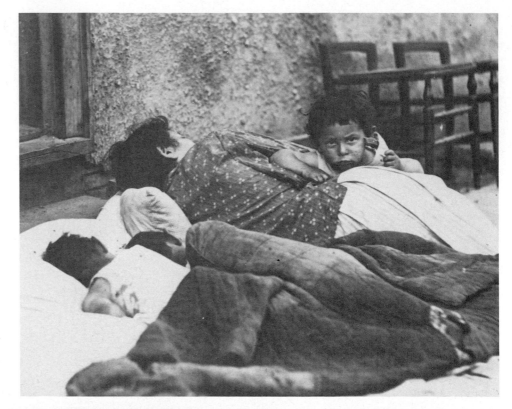

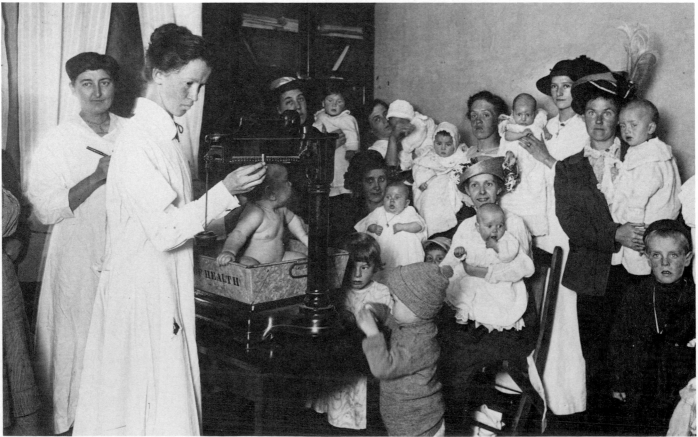

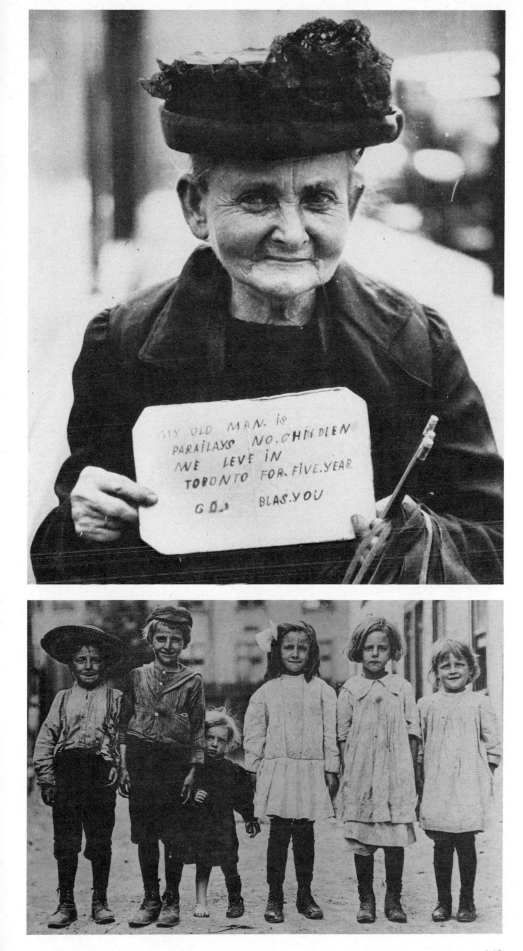

Left: The poignant sign held by this pencil seller in an Edwardian Toronto street reminds us that in an age without government pensions and health care, having no children meant having no support when one grew old. CTA James 676

Below left and below: John Joseph Kelso, Ontario's first Superintendent of Neglected and Dependent Children, did much to document and relieve the appalling conditions shown in this pair of photos from the Public Archives' Kelso collection. His monument is Ontario's child welfare system. Unlike so many of his day, Kelso understood that it was not enough to treat individuals, that social conditions themselves had to be changed. PAC C4244, PA118220

Right: The end of an era came in 1912 with the demolition of old Government House at King and Simcoe streets. The vice-regal residence's drawing room was photographed just before the building came down.
PAC PA29991

Below: Mr. and Mrs. Goldwin Smith bequeathed the Grange to the City of Toronto to be used as an art museum. The first complete section of the galleries opened to the public—eight years after Goldwin Smith's 1910 death—on April 4, 1918, as war still raged in Europe. Notable among this gathering of artists is a natty Wyly Grier seated third from the right.
MTL T13175

larger stadium was built to seat 15,000. The Royal Alexandra Theatre also opened its doors in 1907, and, thanks to the generosity of Andrew Carnegie, the citizens acquired a public reference library. The Toronto Symphony Orchestra was founded in 1908 with 70-80 professional players and Frank Welsman as conductor. A 1905-1906 commission chaired by Sir Joseph Flavelle and including Sir Edmund Walker restructured the University of Toronto, making it independent of the government, and several new buildings were added partly by Massey funding. The new Toronto General Hospital was ready in 1913, and, after many years of planning by its first director, Dr. Charles T. Currelly, the Royal Ontario Museum was opened in 1915. While these plans were being made, Sir Edmund Walker persuaded Harriette Elizabeth Smith, widow of Mayor William Henry Boulton and wife of Professor Goldwin Smith, to will the Grange to the city along with six acres of land as a municipal art gallery; the Art Gallery of Ontario dates its beginnings from when the will came into force in 1910. The city now also had a small zoo in Riverdale Park and a properly organized playground system.

As World War I loomed, Toronto had achieved maturity, greatly developed its institutions, and extended its communications and its market on a nationwide basis. It had also moved well ahead on the route to becoming English Canada's cultural capital.

Internationally renowned philanthropist Andrew Carnegie arrives to an official welcome at City Hall in April 1906. Five years before, because its monetary situation was so bleak, the Library Board was forced to sue the city for funds. It was Carnegie's 1903 grant of $350,000 that saved the system. Later it was through Carnegie's help that the new library at College and St. George opened in 1909. Tax reforms eventually rescued the libraries.
MTL T13181

Left: J.W. Gorman's trained "diving horses" regularly exhibited their peculiar talents at the amusement park at Hanlan's Point. This performance took place in 1908. CTA James 192

Opposite page, top: One of Toronto's scenic wonders is Scarborough Bluffs, photographed about 1909. One wonders, as well, how the cloned pair made their way to the pinnacle. CTA James 1537

Opposite: Torontonians enjoyed spending a day at the Toronto Islands. In this 1910 photograph two young mothers pose seated atop driftwood logs while the rest of their party look on. CTA James 688

CHAPTER XII

FROM ONE GREAT WAR TO ANOTHER

1914-1945

By 1914 the world had passed through so many serious crises that the Serbian nationalist's assassination of the Archduke Franz Ferdinand, the heir to the Austrian throne, did not seem particularly dangerous, especially since the crisis evolved slowly. The exhibition and post office authorities, planning the special cancellation banner for the 1914 Canadian National Exhibition, chose the theme of 100 years of peace. Possibly, like the belligerent powers, they thought the war would be a short, sharp conflict lasting only a month or so. Unfortunately the estimate proved to be sadly wrong.

When a *Globe* bulletin at 7 p.m., August 4, announced the war, the citizens cheered for King, Britain, and Victory, and sang the national anthem and "Britannia Rules the Waves." To many the war may have seemed to promise relief from the severe depressions of the last few years: as in the Boer War, volunteers quickly poured into the University Avenue armouries to get into the action. By the end of August volunteers were on their way to the training camp at Valcartier, Quebec, or temporary camps hurriedly installed under canvas at such places as Oshawa. The 1914 exhibition over, the exhibition buildings became a winter training centre. All the old Toronto regiments were there, such as the Queen's Own Rangers, the Royal Grenadiers, and the 48th Highlanders, ready to be sent in the first Canadian contingent. Others followed as large numbers continued to join the army. During the war Toronto provided the strength for three divisions. Women, too, were active, many volunteering for nursing duty and others preparing supplies and bandages for the Red Cross.

Previous page and below right: Torontonians flocked to the colours from the outset of the First World War, and eventually some 70,000 served. Recruiting drives became commonplace. A 1916 photograph of a rally outside City Hall (leaning on the car wearing a straw hat is Mayor Tommy Church) is typical. However, volunteers were needed for more than fighting. The Number One Construction Battalion scoured the streets for recruits going "To Berlin." The Berlin indicated was certainly not Berlin, Ontario; when war broke out, the citizens of that community voted to change the name of their city to Kitchener. CTA James 721, 730

Opposite page, top left: A plane swoops low over University College, whose playing fields are jammed with the tents of Royal Flying Corps cadets. CTA James 752

Opposite page, top right: Photographer William James identified his 1916 photograph of a man—probably too old to be fed to the cannons—making his way down a snowy Toronto street as "Rag Picker." CTA James 616

Opposite page, bottom: Canada had been at war for exactly two weeks when the Toronto Women's Patriotic League formed on August 18, 1914. The women viewed the provision of "soldiers' comforts" as an important part of their job: the volunteers in this photograph—taken in 1917 at the University of Toronto's Physics Building—are rolling cigarettes for men at the front. CTA James 873A

Manufacturing saw the war as a solution to the economic problems, and labour hoped for employment. Early in the conflict Prime Minister Robert Laird Borden began pushing the British and French governments for munitions contracts. Sir Joseph Flavelle, one of Toronto's leading business figures, became chairman of the Imperial Munitions Board, and by 1915 munitions manufacturing had begun in the city. One particularly active company was the American Curtiss aeroplane manufactory, whose training school prepared 54 men for the Royal Flying Corps and the Royal Naval Air Service. A Curtiss seaplane base was established at Hanlan's Point on the Toronto Islands. In 1917 Curtiss' Toronto plant was taken over by the Imperial Munitions Board and became Canadian Aeroplanes Limited. Working on a 24-hour basis, the plant turned out 2,900 aircraft for the Empire and the United States during the war years.

There were immediate efforts, both public and private, to raise funds to aid the soldiers overseas and their dependents, as well as those who returned sick or wounded. The Canadian Patriotic Fund received subscriptions of more than $7.6 million. The City Council paid $1,000 to the family of each Toronto soldier killed in the war. Some employers in the city continued their workers' salaries in full or in part while they were in service. Such assistance was badly needed because of the wartime increase in the cost of living. By 1918 only 36 percent of single-family homes were occupied by their owners, and doubling or tripling of families became common to meet the rents.

The city's mayor, Thomas L. Church, who won the record number of seven elections beginning in 1915, was the perfect wartime leader for Toronto: the city, the Empire, and the Argonaut football team were the things closest to his heart. Something of a colourful dresser, in summer he always wore a straw boater hat at a jaunty angle. He was partially deaf, but this could be a convenience, particularly when he was being interrupted. Church had that perfect talent for a politician: an uncanny memory for names and faces. It was said that he knew every soldier from Toronto on sight, and he saw virtually every one of them, for he was always present to greet both the departing and arriving troops. While they were away he did his best to give their families his personal attention, often being the first to call at a bereaved home to offer help.

Then in November 1918 Germany collapsed. In Toronto peace came to the accompaniment of steam whistles and the ticker tape that Church ordered to celebrate the victory. A year later, in August 1919, the Prince of Wales arrived in Toronto, making a 20-mile drive through the city to the cheering of thousands. It took a few years longer for an appropriate war memorial to be erected in front of the City Hall. The Cenotaph, a copy of the one in London, England, was finally ready in 1925 and was officially dedicated by Field Marshall Earl Haig. Yet for all the disruption of war, Toronto in many ways was still very much the same city. Prohibition, enacted by Ontario in 1916, did not fare well, but the Puritan Sunday continued to flourish. Basically the city was still a sprawling, comfortable village.

POLITICS AND SERVICES
City Council politics continued along much the same path in the postwar period, with the Orange Order's place behind the government remaining powerful. City services were particularly marked by changes in transportation and communications. The most noteworthy development was the final transfer of the street railways to the city in 1921 and the establishment of the Toronto Transportation Commission, now the Toronto

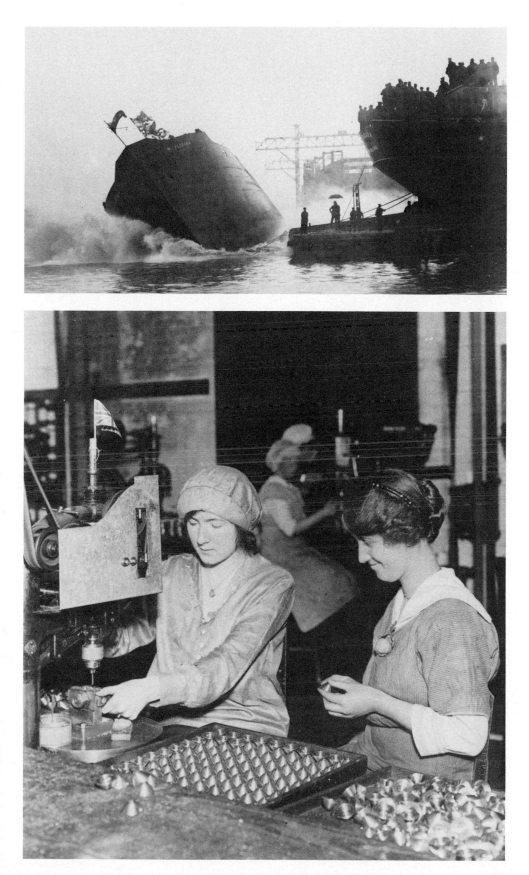

During the war there were a number of ways that Torontonians "kept the home fires burning."

Opposite page, top: Fund raisers—like the apron sale pictured—were held, with profits going to the war coffers. CTA James 872

Opposite page, left: This Toronto munitions factory produced shells for the gluttonous Western Front. It was photographed probably early in the war, since the workers are still all men. CTA James 850

This page, top: The S.S. Floraba was launched on a rainy day from the lists at the Dominion Shipbuilding works on the lakeshore at the foot of Spadina. CTA James 864

This page, left: By the time this photograph was taken in 1917, it was common for factories to be staffed almost entirely by women. Here workers are pictured threading screw holes in the manufacture of fuses for shells at the Russell Motor Car Company. PAC PA24639

The war to end all wars itself ended on November 11, 1918, and, as these photos show, Torontonians joined allies around the world in victory celebrations. In an Armistice Day parade a tank gratified Queen's Park spectators by crushing a car (opposite page, top left), and on King Street the crowds went wild with ticker-tape and talcum powder (opposite page, bottom). If people had been "war mad," wrote one Toronto reporter, they now became "peace mad." Weeks and months later the soldiers came home (right), some to decorated houses like this one on Markham Street (opposite page, top right). Some, of course, did not come home at all: of the 70,000 that Toronto had sent to war, 10,000 would not be seen again. CTA James 733, AO S15118, PAC PA 7481, MTL 981-28

Right: Water is as important to the functioning of a city as is blood to the human body. In the late 19th century Torontonians bought bottled water to avoid using the putrid stuff that was pumped from Toronto Bay—at one and the same time source and sewer. Eventually huge pipelines reached further and further out into Lake Ontario. A pipe and reservoir, part of that system, were photographed in 1922. CTA Toronto Water Works 1002

Below: The demise of the horse seems imminent in this 1928 photograph. Actually, horse-drawn wagons delivering bread and milk were a common sight in the Toronto vicinity until well after the end of the Second World War. CTA DPW 32-817

Opposite page: A number of elements make this photograph of a gas station near the corner of Gerrard and Yonge streets a little jarring for the modern viewer. Of course the prices, 10 cents a gallon for gasoline and 10-15 cents a quart for motor oil, are ridiculously cheap. More distressing is that the service station is just another in a row of shops: thus customers stopping at curbside for gasoline must have caused traffic chaos. Moreover where was the station's gasoline reservoir located? Doubtless it was below the public sidewalk and/or the street. Modern regulations require that these functions be kept well away from public areas. CTA DPW 1-1442

156

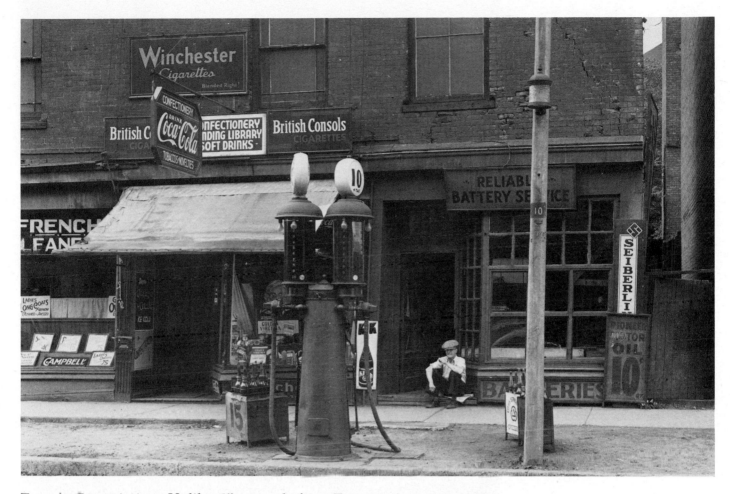

Transit Commission. Unlike 30 years before, Torontonians were more than ready to run their own streetcars. After a plebiscite an act of the Legislature immediately set up a three-man operating commission. In what now seems a strange anomoly, the TTC continued to pay taxes to the city, although it was fully publicly owned.

A consolidation and modernization program was immediately begun and before the year was out 575 new steel streetcars were added, which could still be seen as late as 1963. Double-decker, solid-tire buses were tried out as a supplement with much less success. In 1923 it became possible to use a single ticket on the whole system. The Island ferries were also placed under the TTC administration in 1927, and in the same year the Gray Coach bus line was incorporated as a wholly-owned subsidiary and the still-surviving Bay Street Bus Terminal was built.

For a suburban bus system to operate, the roads had to be improved, and highway commissions to build better roads to York County and Hamilton were set up with the city and province sharing the cost. A concrete road, narrow but still a great improvement, was built to Hamilton, a beginning of the Ontario highway network of today. With more than 10,000 suburbanites in both Etobicoke and Scarborough and nearly 60,000 in the three Yorks (the township had now been divided), construction had to continue, as did the paving of streets inside the city.

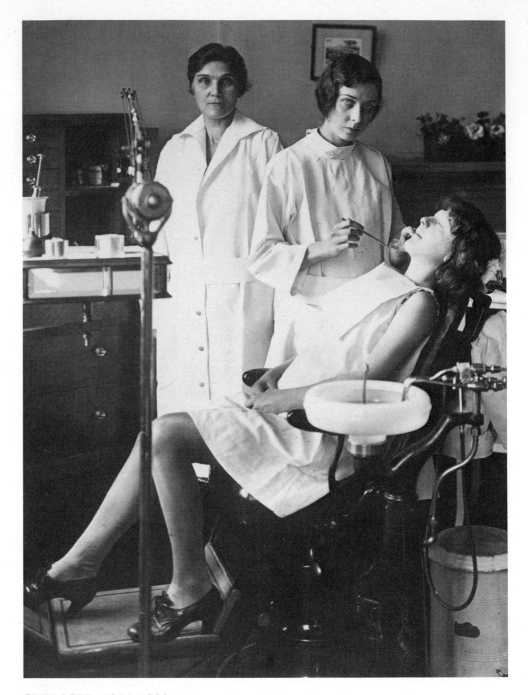

CITY LIFE, 1914-1929

The religious pattern gradually changed in Toronto during the war years and the prosperous Twenties. In 1921 the census showed the Church of England still had a substantial lead in membership with the Presbyterians second and the Methodists third, but both the Catholics and Jews were increasing their numbers. The churches were filled, holding two services on Sundays, and they continued to be active in both community and missionary work. Most supported the closed Sunday legislation despite the changed atmosphere of the postwar world. In 1925 the union of Methodist, Congregational, and most Presbyterian churches took place, forming the United Church of today. In Toronto, as elsewhere, the union caused a great deal of controversy when, at the last minute, the Presbyterians decided to hold votes for union in each congregation rather than joining as a body as had been arranged. The continuing Presbyterians held on to Knox College in the University of Toronto, and the new

United Church built Emmanuel College on the grounds of Victoria College.

The University of Toronto underwent a period of expansion under the long presidency of Sir Robert Falconer (1907-1932). In the postwar period the number of students rose to 4,800 before dropping again, and the faculty increased to nearly 600. In the early 1920s a number of buildings were erected, including Simcoe Hall, the Soldier's Tower on Hart House, another Massey gift which had itself been completed just before the war, the Ontario College of Education, and Trinity College, which had federated with the university and now moved up from Strachan's Queen Street West location. The most significant scientific development at the university was the discovery of insulin in 1921 by a four-man team under the active leadership of Dr. Frederick Banting, who was later knighted for his work. Banting and Professor John J.R. Macleod, who had provided the research funding, received the Nobel Prize in 1923 and divided it with the other two members of the team: Charles H. Best and Dr. J.B. Collip.

In the arts the Toronto Symphony Orchestra, suspended during the war, was refounded in 1924, and the Hart House Quartet was established the same year. By that time Toronto had a resident composer in Canon Healey Willan, an English organist who settled there in 1913. He was a prolific composer, some of his work being prepared for the new radio media. In 1927 Mazo de la Roche made literary history when her novel *Jalna*, the first in a series of 12, won the *Atlantic Monthly* prize of $10,000. The Group of Seven artists were busy in the city in the wintertime, and during the war several of them built the Rosedale Ravine Studio, which may still be seen, leaning at a slight angle, on the east side of the Yonge subway tracks just before the train enters the tunnel for the Bloor Street station. Such artists as J.E.H. MacDonald, A.Y. Jackson, and Lauren Harris had their quarters there.

The professional theatre had flourished through the war, and it continued to do so in the 1920s at the Royal Alex, Grand Opera House, and the Princess. By the war's end a serious rival to live theatre appeared with the advent of the movies. Some of the new movie theatres, such as Shea's Hippodrome on Bay Street, where the civic square now spreads, and Loew's Yonge Street, combined vaudeville and movies, and Loew's had the elegant Winter Gardens upstairs for higher-class entertainment. There were also the Tivoli on Yonge Street and the Uptown near Bloor, which showed the first partial-sound movie *Mother Knows Best* in 1927. Most major theatres had an orchestra, or at least a piano, well before that. The first full-length talkie to appear in the city was Al Jolson's *The Jazz Singer* in 1928. Burlesque was available at the Star and the Gaiety.

In 1922 an all-summer fun park opened at Sunnyside on the lake shore at Parkdale. It shortly drove its older, eastern rival at Scarborough Beach out of business and continued to operate until demolished to make way for the Gardiner Expressway in 1956. Under the imaginative direction of impressario Sol Solomon, Sunnyside brought in the latest types of amusements to please the crowds: a roller coaster; merry-go-rounds, both high and low speed; games of chance; and, of course, lots of peanut and ice-cream stands. The Miss Toronto contest was held there for some years, and there were other special events like flagpole-sitting and the burning of an ancient sailing ship, which attracted some unfavourable publicity, although it provided a good show for the children. Solomon ran into trouble with the Lord's Day Alliance when he offered $25 prizes for the best-dressed Sunday strollers; this promotional scheme was quickly stopped by court order. Sunnyside's activities were supplemented by the boardwalk, which stretched westward to the Humber River and was the scene of the often frigid Toronto Easter parade. The new municipal swimming pool was located part way along its course.

There were 2,054 acres of parks in the city by 1929, including the 60-acre Dentonia Park given by Mrs. Susie Massey in 1926. The exhibition prospered with attendance passing one million in 1928. The playgrounds, although there were never enough of them, had good facilities for baseball, tennis, skating, and ice hockey. Seventeen-year-old George Young of Toronto made history in 1927 when he went to California to compete in the Catalina Island swim and, possibly fortified by experience with Lake Ontario, was the only one of 102 contestants to finish. He picked up the $25,000 William Wrigley, Jr., prize. The next year the Wrigley Marathon swims were begun at CNE, setting a tradition that lasted to 1965. Baseball came into its own when the Maple Leaf Stadium was opened in 1926 and the Maple Leaf baseball team proceeded to win the little world series. The beginning of the Olympic Winter Games at Chamonix in 1924 gave Toronto a chance to shine in Canada's national sport. The Toronto Granites carried off the first prize, a feat that was repeated in the 1928 Winter Olympics at St. Moritz by the University of Toronto Graduates and carried on by other Canadian teams later.

Sports were particularly popular in 1920s Toronto. Not only did the Maple Leafs win the Little World Series in 1927, but many Torontonians played amateur baseball, seen here at Riverdale Park about 1920. CTA James 2217

Flappers were all the rage from about 1925 through to the beginning of the Depression. Featuring bobbed hair, cloche hats, short skirts, ravishing scarlet lips, and a (particularly daring) public cigarette, the style was universal, cheap, easy, and fun. The age of mass production had really arrived. CTA James 1902

Opposite page: Sunnyside was built by the Toronto Harbour Commission in the 1920s. For three decades the amusement park attracted crowds until most of it was razed to make way for the Gardiner Expressway. All that remains is the old Palais Royale Dance Hall and the splendid, recently refurbished Sunnyside Bathing Pavilion. PAC PA98386

The Arts and Letters Club was a focus of Toronto cultural life. Adding to the smoky ambience circa 1921 are, around the table from left to right, artists Frederick Varley, A.Y. Jackson, Lawren Harris, Barker Fairley, F.H. Johnston, Arthur Lismer, and J.E.H. MacDonald. AO S12842

The advent of radio brought another source of entertainment. Radio station CFCA led the way when it began broadcasting on March 28, 1922, under the auspices of the *Toronto Daily Star*. Three years later 39-year-old Ted Rogers devised a plug-in radio that operated on ordinary household electrical supply instead of batteries. The Rogers-Majestic batteryless made his fortune, and radio station CFRB, which he started, remains one of the most successful stations. CFRB began broadcasting in February 1927 with the Jack Arthur Orchestra playing from the studios of the Ryan Art Gallery, and before long Foster Hewitt was reporting the hockey games from the Mutual Street Arena. Both programs were on the way to becoming Canadian institutions.

In addition to the ordinary forms of entertainment, two unusual events of the period provided Torontonians with endless opportunities for gossip. The first was Toronto's most celebrated mystery: the disappearance of Ambrose Small on December 2, 1919. Small, the wealthy owner of the Grand Opera House and a string of theatres, matched his name to his size, hiding an unimpressive appearance behind a droopy moustache. He loved anonymity and even ran his beloved race horses under another name. By many reports he had a decidedly mean disposition. Small was also extraordinarily frugal; leading ladies at his theatres were often presented with only a small box of chocolates as a token of thanks after successful performances. On the day of his disappearance, he had sold his theatre chain for $1.75 million in the morning, deposited the down-payment cheque for one million dollars in the bank, lunched with his wife, and then returned to the Grand Opera House where he spent the afternoon. At 7 p.m. he purchased the paper from his usual newsboy and then vanished from the face of the earth. He was not carrying any large sum of money with him.

Several days later his long-time secretary, John Doughty, also vanished together with $105,000 from a safety deposit box. He was later picked up at an Oregon lumber camp, brought back to Toronto and tried for both theft and conspiracy to kidnap, but convicted of theft only and given four years. It seems that he had taken advantage of an apparent opportunity, rather than playing any role in Small's disappearance.

In June 1920 Mrs. Small offered a reward for Ambrose's return: $50,000 alive or $15,000 dead. But in spite of rumours and reports that surfaced over the years, no one ever came forward with solid evidence about him, and no good reason for the disappearance was ever advanced. As the years went by, Small's ghost was seen walking through his old theatres like Queen Anne Boleyn at the Tower of London. People watched anxiously as the Grand Opera House was demolished but the hoped-for ghost or corpse did not materialize.

The other diversion for Torontonians was the Charles Vance Millar will, which was admitted to probate in the mid-1920s. Millar, a decidedly cantankerous old solicitor with no heirs, took the opportunity of getting even with everything and everybody he disliked in a will that kept the city amused for a decade. For example, Millar had been a leading horse owner, so he left shares in the Toronto Jockey Club to Methodist clergy-men who opposed racing as an evil. However, they sold the shares and used the money for worthy purposes, which would have hardly pleased him.

Millar's greatest bequest was the sum of $500,000, which he left to the Toronto woman who had the largest number of children during the 10 years after his death. This set off what was to become known as "the Millar Stork Derby." Deliberately or otherwise, the will failed to include instructions on certain important points, such as whether the mother was to be married and whether there was to be one father, one father per child, or any number of fathers. For a decade the city kept anxious watch, and then, with the 10 years up, two years of litigation ensued while the courts tried to sort out which families qualified and who was the winner. They finally ruled for virtue, only allowing legally married women to qualify, and in October 1936 the bequest was divided between four mothers with nine children each. Like the Small disappearance, the Millar will saga has remained alive with follow-up articles periodically appearing on the recipients.

The paper that most razzled and dazzled Toronto in the twenties was The Star, *and two of the most substantial* Star *fixtures were the very capable Gregory Clark and globe-trotting (and here gun-toting) Gordon Sinclair. CTA James 1796*

BOOM AND BUST

Although some munitions workers received their final pay cheque within a week of the war's end, Toronto's change to a postwar economy was smooth and the wartime momentum continued. It took two years to

This series of photographs shows the evolution of the waterfront in the 1920s. In the first photo (right) the 1910 Harbour Commissioners building is isolated, surrounded by lake steamers and pleasure yachts moored in the foreground. Iceboats dot the harbour in winter (opposite page, bottom right), although one lake steamer pictured (opposite page, bottom left) has broken its way through to dock at the foot of Yonge as late as December. By 1926 fill operations were going on in earnest (opposite page, top), landlocking the Harbour Commissioners building.
AO S5974, CTA James 448C, MTL T30246, PAC PA87303

catch up with demand; then the continental economy went from postwar recovery into a period of overproduction that was to last nearly through the 1920s. With the economic boom prices remained high and wages lagged, but basically prosperity continued. There were setbacks, such as the collapse of the 16-year-old Home Bank, thanks in part to the borrowings of Pellatt and his friends. In one sweep this led to half of the $15 million depositors' loss from bank failure that had occurred since Confederation.

Generally the city also continued to prosper. The harbour expanded and roads improved, auto manufacturing exceeded that of Montreal, and new buildings rose on Bay Street, which began to turn into a "canyon." The most impressive commercial development was the Royal York, which replaced the once elegant Queen's Hotel opposite the newly opened Union Station in 1927. Officially opened by the governor-general with magnificent ceremony, the Royal York had all the latest amenities, such as running water in all its 1,600 rooms, and with an addition became the largest hotel in the British Empire.

By the mid-1920s a major era of speculation was underway. This was partly fuelled by the loose stock market regulations of the period, which

The second time that the Prince of Wales visited Toronto, in 1927, he was accompanied by his brother Prince George, Duke of Kent. The occasion was the Golden Jubilee of Canadian Confederation, and the visit was commemorated in Toronto by the opening of the Princes' Gates at the Canadian National Exhibition, seen here in a 1931 photograph. Through the arch one can see the grand facade of the 1928 Electrical Building (now demolished).
PAC PA52988

allowed the purchase of stock on the very limited margin of 10-percent down payment. Locally the boom was enhanced by a northwestern Ontario gold rush. New mining magnates appeared, such as Toronto lawyer James Y. Murdoch, president of Noranda from 1923, who eventually headed up 21 other companies and became a director of 35 more. It was no accident that one of the largest of the new Bay Street skyscrapers was named the Northern Ontario building. By 1928-1929 speculation had assumed wild proportions, stocks were selling at a fantastic multiple of company earnings, and many investors lacked any idea of what they were purchasing. Despite economic indications that world production had exceeded demand and a general decline was beginning, the stock market continued to rise, peaking in New York on September 3, 1929.

A little more than a month later, the markets were showing minor price declines but were rebounding. Then on Black Thursday, October 24, came the first real setback. This was followed by a partial rally, and on an even blacker Tuesday, the 29th, the bottom fell out. The ticker tapes of the exchanges ran hours behind the transactions as investors tried to get out or were sold out when they could not meet their margin calls. In Toronto the Stock Exchange registered 330,000 shares sold; in Montreal, still the largest exchange in the nation, 500,000; and in New York, the financial nerve centre, an unprecedented 16 million. Through November the market continued to slide and generally kept on that course until 1932. The boom was over and the Great Depression had arrived.

Many of Toronto's Victorian and Edwardian districts had assumed an air of settled propriety by the 1920s. In this autumn 1924 view of Markham Street south of Bloor, note the carriage step-stones in front of each house—very few examples of which remain today. CTA James 7186

THE GREAT DEPRESSION

The collapse of the stock market did not cause the Great Depression; rather the market crash came as an early casualty of the underlying conditions and an economic indicator of the troubles to come. For the next decade the Depression dominated everything, until it was pushed aside by an even more dramatic world conflict. For many of the now middle-aged generation, it was to instill ideas of frugality that have never been shaken. The fact that it seemed to hit so suddenly in an era of prosperity only intensified the Depression's blow.

Toronto, as a major manufacturing and exporting centre, was severely affected by the worldwide economic collapse. Also, many of the city's national markets like the prairie provinces were among the areas worst hit. There Nature sent a drought that, allied with the declining economy, wiped out all traces of prosperity in a cloud of dust. The declining standards of the Depression are best shown by a few statistics. Building permits dropped from $51 million in value in 1928 to $4 million in 1933, the worst year. The consumer price index fell by 17 points from 1929 to 1933. City revenues dropped drastically: in 1931 Toronto tax arrears were $5 million, and by 1932 the city had a deficit of over one million dollars.

In May 1933 Canadian unemployment reached 32 percent. Such high figures, together with a basic lack of relief services for the unemployed and general world unrest, naturally led to demonstrations. Toronto was not immune, and the provincial and city police stopped demonstrators around Queen's Park and rounded up Communists with a zest that some claimed limited freedom of speech. The *Telegram, Mail & Empire,* and the *Globe,* however, all agreed the police action did not infringe upon freedom of speech.

With the Depression even those who were not let go from their jobs often had their wages reduced; usually the less skilled the worker, the larger the reduction. To cut down costs, employers took advantage of any natural reduction in staffs, and promotions were deferred. Those who were still receiving wages were comparatively not too badly off with the reduction in the cost of living. The real problem was the increasing num-

*The prices in this 1930 shop
seem a bargain until one
remembers that $15 to $20 was
considered a good weekly wage.
The variety of local produce
suggests that the scene is
probably from late summer.
CTA James 339*

ber on relief. The provincial government appointed a commission on unemployment and relief in Ontario, which in 1932 reported on the growing problems of the last three years, but the institutions for aid, or the will to implement it, were as yet undeveloped. The Toronto House of Industry provided food parcels, and after 1933 the Department of Welfare issued vouchers for both food and clothing. A subsistence living was thus provided in most cases.

The number of single male transients who had come to the city from even worse-off areas in the search for nonexistent work further strained the system. From 1931 to 1936, no fewer than 23,000 of the 44,000 men registered for relief were transients. To provide accommodations the once-elegant St. Lawrence Hall was fitted up with steel bunks and became a flophouse. Less fortunate individuals lived in tarpaper shacks on garbage dumps or in underground burrows along the downtown rail tracks. Men begged in the streets and circulated through the residential districts searching for odd jobs or handouts. They soon developed a system of chalk markings to indicate which houses had generous occupants. When the Tory government was defeated by Liberal Mitchell F. Hepburn in 1934, the list of the unemployed was swelled by a goodly number of civil servants.

Housing, too, was a particular problem. Prices had been rising steadily since World War I, and although the Toronto Housing Commission had built some low-rent homes, these were not nearly sufficient, and with the Depression many of the occupants found that meeting even the low payments was difficult. Apartments had become more abundant, but their rents were still beyond the reach of most of the unemployed. When Lieutenant-Governor Dr. Herbert A. Bruce set up a commission on housing in 1934, it reported that of the 1,332 dwellings inspected 96 percent were below the acceptable standard of amenities and 75 percent were below the standard of health.

Evictions for nonpayment of rent were frequent; a family could return home to find all its belongings piled on the front lawn and the door padlocked. Even in well-to-do residential districts that were beginning to decline, such as the once-affluent South Parkdale, the sight was common. Children going to school might see one or sometimes even two sad piles of belongings on front lawns; occasionally these remained for a couple of days before the people evicted were able to remove them. Landlords ordering the evictions were often themselves in difficulty, counting on the revenue from the apartment or house to pay their own rent or mortgage. Suspension of electric and water services were even more frequent and a good deal less obvious to the passer-by.

After the mid-1930s the economic situation began to improve. In 1936 there was a definite upturn in the economy that lasted through much of 1937, only to be succeeded by a return of hard times at the end of that year. Although the situation improved again in 1938, it was the outbreak of war the next year that brought the turnaround.

As if economic troubles were not enough, Toronto experienced some of its worst weather during the Depression era. In 1933 only 23.84 inches of rain fell, the all-time low in the city's history. This was followed by one of the coldest periods on record in February 1934, and then July 1936 saw one of the worst heat waves with accompanying high mortality. Thousands slept by the lake shore and a humorist fried an egg on City Hall steps. The city had to wait until December 11-12, 1944, for its worst snowfall: 20.5 inches in 24 hours. Toronto even experienced one of its extremely rare earthquake shocks on November 1, 1935. Striking at 1:04 a.m., its epicenter registered 6.25 on the Richter scale. At Toronto it awakened the citizens, but did little damage.

POSITIVE CHANGES IN A DEPRESSION SOCIETY

Few improvements in services could be expected, but in 1938 the Toronto Transportation Commission introduced the new President's Conference Committee streetcar at CNE. An extremely comfortable vehicle, it long provided, and still provides, excellent service for the citizens, with far better padded seats than its successor.

Culture and education could hardly flourish during the Depression era, but Toronto's institutions managed to carry on in spite of restrictions. The city lost McMaster University to Hamilton in 1930. The Royal Ontario Museum, which stands east of McMaster's old Bloor Street location, did manage to get funding for a major expansion, which included the University Avenue wing with its magnificent rotunda. Another major attraction for both citizens and tourists opened in 1937

171

This 1929 photograph, taken high above University Avenue looking east across the grounds of Osgoode Hall and commercial buildings south, shows workmen hoisting into place the uppermost row of stones capping the Canada Life building. The narrow working ledge and flimsy guard rail contribute to the feeling of vertigo—and where is the photographer? CTA James 3182

when the Kiwanis Club of West Toronto took over Casa Loma from the city, which had seized it for taxes, and opened it to the general public. The castle, although by then somewhat battered from neglect, became an immediate hit with young and old. A great loss to the city was the closing of the 1915 French chateau-style Government House, Chorley Park, which was shut down as an economy measure in 1937. It was eventually pulled down, leaving Ontario and Toronto without suitable quarters for official receptions and visiting dignitaries.

Professional sports fared better. In 1927 Conn Smythe, who had been fired from the New York Rangers, managed to raise the purchase price of $160,000 for the St. Pats, which he renamed the Maple Leafs. He was soon planning the Maple Leaf Gardens, and in 1931 the 12,586-seat, $2-million arena was built in five months. The Maple Leafs proceeded to take the Stanley Cup from the Rangers in three straight games in 1932.

In 1934 Toronto, despite its somewhat beleaguered finances, celebrated the centennial of its incorporation. In 1932 the city began the restoration of Fort York, one of the earliest and probably most creative restorations that Ontario has witnessed. With Bathurst Street cutting across the original site and the railway tracks running to the north, reconstruction would have been impossible, but the new earthworks that were added were considerably more impressive than the originals. By the 1950s almost everyone was certain that the entire fort dated from Simcoe's regime.

On March 6, 1934, a flaming rocket fired from the exhibition grounds gave the signal for the lighting of 200 barrels of resin and tar on Hanlan's Point, and the festivities began. Canon Henry J. Cody, president of the University of Toronto, led thanksgiving prayers for the city, and the distinguished visitors who joined in included Prime Minister William Lyon Mackenzie King, Willoughby J. Cole of Southampton, England, a descendant of Governor Simcoe, and Colonel Gabriel de Taffaneul, Marquis de la Jonquière, a descendant of the marquis who ordered Fort Rouillé built. In a good neighbour gesture, President Franklin D. Roosevelt sent a gunboat bearing the mace from the Legislature that had been captured in 1813. It was duly received by Lieutenant-Governor Bruce, although no one was quite sure what to do with the rather primitive artifact. The ceremonies continued for some weeks with fireworks, parades, and a Victoria Day pageant including floats of the national groups comprising Toronto's population.

BUSINESS AND DEVELOPMENT IN THE DEPRESSION ERA

Many business plans fell victim to the Depression, and those developments that took place were largely a completion of pre-Depression projects, such as the 36-storey, 476-foot Bank of Commerce tower, then the highest building in the Commonwealth and now part of the Commerce Court complex. For years there were a couple of partially completed skyscrapers in the central business district, the frameless windows of the upper storeys of one structure staring northward to the City Hall. The

most magnificent unfinished project was Eaton's plan for a new store at College and Yonge streets: a 40-storey masterpiece of the then-popular Art Deco style designed to capture the crosstown trade along the College-Carleton access, just as the original Eaton's had profitted from that along Queen Street. A combination of Depression, quicksand, and the lack of potential tenants considerably cut down the portion that was completed, and a much reduced building occupying only part of the site opened in 1931. With World War II and the transfer of the main crosstown access northward to Bloor Street, the building was never finished but has become the still-gracious College Park of today.

The great commercial change of the 1930s was the spread of the chain store. Suddenly the family grocery or shoe store became part of a great chain, and with the transformation some personalized services disappeared. Many stores refused to join chains, and while some were squeezed out, others managed to continue as local corner stores or became more specialized. In communications, the radio, now smaller and more convenient, was by the late 1930s standard equipment in most homes, and people talked of the coming of television, which was making its appearance in England. In 1936 George McCullagh bought the *Globe* with money provided by William H. Wright, a leading mining magnate.

Soon McCullagh also purchased the *Mail & Empire* and amalgamated the two, leaving Toronto with just one morning newspaper. The Malton (Toronto International) and Toronto Island airports were built in 1937-1938 and Trans-Canada Air lines, now Air Canada, was formed in 1937.

Thanks partly to strict controls, there were no bank failures in Canada during the Depression. The Toronto Stock Exchange took its modern form when it amalgamated with the Standard Stock and Mining Exchange in 1934. In 1937 the exchange moved to Canada's first air-conditioned building at 234 Bay Street, which it occupied until 1983. Another magnificent example of the Art Deco style, the Stock Exchange included all the latest technological gadgetry and utilized the post system where stocks were traded at set places on the floor.

By the late 1930s construction on Canada's first superhighway, the Queen Elizabeth Way, was proceeding well. It was finished, complete with night lighting, superb landscaping, and Imperial Roman-style bridges, in time for the Queen to open it in May 1939 during the first Canadian visit of a reigning sovereign. The royal visit, with its ceremonies at the Legislature, motorcades, presentation of the Dionne quintuplets, and George McCullough's horse Archworth winning the King's Plate at the Woodbine, made a great impression on Toronto.

WORLD WAR II AND THE CITY

While the world economic picture was improving somewhat, the world political situation was degenerating. Then in 1939 Poland was threatened by Germany, and Britain and France sent an ultimatum to Hitler when he invaded that country on Saturday, September 2, 1939. A warm, pleasant Labour Day weekend hardly seemed a time when the world would again be thrown into a fearful conflict, but the next morning many a minister climbed into his pulpit and announced that, as there had been no answer to the ultimatum, a state of war now existed between Britain and Germany. That very evening the war was sharply brought home to the city when the liner *Athenia* was torpedoed by a German submarine a hundred

Above: In 1939 Torontonians welcomed the new, shy, stuttering King George VI, and his friendly, radiant Queen Elizabeth. Simpson's, at Queen and Yonge, was particularly enthusiastic in its declarations of loyalty. AO S14190

Above left: The royal visit was also the occasion for the opening of Canada's first superhighway—the Queen Elizabeth Way, linking the city to the Hamilton area and thence to Niagara. The photograph shows the intersection of the new road with Highway 27, and indicates how efforts were made to create a garden setting. There were no cloverleafs in the garden yet. AO RG14 B-10-2

Opposite page: In the near half-century since this photo of Yonge Street looking north from Queen was taken, most of the shops have migrated, although the facades of buildings on the right-hand side of the photo largely remain. AO Acc. 14900-62

Above: Posters by the thousands changed the face of Toronto. Not simply to recruit, the images reminded citizens that in total war home was a vital front. PAC C87120

Above right: As in the First World War, women moved into factories. Here Veronica Foster, the "Bren Gun Girl," takes a break from the production line at the James Inglis, Ltd., plant in May 1941. The Toronto plant turned out 100,000 Brens during the course of the war. PAC PA119766

miles west of the Scottish Hebrides. Among its 1,400 passengers were 200 Torontonians.

Although Canada did not officially declare war for nearly a week, that first weekend more than 1,000 recruits flocked to the colours and guards were placed at hydro installations and other danger points. As the year's exhibition closed, CNE was turned over to the troops for the duration, becoming the Manning Depot, which processed thousands of soldiers. Soon thousands of British children were being moved to safety in Canada, many living with Toronto families as "war guests." With its solid industrial base, the city promptly became a centre of Canadian war manufacturing; by 1943 slightly more than two-thirds of the workers were engaged in the war effort and many new jobs had opened for women. Several plants made ammunition, the aircraft industry expanded rapidly, and there was heavy industrial involvement in chemicals, precision instruments, electrical apparatus, shipbuilding, and explosives.

Once again there were all the problems of housing shortages, compounded by the fact that, as a city committee reported in 1942, so little had been done for the past two decades. The Toronto Transportation Commission's streetcar system was almost hopelessly swamped with riders as automobile manufacturing ground to a halt, gas rationing limited driving, and tires became difficult to replace. In 1939 the system had carried 150 million riders; by 1939 its traffic had increased to 303 million. The bicycle came back into its own as a method of transportation, although limited in value by Toronto weather, and for that long-time source of transportation power, the horse, the war provided a last reprieve. By the 1930s horse-drawn vehicles had almost disappeared, but bread-and-milk carts were still making their daily deliveries and vegetable waggons drawn by horse went from house to house. Horses were regularly used for policing, and even the occasional rich eccentric

176

had horse-drawn carriages. With the end of the war, and with declining home deliveries of many products, the horse took its final bow on the streets except for police control and ceremonies.

As the war progressed the city's life-style changed. At the outset Toronto's residential streets lost one set of the lights that usually ran down both sides. Before the war was over there were electricity shortages, and dimouts became a way of life. There were also shortages of various foods. Canned goods were sometimes difficult to find, and when something special came into the grocery stores, it frequently did not go on the shelves but rather was hidden under the counter to be slipped in with regular customers' purchases.

In 1945 Germany and then Japan capitulated, and once again the fortunately undamaged city turned its mind to reconstruction. The problems facing Toronto were enormous, even if it did not have the rebuilding and refugee difficulties common to the cities of Europe. As a result of the Depression and war, to say nothing of prior neglect, there were countless matters to be settled in housing, transportation, and planning. Beyond these were the underlying complexities of economic reorganization for peacetime and the question of what should be done about governmental organization and services for the metropolitan area.

THE CRIPPLED CHILDREN
OF TORONTO
WELCOME.... Our Queen

CHAPTER XIII

A NEW GOVERNMENT AND A NEW AGE

1945-1967

The pre-eminent problem facing Toronto in 1945 was the overall future planning of the government of the metropolitan area. There had been no annexations since 1914 and Toronto was now surrounded by a group of urbanizing townships. The percentage of the population in the central city was constantly decreasing: it remained under 700,000 while the suburbs increased from 220,000 in 1939, to 265,000 in 1945, to 508,000 in 1953, when Metro came into force.

The problems of adjusting the interests and needs of Toronto and the 12 municipalities that were to be combined to form the Metropolitan Toronto of today were considerable. Some of the villages were as large as cities. The services available were uneven, particularly water supply, sewage disposal, and access to transportation. Many received some of their services from the city itself. Most of the population worked in the city or did work that was dependent on it, yet the suburban population did not share in the costs of solving the problems of the metropolitan centre, such as poverty, slums, and crime. Attempts to regulate inequalities were made by various intergovernmental agreements and agencies, but these were inadequate. By 1945 all the governments—provincial, city, and suburban—agreed that change was needed, yet the province, which would pass any new legislation, had to tread warily for fear of a political lashback. None of the municipalities wanted to give up their independence, and the Toronto area included a great number of provincial ridings.

Negotiating a metropolitan government proved to be a long and complex process. When the parties could not agree, the Ontario Municipal Board opened hearings, which led to the preparation of the three-million-word Cumming Report of 1953, with its 300 exhibits. This document studied the system and laid the basis for the future metropolitan government. It called for a federation of the existing municipalities with a metropolitan council for overall services, while the individual municipalities retained some power in local matters as they desired. The result was the Municipality of Metropolitan Toronto Act of 1953. This established a Metropolitan Council consisting of 24 representatives, 12 each from the city and suburbs, plus a chairman as chief executive. The first chairman was to be appointed by the provincial government; subsequent chairmen were to be elected by the council. The result has been a dual leadership for Toronto with an appointed chairman for the whole area and an elected mayor for the city itself.

Under the act, powers were divided into four categories. A metropolitan government assumed the tasks that needed overall regulation: assessment, borrowing, transportation, and justice. Other powers were shared: Metro supplied the water, although it was distributed by local authority, and sewage disposal also became a Metro responsibility. Further powers were divided between the two levels: taxation, education, parks, health, welfare, housing, and community services had both metropolitan and municipal departments administering them. Fire, police, garbage, traffic, and hydro distribution remained with the municipalities. The system was not perfect, but it was a workable compromise for the new 245-square mile entity with its 1.25-million population, and it set the precedent for other metropolitan areas, such as Winnipeg and Montreal, when they adopted metropolitan governments.

POLITICS AND SERVICES

The outlook of the City Councils continued to be basically conservative, pro-business and pro-development. They strongly emphasized municipal economy. In the late 1950s the province removed the property qualification for voting in all municipalities. In 1966-1967, under a revision of the act, the number of municipalities was reduced to Toronto and five boroughs, the city proper absorbing Swansea and Forest Hill.

In 1950, nineteen Toronto business firms that had been in operation for more than a century presented the mayor with a chain of office, adding a touch of dignity along the lines of the English system. Under their mantle of dignity, however, many of the modern mayors have been controversial, as have some of the metropolitan chairmen. When Mayor Leslie Saunders, the last outstanding proponent of the Orange Order, went down to defeat before Nathan Phillips, who became Toronto's first Jewish mayor, the change was symbolic of how much Toronto itself had changed.

Phillips, who held office from 1955 to 1962, was a *bon vivant* who was frequently in trouble with the newspapers for neglecting city business to enjoy ceremonial, athletic, or ethnic occasions; he hated missing a good banquet. Nevertheless, Phillips captured the imagination of the electors who returned him for four terms, the record number of years in office. A man of great determination, he must receive credit for the impressive new City Hall with its 12-acre square, which is appropriately named in his honour.

The outstanding figure during the formative years of Metro was Metropolitan Chairman Frederick G. Gardiner, "Big Daddy" as he was called, sometimes lovingly. A lawyer and former reeve of Forest Hill, from 1953 to 1961 Gardiner ran Metro as his personal principality and laid his stamp decisively on the new governments. It could be argued that he was too concerned with the exact fractions of the interest rate on debentures and that he favoured throughways too greatly over subways, but Gardiner had the energy and force of personality to set the system in motion. The Gardiner Expressway was one of his achievements.

With the planning functions for Metropolitan Toronto split, there were two planning boards. The Metro Planning Board began to lay out future plans for Toronto itself and for coordination with the five adjacent fringe townships of Markham, Pickering, Toronto Township (now Mississauga), Toronto Gore (now in Brampton), and Vaughan, as well as the waterfront development. In the city, by 1956, planners were coming to grips with the problems arising from the increasing numbers of high-rise buildings and the spot zoning that permitted large apartment buildings in residential neighbourhoods. It recommended the establishment of zones of high and low density. School planning adopted a common standard of education. In the 12 years after 1953, to accommodate the post-war baby boom, 250 new public schools were built in Metro Toronto and additions made to 500 others. In 1957 the police forces of all the municipalities were amalgamated to correct existing imbalances, and an appointed Metropolitan Board of Police Commissioners was established.

TRANSPORTATION FOR A NEW AGE

One of postwar Toronto's greatest problems was updating its communications network. Car production returned to normal after the war, and by the late 1940s most major Toronto streets were becoming congested and Yonge Street was virtually impassable. Outside the city, the highway system was progressively unable to handle the load, especially on the Toronto-Hamilton corridor.

In 1955 the Parking Authority was formed by provincial legislation, and in 1963 the 600-odd traffic lights were regulated by a $3-million computer in what was the most advanced traffic-control system in the world. These changes did not come any too soon: by 1967 one in three Torontonians owned a car. Although the battle between public transit and expressways was underway by that time, fortunately in Toronto the automobile boom was not automatically followed by the collapse of the public transit system.

Much of the credit for the system's survival was attributable to the efficiency of the Toronto Transportation Commission, or Transit Commission as it became in 1954. The TTC introduced the trolley bus in 1947,

which used overhead wires but had the flexibility of being able to pull out of the way of traffic. It proved a success. In 1954, under Metro, the commission purchased four suburban bus lines and by 1967 buses were carrying 40 percent of the traffic. The abolition of streetcars was considered but fortunately not implemented.

The buses helped with the traffic problems, but any solution for the volume required more drastic action; the contest was soon underway between expressways and subways. Toronto had already adopted a combination of the two systems prior to Metro. In 1946, backed by an overwhelming vote, the City Council had agreed to proceed with a Toronto subway. The first line was to stretch 4.6 miles from the Union Station northward on Yonge Street to Eglinton Avenue (much the same as the 1912 plan).

Work was started on the subway in 1949 to the skirl of bagpipes, and Yonge Street shortly became a complete shambles; after a few years the citizens began wondering if the subway would ever be completed. But in March 1954, after five years and $64 million, Premier Leslie Frost opened the 12-station, 104-car line. More than 100,000 Torontonians crowded onto their new attraction on the first day. An added bonus was the removal of the tangle of overhanging wires and signs on Yonge Street.

The need for an extension of the subway system soon became apparent, but ran counter to the belief of Chairman Gardiner and the traffic departments that financing priority should be given to throughways. The result was a hiatus in subway building until the chairman's retirement. Then the two-mile University Avenue subway was opened in 1963, and the Bloor-Danforth subway in 1966. At the same time a four-mile extension of the Yonge Street subway to Shepherd Avenue was being planned.

The expressway system was growing simultaneously and the access roads to the city were being improved. The great changes for Toronto were the building of four-lane Highway 400 north to Barrie and four-lane Highway 401, now the Macdonald-Cartier Throughway, which was intended as a bypass across the northern part of the city, not an in-city traffic artery. Its construction pointed up the difficulty of keeping ahead of traffic growth and urban sprawl; soon the four lanes were being increased to 12.

The idea of a network of throughways cut through the city quickly ran into public opposition: everyone wanted faster roads, but no one wanted them running through their own neighbourhood or spewing out vehicles onto their local streets. The problem of downtown parking, despite the efforts of the Parking Authority, remained acute and would inevitably be exacerbated by in-city throughways. Further, the extension of throughways would have called for demolishing a great number of dwellings. Soon citizens' groups were up in arms. In the end, a much-truncated system was built: the Gardiner Expressway along the lake shore in the late 1950s, connecting the Queen Elizabeth Way and Highway 401 in the east, and the Don Valley Parkway, which was opened in 1961. However, the Spadina Expressway has never been completed, and an east-west crosstown expressway slashing through the middle of the city was never started.

By the mid-1960s the Ontario government came up with the idea of commuter trains using the existing rail line, with large, free parking lots at the suburban stations. The result is the GO (Government of Ontario) train system, which opened from Oakville in the west to Pickering in the east in 1967 and has now been extended considerably. With these communication lines laid down, Toronto has developed an expandable system of transport for the inner city and good communications with the suburbs and the southern Ontario hinterland.

Great changes also took place in Toronto's broader communications, particularly by water. By 1956 Toronto's port had been expanded by the addition of a 26-acre dock site capable of handling the larger ships that would be coming through the new St. Lawrence Seaway. When the seaway opened on June 26, 1960, the Great Lakes were at last accessible to oceangoing ships, as the early merchants had dreamed; Toronto and the other lake cities became ocean ports.

Air traffic was also growing at a rapid pace, and Toronto's old Malton Airport, soon renamed Toronto International Airport, became hopelessly inadequate, especially after the advent of jet aircraft in 1960. In 1964 the first new terminal was opened at a cost of $42 million. Planned to serve 2.5 million passengers yearly, it almost immediately had more than 3 million, far more than any other airport in Canada.

THE FACE AND LIFE OF THE NEW METROPOLIS

The creation of Metropolitan Toronto came at a time of changing retail patterns, in which an increasing number of shoppers drove to plazas instead of walking to the traditional stores lining the main streets. In the new sections of the city, of course, such streets did not exist. At the same time new high-rise buildings were appearing with increasing frequency. In some of the older residential districts, some streets like the once-elegant Jameson Avenue in South Parkdale were totally demolished; on other streets new apartments began springing up surrounded by older homes, which were completely under their shadow. In the downtown area many older buildings were coming down to be replaced by high-rise construction. One of the first city centre superdevelopments was the 1964

The great boom of the 1950s resulted from domestic spending — not from an increase in exports. Europe's economic recovery and American competition meant bad times, for example, for the wheat farmers of the Canadian West. Unhappy repercussions followed for manufacturers of farm implements. Here laid-off employees at the Massey-Ferguson plant at Toronto line up to receive benefits in July 1956. PAC PA93792

Toronto-Dominion Centre, a large banking plaza with two towers, one of them 55 storeys high. When opened in the late 1960s, the highest tower at 740 feet was the tallest building in the Commonwealth; Toronto was still in the lead.

The most spectacular development, and the pride of the citizens, was a badly needed new City Hall to accommodate the expanded city and Metro governments. Mayor Nathan Phillips fought the battles that made it possible. He pushed for an international competition for the building's design, and the voters, after an initial rebuff, finally approved the plan. The international contest drew 532 entries from 42 countries. The winning design of Viljo Rewell of Helsinki, Finland, has given the city a building that has attracted international attention. When opened in 1965 the hall and square in front of it, which was appropriately set between Osgoode Hall and the old City Hall, had cost $30 million. The city then expropriated the area to the south to control its development and assure compatible future design.

Planning for the new City Hall made Toronto's civic leaders aware of a problem that has faced all cities in the last 30 years: while building for the future, what should be done about preserving the past? On the one hand, a burgeoning city needs new business and commercial space; on the other hand, it has an obligation to preserve what is beautiful or has historical interest. The difficulty has been to strike a balance between preservationists and developers. Today cost-estimate studies frequently indicate that servicing new high-rise developments can outweigh the tax revenues that they generate. Also, it is increasingly clear that buildings from the past can add variety and charm to any city. Although Toronto suffered the loss of some important structures, many of its major buildings have survived. The Toronto Historical Board deserves great credit for its part in recording the city's heritage and fighting to save the important monuments.

Preserving St. Lawrence Hall, fortunately, was not controversial, and the City Council agreed to its restoration for a Canadian Centennial project in 1967. The great preservation battles in Toronto raged around two buildings: the old City Hall and Union Station. With the new City Hall available, Eaton's store to the east quickly planned a new development that would take over the City Hall's site. The City Council approved demolition, but public reaction in support for the "old horror" was sharp and astonishing. In the end Eaton's dropped the proposal as "insufficiently profitable." The old City Hall was finally leased to the province for law courts and given a thorough cleaning. Ten years later Eaton's came forth with a new plan and now the city has both the old City Hall and beside it one of the finest indoor shopping malls on the continent. A parallel battle took place over Union Station, which remains as the great entrance gate to the city and, with its vast pre-World World I expanses, is ideally suited to the increasing numbers of people using train, commuter train, and subway facilities.

During these years two of Toronto's worst disasters occurred: the burning of the SS *Noronic* and Hurricane Hazel. The *Noronic* was a cruise

ship that carried passengers from Chicago and Detroit to the Thousand Islands and back. Built 36 years before at Port Arthur (Thunder Bay), it had once been one of the queens of the Great Lakes. On September 16, 1949, it docked in Toronto Harbour so the 542 passengers could explore the city and shop. About 1:00 a.m. on the 17th, some passengers smelled smoke and the crew members were warned; yet no alarm was given until 2:38 a.m. By the time the fire department arrived the blaze was completely out of control and many of the passengers were already asphixiated or trapped. When the toll was taken, 119 had died. Compensation of $2.15 million, then a vast sum, was paid to the families. The hulk was towed to Hamilton and scrapped.

Hurricane Hazel arrived five years later on October 15, 1954. For years Ontario had enjoyed the illusion that such phenomena as hurricanes and tornadoes stayed south of the border in the United States, and there had been no effort to prevent new housing developments from spreading onto the flood plains along the rivers. The stage was ripe for disaster.

The weather office failed to give any proper warning. Their bulletin, which came out several hours after the heavy rains had started, did not mention a hurricane and was so watered down that it was meaningless. The result was an unprepared city and hinterland when the partially exhausted storm hit. Within a few hours the Don and Humber rivers were rising rapidly, and to the north of the city near Lake Simcoe, the Holland Marshes were flooding. The hurricane struck particularly heavily on the Humber, where Raymore Drive with 38 of its sleeping inhabitants literally disappeared.

In the end 81 people died, including 5 firemen killed while attempting a rescue. Some $25 million in damage was done across the city. However, the hurricane had one positive effect. Building on the flood plain ceased, and this, in turn, opened new parkland for the city.

Socially Metropolitan Toronto was a very different place from the Victorian city that had survived until the war's end. Some might have said that the city was going to hell. In 1947 cocktail bars were opened, and three years later the issue of allowing public sports events on Sunday was put to the vote and won decisively after a hard-fought contest. Ten years after that, in 1960, Sunday movies, plays, and concerts were also approved by the voters by a majority of two to one. In 1968 came a

Many women immigrants, especially those who had difficulty with English, found work (for long hours, with low pay) in Toronto's textile industry in the postwar period. The industry remains comparatively labour intensive, and—in terms of the workers— inadequately organized. PAC PA117582

further relaxation of the Sabbath rules permitting the opening of CNE and the race-tracks. While Toronto was hardly a wide-open city, something of a balance was being struck: a reasonably quiet Sunday with reasonable facilities for entertainment. After an equally sharp contest, flouridation was approved by a narrow margin in 1962.

The ethnic picture of the city was also changing. The census of 1931 showed that, although non-British groups formed one-third of the population, most Torontonians had British origins. There were sizeable contingents of Germans, Italians, Greeks, and Slavs, and by 1939 Chinese had settled around Elizabeth Street, just west of the old City Hall.

By 1941 fifty-nine percent of the population was still British-born or descended, but with the war's end New Canadians from the Continent began to pour into Toronto supplemented by many arrivals from other parts of Canada, including French Canadians, and the increasing rural-to-urban migration. The Italian community by then was particularly strong, numbering some 300,000 and providing much of the labour for the building of the new city. Germans, Poles, and Ukrainians also increased their numbers. At the same time the older, established Toronto families were moving out to the new suburbs; the result was a considerable change in the ethnic mix of the city itself.

The variety of languages and cultural expression brought a new liveliness to Toronto. With the European love of public parks, recreation grounds like High Park, which had been deteriorating, were cleaned up and became pleasant areas for socializing and relaxation. At the same time, the process of assimilation was taking place as a new generation grew up, moved through the educational system into the universities, and intermixed and intermarried with the older settlers. With the large ethnic vote, provincial legislation on employment discrimination was soon enacted.

The position of the churches in the postwar period, as in earlier times, is difficult to estimate. By 1961, however, the Catholics were definitely the largest denomination, the United Church second, and the Anglicans third. In 1945 Catholic Archbishop James McGuigan was elevated to the College of Cardinals by the pope. A native Canadian and strong supporter of Britain and the war effort, his triumphal return from the ceremonies in Rome was greeted with cheers.

The postwar period saw a great increase in the numbers seeking higher education because of the volume of returning soldiers who were given government support. The level fell after 1950, but the baby boom soon came along, elementary and secondary education expanded, and by the 1960s the universities, too, were undergoing unprecedented growth. Ryerson Institute became Ryerson Polytechnic Institute and began a very considerable rebuilding of its campus. The University of Toronto spread out, opening a new campus extension west of St. George Street. In 1962 it purchased 202 acres in Scarborough and 180 acres in Erindale for satellite campuses. These were opened in 1967. Graduate education at Toronto also increased rapidly, and former Governor-General Vincent Massey built Massey College as a scholarly community in 1962. Meanwhile, York University had been established in 1960 and five years later moved to a 475-acre campus in the northwest of the Metro area as its principal headquarters. New health-care facilities were also built and others enlarged. Sunnybrook Military Hospital opened in 1946 to take care of veterans and expanded as a University of Toronto research centre, and other hospitals—the Toronto General, the Sick Children's, and Mount Sinai—underwent reconstruction.

There was a vigorous growth of Toronto's cultural institutions, partly thanks to the help of the new Canada Council, which had been created as the result of a report by a Royal Commission headed by Toronto's Vincent Massey. The Royal Ontario Museum and the Art Gallery of Toronto (now Ontario) hosted major international exhibitions. Thanks to a gift from R.S. McLaughlin, the Royal Ontario Museum was able to add the McLaughlin Planetarium to its facilities. Smaller museums were established, too. The surviving building of the 1841 Stanley Barracks opened as the Marine Museum in 1959, and a year later William Lyon Mackenzie's last home was deeded to the city as a memorial to the first mayor.

The performing arts also flowered. The Canadian Opera Company and the National Ballet of Canada opened in 1950-1951. The city's first major theatre—the $12,000 O'Keefe—opened in 1960 with the world premiere of *Camelot*. The old Royal Alex was saved from demolition three years later when it was purchased and refurbished by Ed Mirvish. Finally the St. Lawrence Centre was approved in 1964 as a city cultural centre, although it was completed only in 1970 after circumventing many political roadblocks. At the same time a host of smaller theatres were springing up, such as the Crest and the Colonnade. CBC FM radio began in 1945 and television appeared in Toronto when CBLT began regular telecasting in 1952, and a second station, the privately owned CFTO, began operations nine years later. In TV, as in radio, Toronto became the centre of operation for the English-speaking division of the Canadian Broadcasting Corporation.

In sports the Argonauts captured the Grey Cup in 1945-1947 and again in 1950 and 1952. The Maple Leafs simultaneously had a winning streak, carrying off the Stanley Cup five times from 1945 to 1951 and winning it again from 1962 to 1964; but after 1964 they joined the Argonauts in the shade. Swimming saw the 1954 victory of 16-year-old Marilyn Bell, who conquered Lake Ontario from Rochester to Toronto in 23 hours and 40 minutes at the time of the CNE. Soccer, introduced by the Italians and other immigrant groups, was quickly gaining in favour.

Thus, by Canada's 1967 Centennial Toronto had grown into a fully developed metropolitan centre with its own hinterland of Ontario and an economic network that spread across Canada. The population of the city by that year was 685,313 and of Metro, 1,887,798; within three years the latter had crossed the two-million mark. Toronto was also becoming the English-speaking cultural centre of the nation; it had well-established institutions, the CNE, and the leading university. The city was poised to overtake Montreal as the predominant metropolis of Canada.

Great advances in medicine accompanied the postwar period. The baby boom's early confrontation with polio had left thousands crippled and hundreds dead. By 1955 the Salk vaccine had been developed and distributed in sweeping campaigns through the schools; the oral Sabin antidote was later used to even greater effect beginning in 1961. By the 1970s the disease was virtually wiped out. This unfortunate youth is in quarantine at J block of the Stanley Barracks in August of 1947. PAC PA93672

CHAPTER XIV

A NORTH AMERICAN METROPOLIS

THE TORONTO OF TODAY

The cosmopolitan city that celebrated Canada's 100th birthday in 1967 by restoring historical St. Lawrence Hall, constructing its own cultural focus, the St. Lawrence Centre, and holding its first Civic Honour's Day, was a far cry from the Sabbatarian Toronto of old. Yet while the metropolitan central area was giving Toronto its reputation as one of the liveliest cities on the continent, under the surface and in the suburbs much of old Toronto survived. The same conservative forces that had dominated Toronto's past remain active in its present; even the reform municipal leaders of the last decade have belonged to Toronto's more affluent classes.

The decade following the Canadian Centennial saw Toronto pass Montreal to become Canada's dominant metropolis. Partly because of its centralized geographical base, partly because of its grasp of Ontario's destinies as both capital and economic metropolis, Toronto had been gradually moving ahead of Montreal for years; after 1967 the pace suddenly accelerated. The causes were diverse. The St. Lawrence Seaway was one: the farther shipping could go inland, the cheaper the shipping costs. With the seaway opening, Toronto, although it captured only a portion of the trade, was definitely the winner from all the canal improvements. Montreal, like Kingston with the earlier, smaller canals, could now watch the ships sailing past its harbour. Also, Toronto has been much more receptive to immigrants of all types, particularly from the former colonies of the British Empire. As well, the rural-urban population movement and the many jobs available have brought far larger numbers of

Previous page: Artist Tom McNeely created this "bird's-eye view" of Toronto in 1973. The sprawling cityscape is viewed looking north up Bay Street. Courtesy, Canadian Imperial Bank of Commerce MTL T10289

people into the Metropolitan Toronto area. It was no surprise that the 1976 interim census showed that Toronto had just edged out Montreal to become the largest Canadian metropolitan area, with 2,803,101 people compared with Montreal's 2,802,485. The 1981 census showed the accelerating trend: Montreal, 2,828,349, and Toronto, 2,998,947.

Yet the seaway, the natural population shift westward and to the cities, and the increase in immigration were only part of the picture. A major factor was Montreal's deteriorating status vis-à-vis Toronto. The new atmosphere of francophone nationalism and socialist outlook that followed the election of a separatist provincial government in Quebec in 1976 meant that North American and British businesses were reluctant to invest large sums there. For individuals, taxes were higher and Quebec's new cultural legislation, which placed limits on education in English, meant that anglophones would be unwilling to have corporations transfer them there. For Montreal, which had long been noted for its charming bilingual atmosphere, insistence on signs in the French language and that business be conducted basically in that tongue were disastrous.

Conversely, while Montreal was becoming more xenophobic, Toronto was becoming more broad-minded. While anglophone Canadian and American tourists were attempting to puzzle out French-only signs in

190

Montreal, in Toronto bilingual street signs were going up in the Chinese neighbourhood and immigrants of all tongues were at liberty to put up signs in whatever language they desired. All this soon made Toronto the major destination for one of the largest hordes of refugees ever to stream across our nation: the anglophones fleeing Quebec. These were unusual refugees, whether individual or corporate: they brought with them not only their skills but also their wealth. Accompanying them were many of the less nationalistic francophone youth seeking greener pastures to the west.

By 1967, even before Montreal's acute problems began, Toronto had about two-thirds of the nation's manufacturing capacity. Of the Canadian total of $230 million worth of cheques written against individual accounts, 33.3 percent were cashed in Toronto compared with 26.4 percent in Montreal. The growth of Toronto in finance is particularly notable. Three of the big five banks have their headquarters in the city and the other two major chartered banks, which have Montreal head offices, the Royal and Montreal, have been switching important parts of their operations—for example, international banking and computers—to the Toronto area. Furthermore, of the 52 recently admitted foreign banks, 43 have chosen Toronto as their Canadian headquarters. Toronto has also been the centre for life and fire insurance companies for many years. The Toronto Stock Exchange in 1981 was trading 1,221 issues of 838 companies with a value of $25 billion, 40 times that of 1937, and the new exchange offices, opened in May 1983, have the world's most advanced equipment.

GOVERNMENT POLITICS AND COMMUNICATION

Municipally the reform forces were gaining influence in the city. When William Dennison, the first New Democratic Party mayor, retired in 1972, the voters returned David Crombie, a Conservative reformer who stressed such issues as delivering more efficient services, giving the taxpayer a better break, and a program of Metro government reexamination, "Reform, Retrench, and Simplicity." When Crombie retired shortly before the end of his third term to go to Parliament in Ottawa, the council elected a senior alderman, Fred Beavis, as mayor. He became the first Roman Catholic to hold the city's highest office.

With the elections of 1978 John Sewell, one of the most radical of the reform group, became the new mayor, stressing Crombie's principles but in a more forceful manner. Although Sewell asserted in his inaugural statement that the council was not there "to pursue our internal differences," that, to a large extent, is what it did for a very fractious two years. Controversial civic issues were carried to the Metro Council, where Conservative Chairman Paul Godfrey, in office since 1973, was often at odds with Toronto's mayor. Concurrently the Toronto voters were reacting to tighter economic circumstances and the usual desire for change after a few years. In 1980 the reform wave broke against conservative rocks, and Arthur C. Eggleton defeated Sewell with a platform of more jobs, homes for all, and safety and security for residences, workplaces,

The Metro Toronto International Caravan is an annual celebration of Toronto's ethnic mix. A Caravan "passport" allows a visitor to wander freely through the world in miniature over a 10-day period OMIT 74050419

Opposite page: The Ontario Legislature at Queen's Park was photographed at night, decorated for the 1967 Centennial of Canadian Confederation. Toronto took a backseat to Montreal which hosted EXPO '67, the world's fair that was the focus of Centennial celebrations. Ontario Place, which opened in 1971, was perceived by many to be a kind of poor boy's replacement. Since then, much of the EXPO site has fallen into decay, and Ontario Place flourishes. Courtesy, Ontario Ministry of Industry and Tourism (OMIT), 5K 2567

Why—one might ask—is this woman smiling? The photograph is taken from the publicity files of the Ontario Ministry of Industry and Tourism and dates from the early 1950s. Is the suggestion that even receiving a ticket is pleasurable in Toronto? Nostalgia isn't what it used to be. AO Acc. 9508-12947

and streets. Toronto had returned to its more Tory approach, but the reform period had left some important legacies.

One of the major developments of the decade was the continuing improvement in transportation. In 1967, to aid in the Yonge Street subway extension, the TTC was finally relieved of the municipal taxes it had paid since 1921 as successor of the old private company. The six-mile-long Bloor subway extensions were opened in 1969, and the second Yonge subway extension to Finch Avenue was announced the same year. That route was opened in 1974. Meanwhile, provincial funding made possible both a Spadina subway and further extensions to the Bloor Street line. The $220-million Spadina subway opened in 1978. The Bloor line is now being extended east to the Scarborough Town Centre and other lines are being planned.

With the decision to retain streetcars on selected routes, the TTC ordered 200 new cars in 1974, and is planning the introduction of a new streetcar route. The provincial government itself extended its GO trains, which by 1967 were running along the lake shore from Hamilton to Pickering with fifty 80-mile-per-hour trains per day. In 1970 the Hamilton service was improved and new lines extended to Barrie and Oshawa. Double-decker trains appeared in 1978. The Spadina Expressway, a continuing source of friction, had remained unfinished.

The expressway's problem of public opposition was repeated again at Toronto International Airport where a 1969 $300-million, 2,000-acre expansion was cut back considerably because of local opposition, although Terminal 2 was opened in 1973. The Ontario government also acted as a brake on airport expansion with the establishment of noise zones over an 80-square-mile area around the airport. Plans for a second, 18,000-acre airport at Pickering, 30 miles northeast of the city, ran into similar problems, and its development has been postponed indefinitely.

The difficulties of the expressways and the airport have been nothing compared with those of an institution long regarded as the most reliable of public services: the post office. In his enjoyable 1967 history of Toronto, Bruce West correctly noted that Torontonians could then pay five cents for posting a letter that would be jet-propelled to Vancouver by the next day, and that they would complain if it did not get there. In the following years there has been the introduction of area codes, the building of a vastly expensive and complex Gateway terminal, and a fire at the old Union Station Post Office, where the belts were not turned off quickly enough and carried burning mail from one section of the building to another. Today, if you deliver it to the central office, the post office has a priority post service that will take your letter from Toronto to London, Ontario—a distance of 125 miles—in one day (no guarantee) for a mere $7.42!

DEVELOPMENT, PLANNING, AND HOUSING

In 1970 Mayor Dennison asserted that "our downtown must be planned to keep our city alive at night." To achieve this Dennison believed in working with the business owners' Downtown Redevelopment Advisory

Agency. Mayor Crombie took a different approach, stressing the importance of neighbourhoods and noting the need to both preserve and innovate. Crombie and, later, Sewell stressed "bringing planning to the citizens" and the desirability of mixed residential and commercial use in the downtown area. Crombie's downtown control measure was a height limit which was fought by the developers but upheld by the Ontario Municipal Board in 1978. This allowed the city to control high-rise development and regulate a mixture of houses, offices, and stores in the central business district.

Toronto is today witnessing an interesting process through which the height bylaw is being modified by transfer-of-development legislation, allowing the owners of historical buildings to transfer the unneeded air space above their structures to other property owners, who then can increase the height limit for their buildings at other locations. This saves the historical buildings and allows more flexible development. A transfer of residential building credits is also possible. In all, the rather tangled legislative pattern is sorting itself out to create a living central city.

Banks have led the way in the redevelopment of the central business district: the Bank of Commerce's Commerce Centre; the Bank of Montreal's 70-storey tower; and the Royal Bank's imaginative, genuine gold-tinted glass towers flanking an opulent central banking hall. The Bank of Nova Scotia is currently planning to retain its 1940s executive offices and build a modern building around them. The evolution of the design of such complexes points the way to a new architecture for our cities: not just a forest of upended, multicoloured four-by-fours, but rather new styles to match the new technology and materials, with surviving historic structures included in the pattern.

Highway 401 links Detroit/ Windsor with Montreal. At one time Torontonians pointed to it proudly as a symbol of progress. Nowadays, however, the definition of "progress" seems to have changed, and the 401 with its sprawling intersections is thought to be merely a necessary evil. OMIT 42060815

One of the most vital links in the continuing rejuvenation of the downtown has been the new Eaton-Fairview Centre, which stretches north from Queen Street along the west side of Yonge Street to Dundas Street, leaving the old City Hall safely standing to its west and the 1847 Church of the Holy Trinity and two historical houses virtually embedded in its arms. The $200-million, 15-acre Eaton's development includes 302 stores in an 860-foot-long, 4-level interior shopping mall with Eaton's own store to its north. It connects with Simpson's to the south across Queen Street and through a network of underground tunnels is joined to the new malls of the banking centres. Now it is possible for Torontonians to walk north from Union Station through some 2.5 miles of underground malls and tunnels to the roofed court yard of the Atrium development north of Eaton's without venturing into wintry weather. Excellent shopping malls also have risen in the suburbs, such as the Yorkdale and Sherway shopping centres. Scarborough and North York have led the way in establishing municipal town centres.

Providing adequate housing has been a constant problem. In the 1950s the Regent Park, a 42.5-acre subsidized housing development, was built. The Ontario Housing Corporation, which took over the assets of the Toronto Housing Authority in 1969, has since extended its operations. Apartment prices escalated during the economic boom of the

Toronto became very much a focal point for Canadian demonstrations in the 1960s. A strong sense of nationalism emerged in those prosperous years which, as it often had in the past, took the form of anti-Americanism. That sentiment is a part of the 1966 anti-Vietnam War demonstration at Nathan Phillips Square, urging withdrawal of U.S. forces. PAC PA93533

1970s; for instance, in the first six months of 1973 they increased by 23.6 percent. As a result provincial rent controls were instituted despite great opposition.

By the late 1960s Toronto proper was ceasing to be a city of private homes as the cost of operating a home rose and more apartments were built. In the 1960s and 1970s the main theme was the migration downtown by the affluent, who were tired of fighting traffic. This resulted in the purchasing and refurbishing of many century-old homes in areas like the once-poor immigrant district of Cabbagetown, just north of the Regent Park development. This white-painting phase of downtown redevelopment saved many old areas from the wrecker, but it did nothing to solve the housing problem for the poor, who were forced to move elsewhere. Recent trends have been to give more consideration to subsidized housing in new developments, particularly downtown, and rent controls appear to be permanently entrenched with the large number of voters affected.

SOCIETY AND CULTURE

Torontonians generally have been rather defensive of their city and its appellation "Hogtown." With the 1960s this attitude began to change, the city was becoming a metropolis, and American tourists were now flocking to Toronto and lauding its joys, its cuisine, its shopping, and its safety. The new pride showed in the 1974 City Council decision to have a Toronto flag. A $500 prize offer resulted in some 700 entries, and the winner was Renato De Santis, a 21-year-old George Brown College design student.

In the late 1960s the city became a northern magnet for the counterculture. Its devotees flocked into the Yorkville area, which was then being rejuvenated as the declining housing was spruced up and boutiques and restaurants made their appearance. For a while the area was one of the more lively sections of the city, but Toronto's flower people were dispersed by conservative opposition and increased rents and costs. Grubby old Yonge Street changed, too, becoming a night place for youth and a centre for the gay community. By 1975 massage parlours and sex shops had proliferated greatly. A police clean-up began, which led to the end of the massage parlours in 1978 after the murder of a 12-year-old shoeshine boy. The later raids on the gay steam baths seemed to many a resurgence of old Toronto morality, designed mainly to embarrass the patrons. Yonge Street has now developed the inevitable pinball machines and a wide spectrum of movie houses.

By the late 1960s half the Metro population was non-British and the non-British were in the majority in the old city. The Italian community was the largest; but there was a wide variety of groups, including an increasing number of Portuguese. Together these new Canadians and now well-established Canadians represented the first major switch in the ethnic character of Toronto since the arrival of the Irish in the 1840s. Except for the expanding Chinese community, virtually all were from a European background.

Then with the new more liberal immigration legislation passed by the federal government, Toronto suddenly became the home of an increasing number of Arabs, Asians, Latin Americans, and West Indians, many from the former colonies of the British Empire. The result was a new diversity with new customs and new religions, and inevitably new strains appeared. After some incidents Metro Chairman Paul Godfrey appointed a task force to look into the matter of racism and violence in 1977. The recommendations were acted upon and the situation has improved. Fortunately, none of the problems resulted in any major confrontations, and the life of the city has been further enriched with the ethnic summer restaurant caravans and parades.

The arrival of new ethnic groups in Toronto has led to a further diversification of the city's publishing scene. Many ethnic journals have long flourished; now they are being supplemented in almost every major language of the world. Toronto is also a favoured place for the initiation of new publishing ventures and continues to be the home of most of the leading Canadian publishing houses. The 1970s witnessed the first major reorganization of Toronto newspapers since the 1930s. When the *Evening Telegram* folded in October 1971, after 95 years of operation, its building was purchased by the *Globe and Mail*, its subscription list by the *Star*, and 60 of its ex-employees went on to found the first Toronto tabloid, the *Sun*, a morning paper to rival the *Globe*. At the end of the first six months' operations, the *Sun* had a circulation of 80,000 and has continued to expand. The *Globe* not only has survived but is generally recognized as Canada's national newspaper.

With the growth of Toronto as a financial and business centre, new financial journals have also made their appearance, such as the long-established *Financial Post's* new *Investor's Digest*, begun in 1968. Possibly the most significant symbol of Toronto's changing status was the founding of its own *New Yorker:* the monthly *Toronto Life*, which first appeared in November 1966 and has never looked back.

Education's most significant shift was the founding of the Ontario system of community colleges in 1965 for training beyond high school in the more technical fields. A large number of these schools are located in Metro Toronto and its fringe municipalities. George Brown College, named for the founder of the *Globe*, serves central Metro. Sheridan is to the west in Mississauga, Humber to the northwest in Rexdale, Seneca to the north in Willowdale, Centennial to the east in Scarborough, and the Institute of Medical Technology in downtown Toronto. Some of the colleges have unusual campuses: George Brown has successfully refurbished some fine 19th-century warehouses, and Seneca purchased the 696-acre Lady Eaton estate in Willowdale, with its 80-room mansion, as its third location.

The universities have continued to expand, the most significant building being the $42-million University of Toronto John P. Robarts Research Library, which was opened as the central university research library for the province in 1973. In 1970 the University of Toronto also acquired the Ontario Institute for Studies in Education, which was de-

signed as the major educational research and curriculum development institute for Ontario.

One of the strangest tales in Toronto's history, and in educational history anywhere, must be the story of Rochdale College, an experimental, residential, student-operated, nonstructured institution, which existed without faculty, curriculum, or even any requirements that the residents be registered students. In the liberal educational atmosphere of the late 1960s, the originators, who soon departed from the scene, persuaded the Central Mortgage and Housing Corporation to provide the funding for construction, and the college opened its doors in 1968. Almost immediately it was in trouble. There was no real research or study evident, except possibly in the mixing, use, and distribution of interesting chemicals. After 14 months financial collapse came when the residents would not pay their rent. Reprieves on foreclosure were obtained through a spiralling number of mortgages, but this money disappeared too. In 1973 CMHC, as first mortgagee, began foreclosure proceedings when payments were $5.8 million in arrears. Permission to evict the tenants was finally obtained after hard-fought, rearguard legal action; in October 1975 the last were removed. CMHC took over and Rochdale began a very different life as a senior citizens' home. For seven years the Toronto newspapers had been provided with a superb topic for discussion and the Toronto police had more than a few lively evenings.

Toronto's educational facilities were greatly expanded by the construction of the Ontario Science Centre as the provincial Centennial project. Announced in 1965, the $30-million complex located in a 180-acre park in the Don Valley northeast of the city was opened four years later and became an immediate hit. In 1974 a new Toronto Zoo followed on 700 acres of Rouge Valley land in Scarborough. Other recreational facilities included the Ontario government's Ontario Place, a $23-million

Growth in education at all levels was unparalleled in the decades after the Second World War. Such expansion was unprecedented at the University of Toronto: new buildings spilled west across St. George Street, filling up the blocks from College to Harbord. Student life was relatively docile—the calm before the storm of the activist 1960s. That serene mood is captured in this sedate 1956 photograph of what was then the men's undergraduate centre, Hart House. AO 8-E-1656

neighbour to the CNE that was constructed on stilts in Lake Ontario in 1970. In 1982, thanks to the generosity of Spencer and Rose Clark, who sold the property for far under its real value, Metro was able to purchase the Guild Inn in Scarborough with its 87 acres and unique collection of architectural fragments from old Toronto.

While these developments were taking place, Toronto's established cultural institutions were preparing for renovation. The Art Gallery of Ontario (formerly of Toronto) was greatly extended, with new exhibits including British sculptor Henry Moore's 300-item collection of drawings and models. The Royal Ontario Museum began its expansion a few years later, opening the first galleries in 1982; equally important, it acquired new curatorial and storage space with all the latest in museum technology. Roy Thomson Hall opened at the same time as the museum to supplement aging Massey Hall, which was retained for its excellent acoustic properties.

The crowning triumph of the new Toronto and the symbol of the city is the new CN Tower, at 1,815 feet the tallest unsupported structure in the world. It was topped in April 1975. The city still lacks an opera house and botanical gardens, although both are under consideration. Sports facilities have also improved with the American League baseball franchise awarded for the Blue Jays, and Chairman Godfrey is organizing the planning for a domed stadium. Thus, today Toronto's cultural, sports, and entertainment amenities and the variety and quality of its hotels and restaurants, which will be rounded out by the new convention centre, make it a most congenial urban focus.

Of course, there have been problems in the last few years. There has been an increase in crime, although the city is a comparatively safe one. Pollution has increased. There have been strikes, and there have been some bombings, the worst being of the 1982 Litton Systems' plant in Rexdale, where 550 pounds of dynamite were used in an attempt to impede production of missile guidance systems. But basically Toronto has been lucky. The worst fire since 1904 began in the old Eaton's buildings as they were being demolished in 1977 and was brought under control thanks to modern equipment; the Sunday afternoon earthquake in August 1980 was so gentle that it was mainly noticed in the upper floors of high-rise apartments. Most fortunate of all, the disastrous railway wreck of a CPR freight train carrying chlorine and propane tanks, which took place in Mississauga on November 10, 1979, due to overheated equipment, did not result in the feared explosion, although 250,000 people had to be evacuated. In a few minutes the train would have been in the heart of the city, where an explosion could have done even greater damage, and evacuation would have involved far more people.

As the sesquicentennial nears, Toronto has thus achieved urban primacy in the nation and the status of a cultural, economic, and financial North American metropolis. Still, it has remained a pleasant place to live, added new facilities, kept a living downtown core, and is reasonably well-governed. Nature may have provided a good base, but Torontonians have built well on it.

CONCLUSION

TOWARD THE FOURTH HALF-CENTURY

Toronto at the age of 150 has reached metropolitan status; it is truly an international city. Toronto's political leaders have been quite confident and basically accurate in their assessments of the present situation. In 1977 Chairman Godfrey announced that the city was "one of the most prosperous, best planned, and best administrated municipalities on the North American continent," and a year later Mayor Crombie asserted that "Toronto has been singled out as a safe, sane, and decent place to live." From a more neutral position and greater distance the *Los Angeles Times*, after reciting some of the joys of the city, added: "On top of this, Toronto works."

Conversely, some academics, with that old-time deprecation of the city they seem to so enjoy purveying—while yet enjoying its amenities—have suggested that Toronto's future will be to become more Ontario-oriented and less national in its role, outlook, and activities. History gives little backing for such a theory: examples of successful metropolitan centres that withdrew into their shells without outside pressure are next to impossible to find. Toronto is enjoying great success in bypassing Montreal in what was once their joint hinterland, which many Torontonians now see as their own just hinterland. It is hardly likely to retreat willingly.

When concluding his excellent Toronto history a dozen years ago, George Glazebrook noted several factors related to metropolitan expansion, among them how a city draws visitors and migrants to itself, and its influences on its neighbourhood and beyond. Toronto's influences on its neighbourhood and beyond are still growing briskly, and barring some unlikely catastrophe, they will continue to do so. As for the first point, the city is increasingly drawing visitors, and although the rural to urban migration has slowed down, as has immigration to Canada, Toronto is a major attraction point for migration within the country. It also continues to grow through a reduced but still rising natural increase.

Toronto itself, or even Metro Toronto, can no longer be seen as an isolated unit when considering future development. A large part of Toronto's success has been directly related to the rich agricultural lands of south-central and southwestern Ontario, and an important factor in the history of the city has been the evolution of the rival and associated towns that grew up in its immediate hinterland. A ring of successful satellites is one of the best assurances a metropolis can have for a healthy future, but, in fact, for Toronto the very success of the satellites and the metropolis itself now presents one of the greatest future problems: the surrounding agricultural land is being eaten up by growing urbanization and such important assets as the Niagara Fruit Belt are in danger of extinction.

In the future Toronto's urban area for practical planning and administrative purposes will have to consist not just of Metro itself and the inner circle of townships that surround it, but really the whole Golden Horseshoe,

199

which stretches westward from Oshawa along what is becoming a pretty continuously built up shoreline through Toronto, Mississauga, Oakville, Burlington, and Hamilton, along the Fruit Belt, and past St. Catharines and Niagara-on-the-Lake to Niagara Falls, where it meets the Buffalo Metropolitan area across the American border. Behind this lake shore belt, inland cities are being drawn into the urban shadow: Brantford to the west, the Kitchener-Waterloo-Guelph conurbation to the northwest, and directly to the north of Toronto, Thornhill, Richmond Hill, Aurora, and so on up Yonge Street to Barrie. The overall planning, policing, water supply, and waste disposal for this area, as well as pollution control, the protection of needed agricultural resources, the transportation network development, and access to recreation, will require much more regulation than has been needed in the past.

A decade ago most of the old counties in the area were reorganized into regional municipalities, a provincial action that was necessary but not particularly popular. Now the need for some overall authority for the Toronto-Hamilton-Niagara region has become urgent. The structure that will emerge is yet to be seen, but without some such organization the result may well be chaos.

The place of democracy in this unit must be considered. Whatever is done, local traditions and loyalties must be taken into account. Individuals want to feel that they belong to some definite area, not to a vast region beyond human grasp. The idea of abolishing the boroughs and creating one base city of Toronto periodically arises; but the numbered wards of such a new city would hardly be units to which individuals could relate with pleasure, any more than the Torontonians of a century ago could relate to the names of the endless saints of their wards. London, England, has retained its local names and, if they are traditional, not hesitated to leave borough boundaries somewhat irregular.

The same could apply here, enabling people to retain a sense of their roots. The provincial government used to show little sensitivity to this issue: it abolished the 18th-century townships when it reformed Haldimand-Norfolk and brought in new names. Then recently it was suggested that the city of Hamilton change its name to Wentworth for more efficient regional organization. This resulted in a well-justified explosion. People not only need elected representatives whom they can know, they also need familiar names for their living places.

There will always be urban problems, but to date Toronto has been both lucky and skillful in avoiding them. With Canadian cities reaching metropolitan size and ethnic complexity later than British and American ones, we are fortunate to have the opportunity to learn from their errors. Toronto, with its ring of prosperous satellite cities, has become a North American metropolitan area through long, quiet growth followed by a sudden burst of development and publicity. Its economic base has long been a successful one; equally important, its cultural base is becoming more significant in English-speaking Canada. The next half-century will bring its problems; but it will also hold many promises for the city.

Modern Toronto's office towers are silhouetted by the setting sun. The city has finally scrambled past Montreal to become—at just over 3 million—Canada's largest.

In 1851 Anthony Reynolds Vyvyan Crease sketched this tranquil watercolour scene of John Street out his drawing-room window. Visible on the left are the Provincial Parliament buildings. Taking place in the background is the ceremonial turning of the first sod of the Ontario, Simcoe & Huron Railway. MTL 1135

"IT'S ONLY A QUESTION OF TIME."
OLD FOGYISM MAY HOLD HER BACK FOR A WHILE, BUT SHE IS BOUND TO COME TO US.

During the late 19th century the feeling was rife amongst a large number of Americans that Canada would inevitably come under "the stars and stripes." This idea was illustrated in J. Kepplen's cartoon It's Only a Question of Time. *PAC C6440*

A woodsy retreat from the frustrations of vice-regal life, Castle Frank was named whimsically by Lieutenant-Governor and Mrs. Simcoe after their son Francis. Its site, rugged and picturesque, was on the west side of the Don River, just to the north of present St. James Cemetery. Francis Simcoe was to die while on active duty during the peninsular wars—at the age of 20. AO Simcoe Sketches 135

Opposite page, top: This contemporary photograph captures the historic St. Lawrence Hall at night.

Opposite page, bottom: An architectural drawing by S.H. Maw illustrates architects Darling and Pearson's scheme for Trinity College's relocation from Queen Street to the St. George campus. The 1914 rendering shows an ambitious knot of Neo-Gothicism; however, the scheme that was finally adopted reproduced the old Queen Street buildings. Hoskin Street runs in the foreground and Devonshire Place can be seen (with stadium) cutting north to Bloor Street. Courtesy, Trinity College Archives

This page, top: The British garrison at Fort York is relived on the site of the original fort every summer. However, all that the present fort shares with the flimsy structure of 1812-1813 is the site, and the boy-soldiers who take pains to re-create the era show much more enthusiasm than their predecessors must have at the dirty and monotonous task of frontier soldiering.

This page, bottom: Dr. Scadding concluded that the upper rotunda and adjacent staircases of Osgoode Hall were reminiscent of sun-dappled Genoese palaces. This view suggests that the claim is not that farfetched.

The light, airy interior of Toronto's new $30 million Metropolitan Library, the work of Japanese-Canadian architect Raymond Moriyama, has been criticized for the wasted space it occasions. Still the public crowds into its 1,100 places daily; the library's one million books seem well accommodated, too. Pictured are a detail of the glass and brick exterior (right) and a view of the atrium (opposite page, top). Photo of the exterior by Ninette Maumus; interior courtesy, Ontario Ministry of Industry and Tourism, 4/4/P

Opposite page, bottom: A reclining, clothed student finds himself among the reclining nudes and other sculptures in the Henry Moore gallery at the Art Gallery of Ontario.

Right: The "new" Chinatown's commercial strip along Dundas Street bustles on a spring afternoon. It is estimated that the Chinese community in Toronto numbers 100,000. Photo by Sandra Martin

Opposite page, top: Scots pipers sweep down Queen's Park Crescent in the annual Canadian National Exhibition Parade.

Opposite page, bottom: The Caribana Parade, the annual festival of Toronto's Caribbean community, features colourful dances and performances.

Opposite page, right: A clump of signs at the corner of Carlaw indicates to the informed stroller Toronto's Greek neighbourhood. Photo by Sandra Martin

Opposite page, top: The old Toronto Stock Exchange, Toronto's first air-conditioned building, closed in May 1983. Action at the new exchange is reported to be quieter and less frantic, "like the lobby of a Holiday Inn" according to one critic. The fate of the old building is undecided.

Opposite page, bottom: This view of Bloor Street, looking east from the roof of the Park Plaza Hotel, is scarcely 20 years old. The changes in that relatively short time have been vast, not only in terms of buildings and commercial establishments or the removal of the streetcars and telephone wires, but also in the spirit of the area. Modern Bloor Street is upbeat Toronto's main street—trendy, expensive, international, and not a little arrogant. AO XS 4310

Left: The lush Hazleton Terrace in Hazleton Lanes is the kind of restaurant, as one critic put it, where "photographers go to shoot Remy-Martin advertisements for Vogue." At high summer most of this oasis is covered with enormous Moorish umbrellas; in winter it becomes a skating rink. Photo by Sandra Martin

Toronto's central core was photographed at sunset looking south to the Toronto Islands and Lake Ontario.

Right: A crowd gathers at Harbourfront to listen to an informal concert.

Opposite page, top: Ontario Place rests on three man-made islands adjacent to the CNE grounds. Two million visitors attend the recreation and exhibition centre each year. An aerial view captures Ontario Place surrounded by shimmering water.

Opposite page, bottom: Toronto's autumns are sharp, glorious, and all too short. Photo by Ninette Maumus

Below: Signs like the one pictured are placed on public lawns—this one at Edwards Gardens—to invite, not intimidate.

PLEASE WALK <u>ON</u> THE GRASS

PRIERE DE MARCHER <u>SUR</u> LE GAZON

METROPOLITAN TORONTO PARKS DEPARTMENT

Following page: Robert Gagen completed his splendid oil painting Temples of Commerce *just before the First World War. The work shows the solidity and muscular business sense of Toronto's downtown core. English poet Rupert Brooke described the same Toronto in 1913: "Toronto, soul of Canada, is wealthy, busy commercial, Scotch, [and] absorbent of whisky." Brooke continued: "One must say something—what must one say about Toronto? What can one? What has anybody ever said? It is impossible to give it anything but commendation. It is not squalid like Birmingham, or cramped like Canton, or scattered like Edmonton, or sham like Berlin, or hellish like New York, or tiresome like Nice. It is all right. The only depressing thing is that it will always be what it is only larger, and that no Canadian city can ever be anything better or different. If they are good they may become Toronto." MTL 15*

CHAPTER XV

PARTNERS IN PROGRESS

BY GORDON PITTS, ASSISTED BY GEOFFREY SIMMINS

An era ended in Toronto's financial life in May 1983, when the Toronto Stock Exchange vacated its home of 46 years on Bay Street for sleeker, more spacious new premises about a block away.

The move—in itself a mammoth undertaking—also is symbolic of the forward-looking spirit that has characterized Toronto's business community from the beginning. As the following corporate biographies indicate, the city's business leaders have seldom shied away from risk taking and innovation, and have adapted successfully to changing times.

The TSE's move was prompted largely by the demands of state-of-the-art technology—which also mirrors what is happening to Toronto's business fabric. Industries once thought to be the stuff of science fiction—computers, computer services, video production, for example—are commonplace today. And firms in more traditional fields have had to adapt to this new wave of innovation if they hope to survive.

Thus, Toronto's businesses are reshaping the character and image of the city, as they have been doing since 1700 when the area was becoming a flourishing entrepôt for the fur trade between Native Indians and the European intruders.

As European settlements were established in the 1800s, Toronto with its natural harbour became a vital link in the commercial highway of the St. Lawrence River and the Great Lakes, along which shiploads of goods moved toward European markets. An ambitious, prosperous middle class emerged, including millers, bankers, accountants, and railroad and shipping magnates.

The 20th century brought several revolutions to Toronto's business community. A more affluent population wanted consumer goods and homes of their own. Manufacturers, retailers, and builders filled the void. And waves of immigrants contributed new entrepreneurs and new types of ventures.

Furthermore, Toronto, which

traditionally had been the runner-up to Montreal as a financial centre, overtook and passed its rival during the 1960s and 1970s. Nowhere is this preeminence more evident than in the towering office buildings of major banks and financial institutions which dominate the skyline—and where thousands of Torontonians work.

Toronto is Canada's centre for banking, publishing, and broadcasting, and is developing an international reputation as well. But it would be a mistake to think that the city's development has been solely the product of big business. As the following chapter shows, a healthy portion of Toronto's success has come from smaller enterprises—many of which have grown phenomenally as a result of their efforts.

Today, in industrial areas, strip plazas, and in offices above shops, often in parts of metropolitan Toronto remote from the downtown core, men and women are chasing their dreams. They, too, are "partners in progress."

THE ONTARIO HISTORICAL SOCIETY

It was a classic David-and-Goliath struggle—the combined might of the Toronto City Council and the Canadian National Exhibition against a band of historical conservationists of The Ontario Historical Society (OHS).

The year was 1905. The city and the CNE were hatching a plan to build a trolley line through the centre of Old Fort York, where soldiers had died in defence of the British Empire in the War of 1812.

The rapidly expanding "Ex," which sought to improve the traffic flow to its grounds, was contributing mightily to Toronto's economy and civic pride. As Gerald Killan writes in his history of the OHS, "Little wonder that, at City Hall, it was firmly believed that what was good for the CNE was good for Toronto."

But the trolley line was not to be, because of the untiring efforts of the OHS and one of its leaders, F. Barlow Cumberland, a Toronto businessman. In 1909 Prime Minister Sir Wilfrid Laurier, whose government had final authority in the matter, prohibited streetcars from running through the fort.

This was arguably the finest hour for the Society since the founding of its predecessor organization, the Pioneer Association of Ontario, in 1888. As envisaged by the Pioneer Association's founder, Canon Henry Scadding, a Toronto clergyman, the Society had become a coordinating body for local historical societies in Ontario.

Besides Old Fort York—the Society came to the defence of that landmark several times—it championed the preservation of other historical sites and the erection of historical plaques and memorials.

It also became the vehicle of a nascent English-Canadian nationalism—a belief that the province had a unique and distinguished heritage, reaching back to the Loyalist settlement of the late 1700s and the repulsion of American invaders in the

The Reverend Dr. Scadding, founder of The Ontario Historical Society. (Courtesy of Archives of Ontario S5677.)

War of 1812.

Over the years the Society has been blessed with worthy leaders, among them James Coyne, who reshaped the Provincial Society into the OHS in 1898; David Boyle, the first secretary from 1898 to 1907; and Brigadier General Ernest Cruikshank, who as president pulled the Society out of its lethargy after World War I.

Their work is continued today by the Society's elected president and executive, its Toronto-based staff, led by an executive director, and about 3,000 members and subscribers. More than 300 local historical societies are members or affiliates of the OHS, which assists them by sponsoring workshops on such topics as heritage conservation, oral history, archival methods, and the writing, researching, and interpreting of the province's social history.

The Society's major contribution has been its publications and that tradition continues, through both its newsletter, *Bulletin*, covering events in the preservation field, and the quarterly *Ontario History*, the only scholarly journal specializing in the study of the province's history.

As former president Gerald Killan has remarked: "Since it was founded in 1888, The Ontario Historical Society has never been more vital, relevant, or credible than it is today."

Historical exhibition poster by J.D. Kelly for The Ontario Historical Society, 1899.

DATALINE INC.

The ability to react quickly to technological and market changes has carried Dataline Inc. of Toronto from a small computer-service bureau with 15 employees to a diversified, national company with 200 people employed in four Canadian cities.

When the Canadian computer industry was in its infancy, two young men saw an opportunity to carve out a niche in a particularly fledgling part of that industry—computer time-sharing. In layman's language, that is the operation of a central computer facility connected by a communications network to a number of widely dispersed clients for whom it performs data-processing services.

The young men founded Dataline in 1968. They hired a dozen others, most of whom had worked with computers as employees or were students at the University of Toronto. A few months later they installed their first unit, a Digital Equipment Corporation DECSystem-10, in an office and computer centre at 40 St. Clair Avenue West.

Dr. Joseph C. Paradi, one of the founders, has been president of Dataline for almost all of its 13-year history. The Hungarian immigrant has a Ph.D. in chemical engineering and is

The original Dataline computer room at the 40 St. Clair Avenue West site with two Digital Equipment Corporation PDP-10 time-sharing computers.

the majority owner of Dataline. He has always looked beyond the company to industry issues, and was three times president (1972, 1982, 1983) of the Canadian Association of Data Processing Services Organization.

Initially, the firm's clients wrote or supplied their own software, or computer programmes, while Dataline provided the data-processing services. In the early years the company displayed particular strength in engineering or statistical processing for corporate and government clients. In 1970-1971 the market for statistical processing burgeoned in Ottawa, and the organization opened its first bureau outside Toronto in the capital city.

Dataline's revenues grew rapidly in the early 1970s and in 1973 the company recorded its first profit. Two years later its most dramatic turning point occurred when its shares began

to trade publicly on the Toronto Stock Exchange.

Having outgrown its St. Clair Avenue West quarters, Dataline in 1975 moved to a building at 175 Bedford Road (formerly the home of a venetian blind manufacturer) that still serves as head office, computer centre, and base for support staff, and operates 24 hours a day. The Toronto sales staff also utilizes offices at 67 Richmond Street West.

In the mid-1970s, with the fast-moving industry demanding more than computer services, Dataline became a kind of computer shopping-centre—providing time-sharing, software packages, support services, facilities management, and consulting.

Today the corporation markets a wide range of software products that include an electronic Cashnet system used by banks, an information system for the oil and gas industry, a trust industry system, and many other large applications.

In the 1982 fiscal year, Dataline reported profits of $203,000 on sales of almost $10 million. This represents a compound growth rate of 23 percent from sales of 630,000 in 1970.

The current data centre, located at 175 Bedford Road, operates six Digital Equipment Corporation DECSystem-10 computers, two IBM 4341 computers, and close to 100 specialized communications computers.

I.P. SHARP ASSOCIATES LIMITED

Ian P. Sharp, president of I.P. Sharp Associates Limited. (Photo by Bruce Cole, Plum Studio Incorporated.)

I.P. Sharp Associates Limited is Canada's largest privately owned data-processing services company—with 60 offices in 22 countries serving 1,500 clients. Six of the eight founders are still with the organization, including its Dublin-born president, Ian P. Sharp.

The software specialists opened for business in 1964 in a basement office near the corner of Lawrence Avenue and Keele Street, decorating the office themselves in exchange for two months' free rent. In its first year the new firm accrued $176,000 in revenues. Growth has since been 40-percent compounded annually, and in 1982 Sharp grossed over $50 million.

From the beginning the organization had an international outlook: Its first contract was in Edinburgh, Scotland. Today 70 percent of Sharp's business is outside Canada.

A contract in 1966 led to the development of its major software product—APL (A Programming Language). This concise and flexible system provided the foundation of Sharp's time-sharing business, which it conducts worldwide through a communications network that serves approximately 8,500 people daily.

This network makes Sharp's software products—or programmes—available to its time-sharing customers. Its major areas of software development have been in communications and large-scale data bases. The company has specialized particularly in products for the financial, aviation, and energy industries, and in the economics field. An important part of its business is providing industry with information, often of an economic nature.

Sharp has been operating almost totally free of memos, telephones, and telexes since 1970 because of its electronic mail system—a product also available to customers. The result has been faster decision making.

In 1967 Sharp and its 25 employees moved from the original office to Toronto-Dominion Centre, then again in 1974 to York Centre on King Street at University Avenue. In 1982 there was another relocation to the Exchange Tower, 2 First Canadian Place, where the firm occupies three floors.

I.P. Sharp Associates Limited plans to grow in response to the demands of its customers. This market-driven approach explains two 1982 initiatives: agreements with representative agencies to distribute its products in Japan and South Korea.

The "bridge" of the I.P. Sharp data centre in Toronto—the focus of activity for its worldwide time-sharing service.

P. LAWSON TRAVEL LTD.

Torontonians are ambitious travellers who make extensive use of travel agencies. And P. Lawson Travel Ltd., Canada's largest travel bureau, obtains a large part of this business.

But although P. Lawson Travel Ltd. is more than 50 years old, its Toronto history is quite recent: It opened its first branch there in 1963 (at 83 Bloor Street West) and moved its head office to the city from Calgary in 1966.

But the company can indirectly lay claim to an important part of Toronto travel history through its 1966 purchase of O.K. Johnson Travel Ltd., which had operated since the 1930s.

The Swedish-born O.K. Johnson built a substantial business from his office at the corner of Bay and Gerrard streets in downtown Toronto. He cultivated a loyal clientele among the city's Scandinavian population and some members of its business elite, including the well-known business-man and horseman, E.P. Taylor.

It is ironic that when O.K. Johnson finally sold his agency, it was to another Scandinavian-Canadian, Peter Lawson, who was born in Denmark. Lawson had formed his own travel, insurance, and real estate business in Calgary in 1931.

In the early 1960s P. Lawson Travel Ltd. expanded rapidly across Canada, and by the mid-1960s had become the first Canadian-owned nationwide travel bureau. Its managers eventually decided that the large Eastern Canadian market required a more concentrated effort and moved the head office to Toronto in 1966. It was first located in the Royal Bank Building at 20 King Street West, shifted to the Toronto-Dominion Centre in 1967, and in 1972 transferred to 2 Carlton Street, its current address.

P. Lawson Travel Ltd. organized one of the first post-World War II tours of the People's Republic of China in 1965. A group of 130 from Alberta and British Columbia made the trip, which had been prompted by the first

The P. Lawson Travel Ltd. office in the Shell Canada building on University Avenue in Toronto.

sales of Canadian wheat to China.

The firm also handles many top corporate travel accounts and is the leading travel agency in Canada in this respect. Professional business travel has become a strong requirement for many companies and P. Lawson Travel Ltd. coordinates and handles all travel arrangements for many leading corporations in Canada.

As befits an industry leader, P. Lawson Travel Ltd. takes a keen interest in travel industry issues. John Powell, its president since 1968, was chairman of a federal task force on tourism in 1979, first president of the Ontario Travel Industry Association in 1976-1977, and first chairman of the National Alliance of Canadian Travel Associations in 1978-1979.

Today the firm's annual sales volume amounts to $150 million and it employs 400 people, more than 100 of them based in Toronto.

P. Lawson Travel Ltd. is also located in Richmond, British Columbia.

REED STENHOUSE COMPANIES LIMITED

In the head office of Reed Stenhouse Companies Limited hangs a massive map of the world, carved up by jagged lines into the various time zones. It's an appropriate artifact because, at any time, in any time zone, a Reed Stenhouse employee might be doing insurance business.

This Toronto-based company is among the top half-dozen insurance and reinsurance brokers in the world with over 180 offices in 33 countries and a worldwide work force of 6,000, including 1,600 elsewhere in Canada and 350 in Toronto.

It assesses the insurance needs of thousands of clients (chiefly corporations, institutions, or governments) and places appropriate coverage with underwriters. With its international scope, Reed Stenhouse arranges virtually any type of insurance quickly and economically on a global basis.

As well, the firm provides many other services, including advice on risk management, loss-prevention engineering, computerized financial risk analysis, and employee benefits, actuarial, and compensation consulting.

Reed Stenhouse's Canadian roots can be traced to a couple of one-man insurance agencies, formed in Toronto in the 1870s by Samuel Shaw and Joseph B. Reed. The successors to these men merged the two agencies in 1905 to form one organization, which became known as Reed, Shaw & McNaught.

The firm embarked on several decades of steady growth in Eastern Canada. In 1958, as it was considering expansion into the West, a Vancouver brokerage, B.L. Johnson Walton Ltd., was poised to spread eastward. The two firms joined to create a national entity.

The merger added a healthy dash of entrepreneurship in James W. (Judd) Whittall, the Vancouver firm's senior partner, who had entered the insurance business in 1936 as a $60-a-month office assistant and retired from

Reed Stenhouse as President in 1979.

In 1968 Reed, Shaw & McNaught merged with Osler, Hammond & Nanton Insurance Ltd., a company which also had its origins in Toronto in the 19th century, and Cronyn, Pocock and Robinson Ltd. of London, Ontario. The new corporation, Reed Shaw Osler Limited, became a public company with shares traded on the Toronto, Montreal, and Vancouver stock exchanges.

The firm moved its head office from 25 Adelaide Street West to the new Royal Trust Tower, part of the Toronto-Dominion Centre complex, in 1970.

By the following year Whittall was involved in merger negotiations with Hugh Stenhouse, Managing Director of A.R. Stenhouse & Partners Ltd., a prominent Glasgow-based broker. Stenhouse wanted into North America; Reed was strong in Canada. Reed wanted an international presence; Stenhouse could provide that. Both wanted to penetrate the United States.

But before the knot could be tied, Hugh Stenhouse was killed in a car accident in 1971. It took time for negotiations to resume, but in 1973 the Stenhouse company merged its brokerage business into the Canadian firm in exchange for 53 percent of the equity and 50 percent of the voting interest in the new entity. A key figure representing Stenhouse was William M. Wilson, Whittall's successor as President and Chief Executive Officer, now a well-ensconced Toronto resident.

To acknowledge the importance of the merger in a more meaningful manner and to lend greater effectiveness to this worldwide partnership, the corporate name was changed to Reed Stenhouse Companies Limited in 1978.

Since then, the corporation has become a force in the U.S. insurance market, while continuing its growth

around the world. In 1982 Reed Stenhouse Companies reported worldwide net earnings of $15.5 million on revenues of $292.5 million. It has attained a strong position in providing services to clients in such fields as navigation, aviation, chemicals, petroleum and natural gas, manufacturing, mining, construction, forest products, retailing, food and agriculture, finance, transportation, and recreation.

Its Board of Directors has included Toronto lawyer John B. Aird, who resigned as Director and Chairman in 1980 when he became Lieutenant Governor of Ontario, and the late John P. Robarts, former Ontario Premier.

Reed Stenhouse is represented at Lloyd's of London, both as a broker and as manager of several underwriting syndicates, and has a syndicate management company at the New York Insurance Exchange.

URBAN TRANSPORTATION DEVELOPMENT CORPORATION LTD.

The latest generation of streetcars operated by the Toronto Transit Commission (TTC) was produced by the Urban Transportation Development Corporation Ltd. (UTDC). Having worked with TTC officials on a preliminary design, UTDC was awarded a contract in 1975 to supply replacements for 30-year-old streetcars. First introduced to regular service in 1979, in 1982 the bright red-and-white cars comprised 196 of the TTC's 350-streetcar fleet.

While thousands of Torontonians now ride the carriers daily, others will also benefit from the results of UTDC's research. In mid-1982 the company, owned by the Ontario government, had about one billion dollars in contracts on the books, including a $650-million, 13-mile rail system for Vancouver by 1986; a $150-million, three-mile line in Detroit for 1985; and, in metropolitan Toronto, a $45-million contract to supply vehicles and services for the new $130-million system line connecting the Kennedy subway station with Scarborough Town Centre by 1984.

UTDC, formed in 1975 to develop and market new transportation technology, was born out of a provincial-cabinet decision to block the Spadina Expressway—which would have sliced through the west-central part of Toronto. Spurred by its increased commitment to public

The Articulated Light Rail Vehicle (ALRV) is a derivative of Toronto's CLRV streetcars. It ran in a demonstration programme on Toronto streets during 1982. The ICTS vehicle (shown on the elevated guideway) is similar to vehicles that will run on the new transit line between Kennedy Station and Scarborough Town Centre. Similar rapid transit systems will run in Vancouver and Detroit.

transit, Ontario sought a system that would operate at a passenger capacity between the streetcar and subway, yet without the high construction costs of the subway. At first, hopes rested on a German system, but it could not meet performance requirements.

UTDC continued research into an intermediate-capacity, quiet, and inexpensive system, and in 1977 the first prototype vehicle for an Intermediate Capacity Transit System (ICTS) ran on the UTDC test track. The

ICTS, which is being supplied to Vancouver, Detroit, and Scarborough, is an elevated, automated rapid transit system running on steel wheels and rails. Noise is low because the train's axles follow the rails through curves, eliminating the squealing noise associated with conventional steel-wheel trains. The system's linear induction motor further reduces noise and provides the precise control needed for fully automated operations.

The organization's original mandate was research, development, manufacturing, and the marketing of its technology. It also assumes principal responsibility for delivering and operating entire transit systems. Together with operating Metro Canada Ltd. (the delivery arm for UTDC products), a research division, an international consulting service, and a marketing company in the United States, the firm is also owner of VentureTrans Manufacturing Inc. of Kingston, Ontario, which manufactures transit vehicles.

From its Toronto head office at 2 St. Clair Avenue West, where about 50 of 450-500 employees work, UTDC's impact is changing the way Toronto travels.

The 480-acre Transit Development Centre is located on the eastern shore of Lake Ontario. There are two test tracks on site used in the development and proving of transit systems and their component parts.

TECK CORPORATION

It's a trek of more than 2,000 miles from the rugged, forested northland of Ontario and Quebec to the mountains and shimmering seascapes of British Columbia on the West Coast. But the path has been well-trod by many Canadians—individuals and companies—in search of new stores of resources.

As business opportunities have shifted westward, so has a company called Teck Corporation. Its origins are in Teck-Hughes Gold Mines Ltd., established to develop a gold mine in the Kirkland Lake area of northern Ontario in 1913. But today, Teck is a Vancouver-based organization with assets in excess of $430 million and vast interests in mining, oil, and gas.

And it is constantly breaking new ground, not just in mining but in an eclectic mix of research and development projects—desalinization, cancer research, fertilizers, and innovative batteries, to name a few.

Along its 70-year corporate odyssey, Teck has had close ties with Toronto. This city was its head office from 1932 to 1972, when it relocated in Vancouver, reflecting the changing focus of its resource activities. Teck maintains a highly visible presence in Toronto, with its spectacularly modern offices designed by Vancouver architect Arthur Erickson occupying the 70th floor of First Canadian Place One.

The story of Teck over the past 25 years is the story of two Keevils, Dr. Norman Keevil, a farmer's son from Saskatchewan who became a university professor, pioneer in aeromagnetic prospecting, and successful mining entrepreneur, and his son, Dr. Norman Keevil, Jr., *Northern Miner*'s 1979 "Man of the Year" and now president and chief executive officer of Teck.

Dr. Keevil, Sr., wasn't even born in 1912, when the Teck-Hughes claim was first staked. A year later, when the mining company was formed, it was

The Drs. Keevil with the Afton mine stockpile in the background.

one of the first in the area, located just west of Kirkland Lake in east-central Teck Township.

In the 1915 annual report, shareholders were told that the mine's operator had stopped work because "he and his associates were paying too much for the property and the mine was not sufficiently promising to warrant their proceeding any further with the work."

However, new operators emerged, and they were amply rewarded as deeper digging uncovered higher grades of ore. Teck-Hughes went on to become one of Canada's best-known gold mines, dubbed "Old Faithful" because of its long, steady production.

As early as 1930, its imminent demise was predicted. But new ore discoveries and improved techniques kept it in operation until 1968. By that time Teck-Hughes had turned out more than $105 million worth of gold, or more than 10 times that value at current prices.

Things didn't always proceed

The abandoned Teck-Hughes mine.

smoothly, however. In 1922 someone in the organization forgot to pay taxes and the claims fell open. The mistake was only discovered when strangers were seen staking the land around the mine offices. Teck-Hughes workers restaked the claims, but weren't entirely successful. After a court

Top: Heavy equipment at work in the open pit of the Highmont mine.

Above: The Lamaque gold mine.

dispute, Teck-Hughes had to pay substantial sums to recover lost claims.

In the early years the firm's executive office was located in either New York or Buffalo, reflecting the dominant U.S. interests in Teck-Hughes. But in 1932 it moved to 32 King Street East in Toronto, where it remained for many years.

As Teck-Hughes' ore body gradually dwindled, the reputation of mining geophysicist Norman Keevil was expanding. In 1954 Keevil uncovered a high-grade copper find on Temagami Island in Lake Temagami in northern Ontario. The deposit was so rich that he had a tombstone company polish the ore surface until it shone—a quality that impressed potential investors in his new venture, Temagami Mining Company Ltd. The find was particularly sweet because Keevil's geophysical research had proved correct in the face of skepticism from a major U.S. mining company that earlier had held the claims under option, but had abandoned them.

Working from his strong financial base in Temagami, Keevil was able to buy a controlling interest in Teck-Hughes Gold Mines Ltd. in 1959. Cash-rich Teck-Hughes became the linchpin in Keevil's control of a number of resource companies—the Keevil Mining Group.

In 1963 Keevil consolidated Teck-Hughes, an oil company that it had acquired under his control, and several other holdings into Teck Corporation. Also that year, Dr. Norman Keevil, Jr., holder of a Ph.D. in geophysics, came aboard as vice-president/exploration.

Subsequently, as executive vice-president, he too showed a bent toward successful acquisitions, with emphasis on picking up undeveloped deposits which Teck would develop into new operating mines during the 1970s.

The two Keevils, and their team of like-minded associates, have in recent years been among Canada's most active developers of new mines across the country—from the Newfoundland zinc mine through the Niobec niobium mine in Quebec to the Afton and Highmont copper mines in British Columbia.

The Bullmoose coking coal mine in British Columbia was still under construction in early 1983. It is a $300-million operation, Teck's most ambitious mine yet, and is itself part of the $2.5-billion "Northeast Coal" megaproject, involving two mining consortia, new railroads and port development, and the entirely new town of Tumbler Ridge in northeastern British Columbia.

But in a sense, the company is coming full circle, back to its gold-mining roots in northern Ontario. The 1980s successor to the Teck-Hughes mine may lie in the Hemlo district, 200 miles east of Thunder Bay, Ontario, where Teck owns an interest in a promising gold property. Expectations are that Hemlo will be the site of the next big gold-mining boom—and Teck Corporation will be part of it all.

225

DALE & COMPANY LIMITED

The transition from square-rigged schooners plying Atlantic routes to communications satellites hovering in space encompasses a tremendous leap in time and technology.

Dale & Company Limited, the Toronto-based insurance broker, has been part of the entire evolution—offering marine insurance in the 1800s, aviation coverage in the 1930s, and insurance for Canada's Anik satellites in the 1970s.

Dale is a major national brokerage with 475 employees, including about 170 in Toronto. It is the principal subsidiary of Dale-Ross Holdings Limited, which also owns DML Underwriters Ltd., Canadian managers of several insurance companies, and Boyd, Phillips & Co. Ltd., marine surveyors and adjusters. Dale-Ross' 1981 premium income amounted to $113 million.

Its origins can be traced to a firm called E.L. Bond, which sold marine insurance in the Port of Montreal as early as 1859. In the early 1900s insurance interests in London, where E.L. Bond had placed some insurance, sent a young man named Robert J. Dale to work with the Montreal firm.

Later in 1909 Dale bought the agency, changing its name to Dale & Company. Under its next owners, Montreal's Ross family, Dale & Company moved far beyond its Port of Montreal roots. Gilbert Ross, president from 1932 to 1952, directed the formation of a national network of branch offices. He was also the first Canadian attorney for the prestigious Lloyd's of London.

From a marine background Dale & Company branched out into automobile, property, casualty and life insurance, pensions, and other areas.

A major contributor to this business has been the Toronto office, which opened in 1909 in the old Royal Bank Building at Yonge and King streets. The office's first major account was the Canada and Dominion Sugar

Robert J. Dale, founder and first president of Dale & Company Limited.

Company. More than 70 years later, this firm, now Redpath Industries Ltd., is still a Dale client.

Less than a decade after the Toronto office opened, it was moved to the Metropolitan Building on Victoria Street. There it stayed until 1968, when it relocated in the new Bank Tower of the Toronto-Dominion Centre—which still houses the branch plus Dale's head office.

Gilbert Ross was succeeded as president in 1952 by his son, Sidney M. Ross, who headed the firm until 1970. Dale became a public company in 1964 and the parent company was named Dale-Ross Holdings Limited. In 1971 the head office was transferred to

Toronto from Montreal. In 1974 Kenneth Gilbert became Dale-Ross' president, a position he still holds.

Sodarcan Ltd., a Montreal headquartered group involved in insurance and reinsurance brokerage, insurance and reinsurance management, as well as actuarial counselling, bought controlling interest of Dale-Ross in 1980. Dale-Ross, though, remains completely Canadian and continued its 120-year-old tradition of professional advice and services.

SWISS BANK CORPORATION (CANADA)

On July 1, 1981, Canada got a new chartered bank, Swiss Bank Corporation (Canada), of Toronto. However, for the country's financial community, the newcomer didn't have a strange face—a predecessor company had been doing business there for more than 30 years.

Before November 29, 1980—when a revised Bank Act was passed by the Canadian Parliament—foreign banks, including the prestigious Swiss Bank Corporation of Basel, Switzerland, could not own chartered banks in Canada. The passage of the legislation allowed a host of foreign-owned banks to open their doors.

For Swiss Bank Corporation, one of Switzerland's three major banks,

founding a new Canadian bank involved the amalgamation and conversion to bank status of two existing subsidiaries: Swiss Corporation for Canadian Investments Ltd., formed in 1951; and SBC Financial Ltd., established in 1970.

Since the turn of the century, the Swiss have invested substantial amounts in Canadian stocks and bonds. Swiss Bank Corporation, because it was channelling so many investment funds into Canada, decided in 1951 to form its own company to

---

Louis S. Wiedmer, president since 1969, has been with Swiss Bank Corporation's subsidiaries in Canada from the start in 1951.

coordinate these activities and achieve better on-the-spot supervision.

Swiss Corporation for Canadian Investments Ltd. (SCCI) was established with a staff of four in Montreal. Its primary duties were buying and selling securities, safekeeping and managing them, providing investment advice, plus other related chores. One of its traders was Louis S. Wiedmer, who rose through the ranks and is now president of Swiss Bank Corporation (Canada).

Over the years the commercial banking business expanded rapidly in Canada. To take advantage of this growth, Swiss Bank Corporation formed a second subsidiary in 1970 in Montreal, SBC Financial Ltd. SBC acted as a near-bank, principally supplying loans to Canadian subsidiaries of Swiss firms.

The two companies existed side by side, with SCCI serving as a security brokerage and SBC as a quasi-bank. However, by 1975 management observed that the banking side was growing much faster than its sister firm. When it became apparent that a revised Bank Act would allow foreign-owned chartered banks, Swiss Bank Corporation recognized that it must apply for full bank status as soon as possible.

SCCI had formed a Toronto office as early as 1968. And over the years, as Toronto replaced Montreal as Canada's financial capital, more and more of the two companies' activities—such as commercial credit, securities, money market, and precious-metals trading—were transferred there.

Therefore, when the conversion to a chartered bank occurred, it was natural for the new entity to be based in Toronto. In mid-1983 Swiss Bank Corporation (Canada) employed 60 people in its head office in the South Tower, Royal Bank Plaza, out of a total work force of 150. Other offices are in Montreal, Calgary, and Vancouver.

SEIKO TIME CANADA

More than a decade ago Rodney H. Smith, an employee of a major Canadian watch distributor, received a telephone call from a former colleague extolling the virtues of a firm called Seiko. He scratched his head and inquired: "Seiko? Isn't that a paint company in Quebec?"

Smith, president of Seiko Time Canada since April 1981, smiles at the memory of his mistake—Seiko is now the biggest-selling watch brand in the world. Its origins in Japan can be traced to 1881 when the Seiko Group's founder, Kintaro Hattori, opened a clock store in Tokyo, and 11 years later began making clocks.

But Smith's lapse was understandable in 1971 because Seiko was hardly a household word in Canada. Its 1972 Canadian sales amounted to $1.6 million, and its Toronto staff consisted of fewer than 10 people.

Since then the corporation has achieved remarkable growth in Canada, built on a base of technological innovation, service, and sales and marketing expertise. Annual sales in 1982 were about $50 million, and it employs 140 people, including 120 in Toronto.

Seiko Time Canada's headquarters is a 26,000-square-foot building at 285 Yorkland Boulevard in Willowdale, containing a warehouse, administration offices, and a team of 20 to 25 skilled watchmakers who repair customers' watches quickly and efficiently. Seiko watches are made in Japan and shipped to Canada by the group's marketing company, K. Hattori & Company Ltd.

One individual who has contributed heavily to Seiko's Canadian success is the former colleague who persuaded Rodney Smith to join the firm—L.E. (Ted) Hatch, who rose from sales manager to president (from 1975 to 1981), then to chairman of the board of the Canadian operation.

Before 1971 Seiko watches were marketed in Canada by an

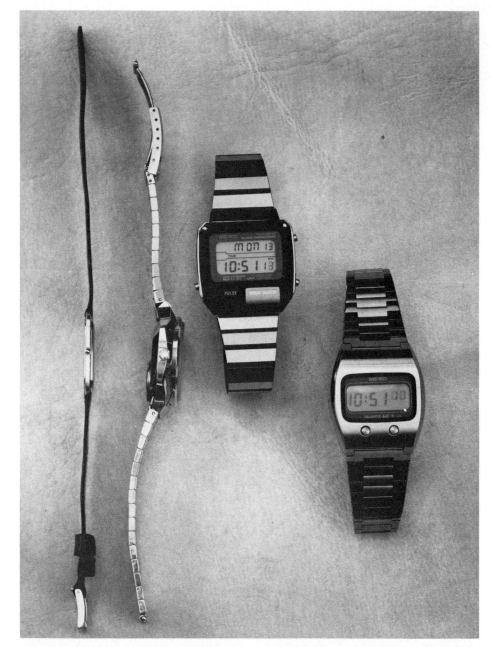

independent distributor. But Seiko had not been successful in the Canadian market. The parent corporation decided to test a new approach, having its own distribution branch in Canada.

Thus, that year a branch of Seiko Time Corporation, the U.S. marketing company, was established at 102 Bloor Street West in downtown Toronto. Seiko lured Hatch, a veteran of 25 years in the country's watch trade, to be sales manager, working closely with

Seiko's first analogue quartz watches were thick and bulky compared to the ultra-thin models available today, as shown on the left. The technology of quartz watches has advanced rapidly, as shown by the two digital watches on the right.

the general manager, Yoshiyuki Narahashi.

After helping get the operation off the ground, Narahashi was recalled to New York in 1974. It was assumed that he would be replaced by someone from K. Hattori, but the parent firm was so impressed with Hatch's performance that he was entrusted with running the Canadian branch.

Over the years it has been the practice of Seiko Time Canada to promote from within. Usually only one Japanese person is on staff at any time, serving in Canada for a three-year period as a liaison with the factories.

The 1970s were a period of breathtaking change in the world's watch industry as large chunks of the market shifted from Swiss and U.S. manufacturers to Japanese firms. Technology also changed as automation and high-technology wizardry increasingly supplanted the handicraft associated with mechanical watches.

Seiko took the market by storm in 1969, unveiling the first commercial quartz-crystal watch, a product much more precise and reliable than its mechanical antecedents. (Seiko, incidentally, is the Japanese word for precision.)

Seiko was also a leader in another product wave, the digital-quartz watch. In choosing a substitute for the hands of a mechanical watch, the company wisely selected the liquid-crystal display (LCD) over the light-emitting diode (LED), a technology that was chosen by other watchmakers but failed to excite the market.

As Seiko emerged as the world sales leader, its Canadian branch also flourished. The operation moved in 1973 from Bloor Street to 109 Railside Road in Don Mills, a Toronto suburb, which was more convenient for import and shipping functions.

In 1975 a Canadian company, Seiko Time Canada Ltd., was incorporated as a wholly owned subsidiary of Seiko Time Corporation in the United States. In the following years the firm moved into the Yorkland Boulevard building.

Seiko Time Canada is reported to be among the top two in Canadian watch sales, and the market leader in watches priced at more than $100. In 1980 it also began to distribute clocks. Seiko sells to fine-jewellery stores and the better department stores.

In 1982 plans were under way for Seiko to cover the entire spectrum of the Canadian watch market. A new company, SC Time Inc., was formed to oversee three operating divisions. One of these is Seiko Time Canada, with its main product lines in the $100 to $400 range.

A second divison is Pulsar Time Canada, with offices at 6630 Campobello Road in Mississauga, just west of Toronto, which will sell medium-priced watches. A third operating arm is Lorus Canada, which—in a dramatic new thrust for K. Hattori—will be entered in the less-expensive end of the market.

After watching the revolutionary changes of the 1970s, president Smith is reluctant to predict the future of the watch trade. All he knows is that Seiko Time Canada will be in the thick of it.

Standing in front of their modern head office in Willowdale are (left) Rodney H. Smith, president of SC Time Inc. and Seiko Time Canada, and (right) L.E (Ted) Hatch, chairman of the board.

COLONIA LIFE INSURANCE COMPANY

Like many young people, Dieter Wendelstadt had an appetite for travel and adventure. So, after completion of his studies in Germany and having achieved his MBA, the enterprising would-be businessman packed his bags and headed for Canada.

Twenty-five years later Dieter Wendelstadt is chairman of the management board and chief executive officer of the COLONIA Group of Companies of Cologne, Federal Republic of Germany, whose German roots reach back 144 years. The group is a large insurance and financial organization with about 7,000 employees and more than $20 billion in assets. In his capacity as chairman of the board and director, Dieter Wendelstadt returns regularly to Canada to visit the wholly owned Canadian subsidiary, COLONIA Life Insurance Company, in Toronto.

W.H. Gleed, the Canadian firm's president, says Mr. Wendelstadt takes special interest in the Canadian operations of COLONIA because of his continuing love for this country. The chairman has always supported the idea that COLONIA should have a strong, tangible presence in Canada—a role filled admirably by COLONIA PLACE, its 15-storey office/retail complex at Toronto's busy intersection of Yonge Street and St. Clair Avenue East.

COLONIA's history in Toronto began on July 1, 1960, with the opening of a branch office at 110 University Avenue. On January 1, 1977, following a major merger of insurance and financial companies at COLONIA in Germany, the Canadian branch operation was transformed into a company incorporated federally as COLONIA Life Insurance Company. The organization formed its own board of directors and management and became a wholly owned subsidiary of the COLONIA Group of Cologne, Federal Republic of Germany.

On March 30, 1977, seven years of planning and building came to fruition when COLONIA PLACE, home of the Canadian company's headquarters, was completed. Because of its prominent location and character, COLONIA PLACE is leased to first-class tenants, both in the office tower and the two retail floors. The mall offers a spectrum of specialty stores for the convenience of the people in and around COLONIA PLACE.

While COLONIA in Canada is a relatively small life insurance company, it has grown impressively. In 1970 annual premium income first reached one million dollars, mostly from life insurance premiums. In 1982 annual premium income exceeded $15 million.

The company does business in all provinces, operating through a brokerage system and selling its products by means of a network of general agents.

W.H. Gleed, who joined the corporation to succeed Dr. Joachim Trabandt as president, continues COLONIA's vigorous commitment to Canada.

Apart from these activities in life insurance, COLONIA is further represented in Canada, writing marine insurance in Ontario and Quebec.

COLONIA PLACE, COLONIA Life's 15-storey office/retail complex at 2 St. Clair Avenue East, was completed in 1977.

WEETABIX OF CANADA LTD.

An artist's drawing of Weetabix of Canada's factory in Cobourg, Ontario, which opened in 1978.

Sitting on the floor amidst boxes of breakfast cereal and a throng of shoppers, Harold Connell in 1967 felt little doubt that Weetabix had a healthy future in Canada. As overseas sales manager for Weetabix Ltd., a British cereal company, Connell was in Toronto to attend a British Week celebration. He brought 300 cases of the cereal to be displayed on the Canadian National Exhibition Grounds.

An institution on British breakfast tables for 35 years, Weetabix—a blend of more than 90 percent whole wheat with malt extract, sugar, and salt—had never been sold in Canada. The firm's board was eager to find out its potential there.

Demand for the product was overwhelming, particularly from former British residents, and within a year it was being sold in Canadian grocery stores, distributed by independent importers. Today Weetabix and its sister cereal, Alpen, account in tonnage for about 1.6 percent of the Canadian cold-cereal market.

In 1969, at age 43, Connell left his position as overseas sales manager at the head office in Northhamptonshire, England, and arrived in Toronto as

North American manager. After running the one-man operation from his home for two years, he moved into a second-storey office in a shopping centre at 6101 Yonge Street in Willowdale in 1971.

In 1971-1972 Weetabix's importers, who had been buying the cereal from the English company and reselling it to retailers, were converted to food brokers who sold the product on a commission basis. This has generally been the corporation's approach, although in Ontario, Alberta, and British Columbia it maintained a sales force from 1974 to 1980 before reverting back to the broker system.

A Canadian company, Weetabix of Canada Ltd., was incorporated in 1975 with Connell as president, replacing the branch office. Two years later, recognizing that high manufacturing costs in England and increased trans-Atlantic freight expenses and import duties were making it too costly to ship cereal from England, the firm decided that a factory should be built in Canada. Weetabix of Canada Manufacturing Ltd. was formed,

opening the Cobourg plant in 1978.

The corporation, which employs 80 people, manufactures about 15 cereals, including about a dozen generic and private labels for retailers in Canada and the United States. Its major sales are in its exports. Weetabix' future in Canada seems assured, following the parent's recent acquisition of a major U.S. cereal company, a move that opens up new avenues for exports.

Harold Connell, president of Weetabix of Canada Ltd., has run Weetabix' Canadian operations since 1966.

231

MAPLE LEAF MILLS LIMITED

Located along the Toronto waterfront, the Lakeside Milling Company Limited (shown here around 1928) later became part of Maple Leaf Mills.

The foundations of Maple Leaf Mills Limited, one of Canada's leading agribusiness corporations, were laid in the 1830s, when hundreds of flour mills dotted the countryside of Upper Canada, now Ontario.

The Welland Canal was completed in 1833, linking Lake Erie and Lake Ontario, and three years later Grantham Mills, a stone structure, was built over a millrace along the new canal in St. Catharines, Ontario.

This was the first step in a long corporate odyssey leading to the modern Maple Leaf Mills. From its flour-milling beginnings, the firm has become a diversified, international corporation. Today it produces and markets animal feeds, seed, and poultry; trades and sells grains; operates country and terminal elevators; mills flour; produces vegetable oil; has rendering operations in several provinces; and supplies consumer food products.

The earliest ancestor of Maple Leaf Mills in Toronto was Queen City Mills, which opened in Toronto Junction (later West Toronto) in 1893 with 35 employees producing 600 barrels of flour a day. The owner, Senator Archibald Campbell, was progressive—the mill generated its own electricity.

Queen City Mills became Campbell Milling Company Ltd. in 1904, and then Campbell Flour Mills Company Ltd. in 1911. Two years later the West Toronto mill's capacity was expanded to 2,000 barrels a day, and more operations were added.

Meanwhile, the West was opening up, railroads were being built, and milling entrepreneurs were gazing beyond local markets. In 1910 two successful millers—Douglas Cameron in northwestern Ontario and Hedley Shaw in the Niagara area—joined forces to form Maple Leaf Milling Company Ltd., based in Toronto.

In 1919 Maple Leaf purchased Campbell Flour Mills and a sister company, Campbell Grain and Feed Company Ltd., including the West Toronto mill. Three years later Maple Leaf bought a controlling interest in Canada Bread Company, incorporated in 1911 to acquire three Toronto bakeries and one each in Montreal and Winnipeg.

The Canada Bread horse and delivery wagon were a familiar sight on Toronto streets until the 1950s. Jim Elliott, a former employee, recalls that during the late 1920s he was paid $18 a week plus 6-percent commission to deliver bread to 220 West Toronto households. While he walked door-to-door, the horse—the same one for 11

Gordon Young Limited is the latest chapter in a long history of the Young family in the rendering business. This 1898 picture shows a business operated by the Young family in the Don Valley.

years—followed faithfully in the street.

In 1960 Canada Bread acquired Dempster's Bread of Toronto (founded in 1898), which has since become the company's flagship brand. Canada Bread's name was changed to Corporate Foods Ltd. in 1969. It is the market leader in Ontario, with 1982 bread sales of almost $90 million. Corporate Foods, now 63-percent owned by Maple Leaf Mills, has 1,100 employees, 700 of them in four Toronto locations.

But back in the 1920s another important strand in the Maple Leaf Mills fabric was being formed. A businessman named Gordon Leitch founded Toronto Elevators Ltd., and in 1928 built a two-million-bushel-capacity elevator on Queen's Quay at the Toronto harbourfront.

Toronto Elevators expanded into commercial feeds (under the Master Feed label) and vegetable oils, and acquired feed and grain operations throughout Ontario. Its Toronto harbour site developed into a sprawling complex.

Leitch and James D. Norris, a Chicago grain broker and part owner of Toronto Elevators, in 1932 formed Upper Lakes Shipping, which became Canada's leading operator of Great Lakes' ships. In the 1940s the two men's interests began to buy shares in Maple Leaf Milling, leading to the 1961 merger of Toronto Elevators and Maple Leaf Milling.

The Canada Bread horse and wagon were a familiar part of growing up in Toronto in earlier times.

By that time Maple Leaf Milling had become a force in Canadian agribusiness. In 1950 it acquired Lakeside Milling Company Ltd., a small milling operation on Toronto's waterfront, founded by Norman Campbell in 1928.

Then, in 1951, Maple Leaf purchased Toronto-based Purity Flour Mills Ltd. (formerly Western Canada Flour Mills, established in 1905), which owned flour mills and feed plants across the country.

Maple Leaf Mills led negotiations by Canadian mills in 1963 for a major flour sale to the Soviet Union. The $65-million deal was considered the largest flour sale ever made, and paved the way for continuing Soviet sales up to the present day.

Maple Leaf Mills was purchased in 1980 by Canadian Pacific Enterprises Ltd. of Montreal. Rothesay Concentrates Company Ltd., a Canadian Pacific subsidiary, was merged into Maple Leaf Mills, thus launching Maple Leaf into a new business area—rendering, or the refining of tallow and grease.

This was followed in 1981 by the purchase of Gordon Young Ltd., a Toronto firm involved in rendering and manufacturing animal feed and fertilizers.

Maple Leaf Mills now employs about 620 people at four locations in Toronto—Gordon Young Ltd., a flour mill at 43 Junction Road, a grocery division on Horner Avenue, and corporate offices in Maple Leaf Mills Tower at 2300 Yonge Street.

But in 1982 a long chapter in the history of Maple Leaf Mills Limited closed when it surrendered its waterfront elevator site, first occupied in 1928. This was the final stage in a federal government expropriation of the Queen's Quay complex which began in 1972.

Maple Leaf Mills Limited—West Toronto flour mill.

CLARKSON GORDON

If anyone were to do a study to determine the company with the greatest influence on the conduct of business in Canada, Clarkson Gordon, one of the country's largest accounting firms, would be a leading candidate.

Clarkson Gordon provides auditing and tax services for a vast number of Canadian organizations, including more than 130 public companies and some of the country's leading financial institutions.

But Clarkson Gordon is actually three entities wrapped up into one: Clarkson Gordon, the chartered accountants; Woods Gordon, the country's largest management consultant firm; and The Clarkson Company Ltd., receivers, liquidators, and trustees in bankruptcy.

Because teams of professionals are assembled from the consulting and accounting areas, it is often hard to tell which employee belongs to which branch of the business. The entire organization in mid-1983 employed 3,100 people in 21 cities, about half of them in Toronto.

Clarkson is rare among the major Canadian accounting firms in that its origins are strictly Canadian—in fact, they can be traced back to 1864 in Toronto. Since 1944 the firm has been associated with Arthur Young International, a worldwide federation of national accounting firms.

Clarkson's founders helped pioneer the accountants' professional associations in this country. The tradition has continued: Since 1902, seven members of the firm have been president of the Canadian Institute of Chartered Accountants, and eight Clarkson people have been president of the Institute of Chartered Accountants of Ontario.

Clarkson Gordon's alumni are so prominent as heads of major companies that the organization has been branded "the unofficial finishing school" for the country's business establishment.

Its professionals have also heeded the call to sit on government commissions, task forces, and in the federal Parliament. Former partner Walter Gordon was a member of Parliament and served as federal Finance Minister in the 1960s. J.L. Biddell, recently retired as chairman of The Clarkson Company, served on the federal Anti-Inflation Board in the 1970s, and another distinguished partner, J. Grant Glassco, was chairman of an important Royal Commission on government organization in the early 1960s, just to name a few of many examples.

Today Clarkson Gordon partners play leading roles in organizations as diverse as the Canadian Cancer Society, Children's Aid, National Ballet School, UNICEF Canada, and the Canadian Opera Company. Retired partner Duncan Gordon was a driving force behind the Hospital for Sick Children.

Clarkson Gordon began as a trustee and receivership business, founded in 1864 by Thomas Clarkson, a native of England, at 83 Front Street in Toronto. He passed the business on to his son Edward—one of 16 children—who

Top: In 1864 Thomas Clarkson founded the firm which became Clarkson Gordon.

Above: Fred Clarkson, around the turn of the century, in Clarkson Gordon's boardroom at 15 Wellington Street West.

developed an accounting practice, as well.

In 1913 a former employee, H.B. Lockhart Gordon, rejoined the firm to form a new accounting partnership, Clarkson Gordon and Dilworth.

In 1913 Colonel H.D. Lockhart Gordon joined the business as a partner.

Gordon was known as "The Colonel" because he was in command of the Mississauga Horse Regiment and saw active service in World War I.

The firm went through several incarnations until 1946, when it became known as Clarkson Gordon & Company, and the trustee practice as The Clarkson Company. There also was geographical expansion with offices opening in Montreal (1922),

Hamilton (1938), Vancouver (1945), and later in other major cities.

Woods Gordon, the management consulting business, began 50 years ago when executives at York Knitting Mills, led by its president, J.D. Woods,

A meeting of the Clarkson Gordon partners in 1982 (from left) included John Cowperthwaite, national director of professional development; Bill Farlinger, chairman of the management committee; Dave Selley, director of national auditing; and Glen Cronkwright, executive and managing partner of the Calgary office.

formed a venture to undertake productivity studies in the textile field.

That organization, J.D. Woods & Company Ltd., attracted the interest—and involvement—of Walter Gordon, then a partner with Clarkson Gordon. In 1939 he brought the two companies together to form a management consulting practice.

During World War II, Walter Gordon conceived the idea of lending the entire firm to the federal government to advise in the effort to conserve manpower and material. In 1959 the organization changed from a limited company to a partnership, taking the name Woods Gordon.

Today Woods Gordon provides advice to government and business management in the general areas of operations management, human resources, financial planning and controls, computers, marketing, and economics.

In the 19th and early 20th centuries, the company Thomas Clarkson founded occupied a number of different locations in downtown Toronto. But in 1913 it found a home in an elegant building at 15 Wellington Street West, which was built in the 1840s and is still standing today. The firm remained there until 1968, when it relocated in the new Royal Trust Tower. By mid-1982 it occupied 11 floors of the tower.

Although Clarkson Gordon carries a deserved reputation as a tradition-rich company, it hasn't been averse to innovation and diversification. In the 1980s, says senior partner Don Scott, the firm is becoming more involved with the owner-operator type of business, while maintaining links to larger corporate clients.

This new orientation requires a broader approach, Scott says. Besides providing an audit certificate, the professional advisor must be prepared to supply ongoing advice in a broad range of taxation, business, and finance areas.

OLIVETTI CANADA LTD.

In the mid-1960s, when the federal government wanted a typewriter that could print the language of one of Canada's original peoples, it went to a relative newcomer, Olivetti Canada Ltd., the subsidiary of an Italian office-equipment manufacturer. The resulting product, used by the Cree Indians, symbolizes Olivetti's commitment to serve the entire range of the Canadian office equipment market.

Olivetti's products are usually less specialized, but no less creative than the Cree typewriter. The company offers a wide variety of items—including electronic typewriters, word processors, business systems, data-processing equipment, personal computers, photocopiers, and calculators.

It is, for example, the world leader in electronic typewriters. And Olivetti Canada is a major supplier of data-processing terminals to the Canadian banking system. In fact, an advanced development group works in the firm's Don Mills head office, designing the basic software for a new line of terminals for the North American banking market.

The product line was much narrower in 1955 when the Olivetti company, founded in Northern Italy in 1908, decided it could no longer ignore the growing Canadian market. Olivetti Canada opened with a tiny staff in an office on Yonge Street, largely distributing printing calculators—it was a pioneer in this field—and later adding machines and mechanical typewriters.

From this base, Olivetti built a network of sales and service branches, agents, and retailers across Canada. In the 1959-1960 fiscal year sales were $1.5 million; by the end of 1962 they had soared to $15 million.

This growth was partly spurred by the parent firm's purchase in late 1959 of the United States-based Underwood company, a typewriter manufacturer. Toronto-based Underwood in Canada merged with Olivetti in Canada to form a much larger unit.

Shortly after the merger, the combined company moved into a new

Olivetti has been supplying typing products to Canadian markets for 25 years. Its latest word processor, the ETV300, utilizes electronic typewriters as keyboard/printers.

head office at 1390 Don Mills Road, still the firm's headquarters.

The 1960s were years of explosive growth for Olivetti in Canada, with sales growing at an annual rate of 25 to 30 percent. During this period Olivetti was presided over by Lanfranco Amato, who came to Canada in 1955 after serving Olivetti in the Far East and Africa. Amato, who became a Canadian citizen in 1960, was president from 1965 to 1973, when he became chairman of the board. He is now a director of the company.

In the late 1970s Olivetti expanded into the data-processing market, an orientation reflected in its large data-terminal business, and successfully launched its line of electronic word-processing typewriters.

One of the leaders in office automation technology, Olivetti Canada today has annual sales in the $55 million area and employs about 600 people nationwide—350 in its 21 branches across Canada, 210 at the head office, and about 40 at its factory on Kennedy Road in Scarborough, where electronic typewriters are assembled for domestic and export markets.

GENERAL MILLS CANADA, INC.

Prior to 1954 General Mills and its many products were familiar only to a minority of Canadians, largely those who lived near the Canada-United States border.

But if General Mills Canada, Inc., still isn't a recognizable name in every Canadian household, many of its brand names are—including Cheerios, Wheaties, Betty Crocker, Lancia, Eddie Bauer, and Monopoly.

The parent company, General Mills, Inc., of Minneapolis, Minnesota, was established by a merger in 1928 of a number of leading U.S. milling concerns. In 1954 General Mills took its first direct steps in Canada, introducing packaged foods and erecting a packaged foods plant at 1330 Martingrove Road in Rexdale, a northwest suburb of Toronto.

The firm started from scratch, convincing retailers to make room on their shelves among the established brands. Its first sales meeting was on June 14, 1954, and the first products in Canada were pie crust, layer cakes, brownies, Bisquick, Wheaties, Cheerios, and Sugar Jets.

Business grew, and in April 1956 the operation was expanded to include a cereals-processing plant. Another expansion in 1967 permitted the manufacture of snack foods.

Today General Mills encompasses much more than grocery products—it is a diversified consumer products company. In 1971 four divisions— Lancia Bravo Foods, Blue Water Seafoods, Parker Brothers, and General Mills Cereals Ltd.—combined to form General Mills Canada, Inc.

Lancia Bravo was formed in 1930 when four Italian immigrants founded the Toronto Macaroni Manufacturing Company to make pasta and noodle products sold under the brand name Lancia.

In 1942 the company came up with a blend of spaghetti sauce, called Bravo, which was widely accepted by both Italian-Canadians and the general market. Toronto Macaroni, now well-established, became part of the General Mills family in 1966 and changed its name to Lancia Bravo Foods in 1971.

Blue Water Seafoods had been introduced to Canada in 1954 when production originated in Newfoundland and merchandise was shipped to Toronto by refrigerated boats. The operation moved to Montreal in 1960 and Blue Water was acquired by General Mills in 1968.

Parker Brothers in Canada began manufacturing its games in North York in 1962. Acquired by General Mills in 1968, the firm built a new plant at Keele Street and Highway 7 in Concord, north of Toronto. This plant was doubled in size in 1976 to meet the increasing demand for its electronic

Although totally developed today, in the early years of General Mills Canada, Inc., its plant in Rexdale was surrounded by vast farmlands.

and board games and modelling compound.

In 1974, a fifth division was added with the opening in Toronto of Eddie Bauer, a retailer of outdoor clothing and equipment. The division now has three stores and a thriving mail-order business.

In its first year, General Mills Canada, Inc., employed about 124 people, and in its first fiscal year recorded sales of about $2.5 million—a far cry from 1,300 employees in mid-1983 and sales of more than $207 million in fiscal 1983.

In 1955 six artists were invited to paint fresh interpretations of Betty Crocker. This illustration, by Hilda Taylor, was selected.

SUNCOR INC.

Large, important corporations often have inauspicious beginnings. So it is with Suncor Inc., of Toronto, one of Canada's leading integrated oil and gas companies with 1982 revenues of $1.5 billion and assets of approximately $2 billion.

In 1919 Major John W. Fourney III was sent by his employer, Sun Company of Philadelphia, Pennsylvania, to follow up on sales of lubricants the firm had made to Montreal-area plants during World War I.

The major opened a Montreal office to sell lubricants and greases. In 1923 Sun Oil Company was incorporated in Canada, and a branch was established in Toronto.

The new business underwent a growth spurt about the time its parent company introduced popular Blue Sunoco gasoline in 1927. The first Canadian Sunoco dealer had opened in 1925 on Queen Street East in Toronto. And in 1931 the firm built its first company-owned service station on the corner of Queen Street East and Berkshire Avenue. Also in the 1930s, the head office was shifted to Toronto from Montreal.

In those early years all Sunoco gasoline sold in Canada was produced outside the country. But that situation was changing. The company's first Canadian oil well was drilled in Nova Scotia in 1944. By the late 1940s the Western Canadian oil boom was under way, and Sun opened a Canadian production division in Calgary. Two oil wells were completed in Alberta in 1950.

Three years later Sun Oil was operating a new refinery in Sarnia, Ontario, linked by a pipeline to terminals in London, Hamilton, and Toronto.

Sunoco introduced its custom-blend pump in 1958. Instead of the standard two-grade system, motorists could choose from six gasoline grades at a single pump, based on different octane fuel requirements for various makes

For almost 60 years Sunoco customers have known that Sunoco service is "a little more personal."

and years of autos.

In the early 1960s Sun Company began to tap the vast oil sands along the Athabasca River in Alberta through a subsidiary company, Great Canadian Oil Sands Limited (GCOS). Sun Company initially invested $300 million in this pioneering venture.

Sun Oil and GCOS amalgamated in 1979 to form Suncor, with corporate offices at 20 Eglinton Avenue West in Toronto. The company has two divisions: The Sunoco Group, with headquarters at 56 Wellesley Street West in Toronto, is involved in "downstream" operations such as refining and marketing; and the

Calgary-based Resources Group incorporates three divisions—oil sands, exploration and production, and resources development. Suncor employs approximately 5,000 employees across Canada with about 1,000 in Toronto.

In 1981 the Ontario government purchased a 25 percent interest in Suncor. The remainder of the common shares are primarily held by Sun Company Inc. of the United States. Suncor's objective is to have majority Canadian ownership and control.

JOHNSON MATTHEY LIMITED

At Johnson Matthey Limited, they like to say that they've made their mark on gold and silver. The company is Canada's leading refiner and fabricator of precious metals, and emblazons its distinctive "JM" logo on the gold and silver bars it supplies to the investment market.

It also can be said that Johnson Matthey has made its mark on the Toronto area in the past 50 years. From two people in a downtown office in 1930, it has grown to become an employer of more than 480 people—at a plant and head office at 110 Industry Street, a precious-metals refinery in Brampton, west of Toronto, and a foundry in St. Catharines.

The roots of Johnson Matthey can be traced to a precious-metals business formed in London, England, in 1817—the predecessor of today's Johnson Matthey group of international companies. Johnson Matthey of London is one of five members of the London Gold Market which, twice a day, sets the price of the metal.

When the London firm decided in 1930 to expand to Canada, it chose Stanley Stilwell, a quiet, capable World War I veteran, to establish an agency.

In 1936 Johnson Matthey purchased Canada Seamless Wire Company at 198 Clinton Street in Toronto, Johnson Matthey & Company (Canada) Limited was incorporated, and it expanded the production of gold and

John Shier, current president of Johnson Matthey Limited.

silver sheet, wire, and tubing for the jewellery business. (One of Canada Seamless Wire's products was the wire window screening for the Royal York Hotel.)

Stilwell was appointed president of the new company, a position he held until his retirement in 1963.

P.R. Mallory & Company Inc. of the United States joined forces with Johnson Matthey in 1946 to form a venture to serve as Canadian agent for both firms. The new entity, Johnson Matthey & Mallory Limited, manufactured Johnson Matthey's precious-metals products and Mallory's lines, which included electrical contacts and timer switches.

To accommodate the expanded business, a new 64,000-square-foot factory was constructed at 110 Industry Street in northwest

Toronto. It opened in 1948.

The corporate marriage lasted until late 1977, when the two parent companies went their separate ways. Johnson Matthey took over the Industry Street plant, as well as its precious-metals refinery, which had opened in Brampton in 1975.

The precious-metals division today supplies a variety of industrial products, such as electrical contacts, silver brazing alloys, and platinum laboratory equipment. In the jewellery area, the firm produces sheet, tubing, and wire for manufacturers.

Johnson Matthey's mint products have been a major growth area in recent years. The company, for example, supplies blanks for the Royal Canadian Mint for its Maple Leaf coins. Growing interest in precious-metals investment has generated a strong demand for Johnson Matthey's investment bars of gold, silver, and, increasingly, platinum.

When the parent company in London, England, decided to expand Johnson Matthey to Canada it chose Stanley Stilwell to establish the agency and serve as its first president.

239

PRICE WATERHOUSE

When Price Waterhouse opened a small Toronto office on May 1, 1910 (its second in Canada), audit examinations represented a minor part of the accountancy practice. More significant engagements consisted of determining the financial standing of companies for credit purposes and keeping the accounts of businesses, individuals, and estates. All work was done manually and the exclusively male professional staff maintained a deliberately low profile.

But what a difference 70 years makes. In addition to vastly expanded audit activities, Price Waterhouse has branched out into taxation, management consulting, and insolvency services. Its clientele includes many of the country's largest corporations as well as a growing number of owner-managed businesses. Almost half of PW's accounting recruits these days are women, and computer techniques constitute an important part of their training. In an increasingly competitive environment, article writing, public speaking, and even advertising have become accepted ways of enhancing the firm's visibility.

It is a scenario that might have caused nightmares for Donald McKenzie McClelland, manager of Price Waterhouse's Toronto office when it opened in 1910 in the Jarvis Building at 103 Bay Street. The son of a Presbyterian minister, McClelland became the firm's first Canadian-born partner and remained, until his retirement in 1948, the embodiment of the accountant's emphasis on discretion, integrity, and quality service. During World War I he was engaged to assist in organizing the staff, procedures, and records of the War Purchasing Commission. When commission chairman Sir Edward Kemp later became Minister of Overseas Forces, McClelland was appointed his financial advisor.

Long before McClelland set up shop in Toronto, Price Waterhouse was already well-established elsewhere.

Clark Kinnear (second from left) and William Simonton (far right) headed the Toronto office in 1962-1972 and 1972-1977, respectively. With them at an informal executive committee meeting are Montreal partner Ian Craig (far left), senior partner Laird Watt (centre), and Vancouver partner Derek Lukin Johnston (second from right).

Sir Nicholas Edwin Waterhouse (1877-1964), son of one of the two English founders of Price Waterhouse, represented the United Kingdom firm when the Canadian partnership came into being in 1914.

Founded in London, England, in 1850, the firm opened its first American office in New York in 1890. Seventeen years later, responding to increasing Canadian business, the American firm opened a branch in Montreal. Its first manager, Roderick Moore, was succeeded in 1911 by A.B. (Steve) Brodie who, with McClelland, provided leadership for PW in Canada throughout its formative years.

The handful of clients referred to the Toronto office by Montreal and New York quickly grew into an impressive list. For example, the sale of a bond issue in London brought PW into contact with The Robert Simpson Co. Ltd., a major Toronto retailer, beginning an association which has remained uninterrupted to this day.

As Canadian business expanded, the firm sensed the need for a distinctly Canadian identity. A separate Canadian partnership was formed in 1914, and 10 years later the Canadian

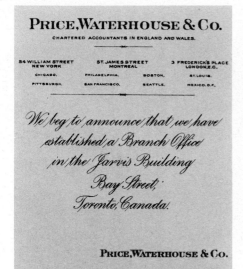

Since its opening as a "branch office" in 1910, the Toronto office has grown into the fourth-largest PW office in the world, with 48 partners and a staff of 640.

Before retiring in 1948, Donald McClelland (centre), partner in charge of the Toronto office for 38 years, got together for a game of golf with his successor James Taylor (right) and Harold Herington, who succeeded Taylor upon the latter's death in an automobile accident in 1950.

and U.S. firms severed their remaining financial links. Today Price Waterhouse in Canada is wholly owned by its Canadian partners, but maintains family-like relationships with other PW firms around the world.

In 1945 PW hired a young chartered accountant, James J. Macdonell, to explore the potential for management consulting services. The experiment was successful and the consulting practice, now Price Waterhouse Associates, grew into an important part of the firm. As for Macdonell, he succeeded another PW alumnus, A. Maxwell Henderson, as Auditor General of Canada.

Price Waterhouse hasn't escaped personal tragedy. McClelland's successor as partner in charge of the Toronto office, James W. Taylor, died two years later from injuries suffered in an auto accident. Upon Taylor's death in 1950, Harold Herington presided over a decade of significant expansion in the firm's Toronto activities. When Herington retired in 1960, Leslie McDonald headed the office until his sudden death in 1962.

Clark Kinnear became partner in charge of the Toronto office after McDonald's death, and held that post until his retirement in 1972. He was succeeded by William Simonton at that time. The current partner in charge of the Toronto office, William Broadhurst, was appointed in 1977—the year that Simonton retired from PW and went on to become a member of the Ontario Securities Commission.

The Toronto office moved in 1916 from the Jarvis Building on Bay Street to the Royal Bank Building at King and Yonge. There it stayed until 1957, when it relocated to 55 Yonge Street. It moved into the Toronto-Dominion Bank Tower in 1967. Since 1975 (when David Higginbotham, the firm's senior partner, was appointed) Toronto also has been the site of PW's national office, with firm-wide responsibility for personnel, continuing education, quality control, and research.

Although PW's recent growth is due essentially to natural expansion, it did merge in 1981 with Jarrett, Goold &

Elliott, a national accounting firm with seven offices across Canada. JG & E was itself the product of a 1974 merger of two firms, one of them Glendinning, Jarrett & Co., with a major office in Toronto.

By 1983 Price Waterhouse (Canada) had grown to 22 offices, 188 partners, and 2,300 staff members, including 1,827 professionals. The Toronto office is now the fourth-largest PW office worldwide with 48 partners and approximately 640 staff members, including 500 professionals. Another 12 partners and 140 staff members work out of satellite offices in Mississauga, Scarborough, and North York.

LABATT BREWING COMPANY LIMITED

A century and a half ago, a young Irish immigrant made his way through Toronto bound for the western part of what then was Upper Canada—to begin an enterprise that today is Canada's leading brewery.

The young man's name was John Kinder Labatt. And although he began his brewery in London, Ontario, its Toronto roots took hold well before the start of this century.

Today Labatt Brewing Company Limited, which is Canadian-owned and -controlled, operates one of its largest breweries at the intersection of Highway 401 and Islington Avenue with 450 employees brewing, packaging, and marketing more than one million hectolitres of beer each year.

In Labatt's era, Toronto was a much different place. Its population was only about 25,000. And just over two million people lived in small, rural pockets strung out across a sparsely populated nation.

Between 1833 and 1847 Labatt became a successful farmer just outside

London. But in 1847, using the money from the sale of his farm, he bought a small brewery on the banks of the Thames River in what now is London's core.

By the time of Confederation in

Labatt's first "bottling agency" was located at 49 Elm Street, Toronto.

The Ontario Brewing and Malting Company which became Copeland and eventually Labatt's Toronto brewery.

1867, Labatt's son, also named John, decided to expand the company's marketing area outside southwestern Ontario. In the 1870s and 1880s the firm developed a product called Labatt's India Pale Ale which, together with its Extra Stock, had wide consumer appeal.

By the 1890s the time had come for Labatt's to compete more seriously in the Toronto market. But the move couldn't be made on a grand scale. Toronto already had eight breweries, most of them in the city's southeastern wards between Yonge Street and the Don River.

The opportunity came in 1897 to buy a substantial brick house, at 49 Elm Street, nearly a block west of Yonge Street, and convert it into a bottling agency. A William Rawlin had purchased the land 30 years before, built the house, and lived there until about 1889. When the new owner had to sell, she wrote John Labatt that he might have it for $4,000, adding that Elm Street "is the only through avenue to the west of the city between Queen and College streets."

The house was renovated to include

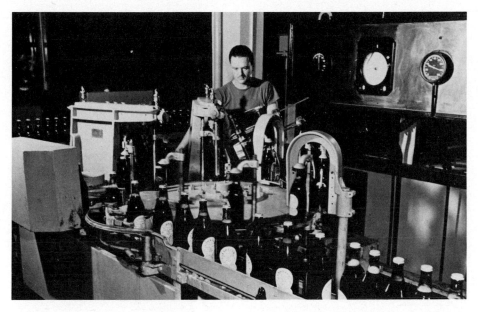

This is the bottling line of Labatt's first Toronto brewery.

an office and an apartment on the upper floor for the company agent—since Labatt's liked its agents to live on the premises. A 12-foot-high basement held bottling vaults running the length of the house. The stable in the rear was enlarged to accommodate four horses and wagons. More than $10,000 was spent on excavations, masonry, brick-laying, carpentry, and ironwork before 1900, when the house became a functioning agency.

Labatt's ale was shipped to Toronto from London in puncheons of 100 gallons and hogsheads of 50 gallons. These were transported to Toronto in boxcars of the Grand Trunk Railway, then carried by team and wagon from the freightyards below Front Street to the bottling vault on Elm Street, where the ale could be poured when ready into smaller kegs or quart bottles for delivery to tavern owners and private households.

By 1911 the space had become too cramped in the prospering agency, and a search was begun for new premises. The company bought the entire south side of Radenhurst Street (lots 7 to 21) for $18,000 in 1913. The street ran east from River Street between Dundas and Queen, ending at the Don Esplanade, a roadway that once had been the bed of

the old Toronto Belt Line Railway and is now the southern extension of Bayview Avenue.

The site lay near the heart of Toronto's brewing industry. A little to the north was the Reinhardt Brewery; to the west was the large Dominion Brewing Company. To the south was the Ontario Brewing and Malting Company. Three others lay farther west—O'Keefe's, Toronto Brewing (later Canada Bud), and the Cosgrave Brewery. Labatt's new location became so identified with the company that a

---

Built in 1970, Labatt's metro brewery at Islington Road and Highway 401 is one of the largest brewing operations in Canada.

request was granted to change the street name to Labatt Avenue—which it remains today.

In 1916, however, with Prohibition in effect, Labatt's withdrew from the Toronto market, closing its agencies and selling its property in 1922. When legal sales of beer and ale resumed at government outlets in 1927 and taverns and beverage rooms reopened in 1934, Labatt's returned to the Toronto market, delivering India Pale Ale by tractor-trailers to the warehouse of the Hardy Cartage Company on Front Street.

By 1946 Labatt's wanted to establish in Toronto a more direct, visible presence, and to reduce the costs of transporting its products. The board of directors decided to make the Copeland Brewing Company at King and Parliament streets Labatt's first brewery acquisition. It was an old plant, dating back to the late 19th century, but after extensive renovations it began turning out India Pale Ale.

In time, the brewery was stretched to capacity, just as tastes were changing toward lighter lager beers. The need for a new, larger plant led to the purchase in the 1960s of land in northwestern metropolitan Toronto, where Labatt's modern brewery now stands. This facility, which utilizes the most up-to-date brewing technology, is evidence of how far the company has come in the 80 years since the bottling vaults and stables on Elm Street.

UNIVERSAL REINSURANCE INTERMEDIARIES LIMITED

To the man in the street, the name Universal Reinsurance Intermediaries Limited may not be familiar. But in the specialized world of insurance, it is instantly recognized as that of a leading Canadian reinsurance broker and reinsurance company manager.

Universal ranks near the top among reinsurance brokers in Canada, serving as an intermediary between insurance companies, both in Canada and the Caribbean, and reinsurance firms worldwide. (Reinsurance companies assume part of the risk on policies written by an insurance company.)

Universal manages the Canadian operations of five European reinsurance companies—Abeille-Paix Réassurances, of Paris; Guildhall Insurance Company Limited, of London; Netherlands Reinsurance Group (N.V.), of Amsterdam; The Nordisk Reinsurance Company Ltd., of Copenhagen; and Union Reinsurance Company, of Zurich. Known as Universal Reinsurance Group, the five reinsurers together in recent years have been topping the list of Canadian reinsurance firms in terms of net premium volume.

All this has been accomplished by a firm which was formed only in November 1973 and in its first month of existence operated out of the apartment of one of its founders.

That is not to say, however, that the new company was short on experience. The founders, including current chairman Sidney Gordon and president Allan Eadie, had been senior executives with another reinsurance broker.

The story of the company's birth is not an unusual one. When their bid to buy the Canadian company for which they worked, and which was up for sale, proved unsuccessful, Universal was formed.

The founders recall there were hectic days. But they remember, too, the "extra effort" put forth by government departments, lawyers, auditors, bankers, and friends within the insurance industry to assist the fledgling enterprise.

Sidney Gordon, B.A., F.I.I.C., chairman.

Allan W. Eadie, B.Comm., C.A., president.

Because of personal contacts in the industry, the founders were able to acquire three major accounts in the first day of operation. Within six months the company had assumed Canadian management responsibilities for three European professional reinsurance companies. By the end of its first year, additional companies had entrusted their management in Canada to Universal.

In 1976 the company began to negotiate reinsurance for insurance company clients in the Caribbean area, particularly in Jamaica and Trinidad. Universal continues to be active there.

As 1982 ended Sidney Gordon was retiring from day-to-day management, while carrying on as chairman. His retirement closes a chapter in a 44-year career in the reinsurance business, which began with his employment at age 16 by brokers at the esteemed insurance exchange, Lloyd's of London, and saw Universal grow from four to 53 people.

Not much will change at Universal. "We've grown every year, and we don't see that stopping," says president Allan Eadie.

KILBORN ENGINEERING COMPANY LTD.

Ken Kilborn resigned as mechanical superintendent at McIntyre Porcupine Mines in northern Ontario in 1947 and embarked on the gamble of his life—forming his own consulting engineering company.

A difficult period followed, until Kilborn Engineering Company Ltd. became securely established. Today the firm employs more than 1,200 people in eight Canadian cities and in Denver, Colorado, including about 700 at the head office in Etobicoke, a Toronto suburb. Kilborn Engineering provides consulting engineering and construction management internationally in such fields as mining, refineries, chemicals, environmental engineering, and public works.

But in 1947, operating from 67 Yonge Street, Ken Kilborn was interested in any work he could find. His first contracts were designing a mining plant in northern Ontario and a Cuban mine project. On another job to design a plant for a Quebec gold mine, Kilborn's client found out there wasn't enough ore to justify the plant. Kilborn tore up the agreement, and, in return, received temporary free office space at 100 Adelaide Street West.

Kilborn Engineering employed seven people in 1949, but mining prospects appeared bleak. Its owner

The former "gambling club" and 1950 office building of Kilborn Engineering Company Ltd.

toyed with the idea of accepting an industry job. But again he gambled, winning contracts with conservation authorities aimed at controlling water flows in Ontario river systems.

Then his office rent increased and Ken Kilborn was forced to move his drafting offices to his home basement, while keeping a small sales office on Wellington Street West. About that time he won an important contract with the Maritime Marshlands Rehabilitation Authority, which was reclaiming salt water marshes along the Bay of Fundy.

In 1950 Kilborn Engineering moved into a building which captured its spirit—a former gambling club at 36 Parklawn Road, complete with a peep hole on the door and a gaming room which was converted to a drafting room. The company flourished on projects in asbestos, the emerging uranium field, and in public works. A new head office building was constructed on the site in 1954.

Suffering from heart trouble, Ken Kilborn wanted to ensure his firm's continuity. He reorganized the business into two operating companies, and employees were given options to buy shares. Kilborn Engineering has

Present offices of Kilborn Engineering Company Ltd.

remained a private, employee-owned corporation since 1954.

Ken Kilborn was stricken with a fatal heart attack in 1959. K.M. Dewar succeeded him as president, serving until 1970 when John Dew, the current president, replaced him.

The company developed expertise in the extraction and refining of potash during the 1960s and participated in the field of potash development in Saskatchewan. And in the 1970s Kilborn Engineering became established in process industries such as oil refining, petrochemicals, and coal beneficiation and liquefaction.

Growth forced the firm to seek new headquarters. Kilborn Engineering moved in 1979 into a new seven-storey glass-and-concrete structure, overlooking Lake Ontario at 2200 Lakeshore Road.

Ken Kilborn, founder and president until his death in December 1959.

245

THE TORONTO-DOMINION BANK

It was late on July 7, 1856, and most of Toronto's 41,000 residents were asleep. But a light glowed from the Bank of Toronto at 78 Church Street, where its president and cashier were signing new bank notes for the bank's opening the next day.

The Bank of Toronto survived that day, and many more, to become a force in Canadian finance. It amalgamated in 1955 with the slightly younger Dominion Bank to form The Toronto-Dominion Bank, one of Canada's major financial institutions and the bank with the longest history of maintaining headquarters in Toronto.

In fiscal 1982 Toronto-Dominion, led by its chairman, Richard M. Thomson, and president, Robert W. Korthals, had revenues of $5.8 billion, after-tax balance of revenue of $255 million, and total assets of $44 billion. It has more than 950 branches, and a presence in major financial centres of North and South America, Europe, the Far East, and the Middle East.

But back in 1857, the Bank of Toronto's single branch recorded profits of $44,000 and assets of almost $900,000.

The bank was formed by Toronto-area flour millers who wanted to capitalize on expanding trade. Its first president, James G. Chewett, had fought with his father's regiment in the War of 1812, then went on to become Deputy Surveyor General of Upper Canada (now Ontario), Toronto Harbour Commission chairman, and city councillor.

In the 1860s J.G. Worts, junior partner to his uncle, William Gooderham, in the Gooderham & Worts distillery, became vice-president—thus beginning the Gooderham family's long involvement with the bank. William Gooderham later became president, as did his son, George, and grandson, William.

The bank's first president, James Austin, had been an apprentice of

The bank's head offices are located in the Toronto-Dominion Centre's 56-storey Bank Tower. (Courtesy of John Harquail.)

printer William Lyon Mackenzie in the 1830s. When Mackenzie led an abortive rebellion in 1837, Austin became involved, and had to flee to the United States. He returned to Toronto in 1844 and co-founded a prosperous grocery business.

By 1955 after decades of growth, both banks were flourishing. But in order to compete effectively with larger institutions, they merged to form a bank with more than $1.1 billion in assets and 450 branches.

Toronto-Dominion moved its head office and Ontario and Toronto divisions into the 56-storey Bank Tower, the first phase of the new Toronto-Dominion Centre, in 1967. The 46-floor Royal Trust Tower was added in 1969, followed in 1974 by the 32-storey Commercial Union Tower.

Today Toronto-Dominion is involved in the whole range of consumer, commercial and corporate, and international banking. Its

Richard M. Thomson, chairman of The Toronto-Dominion Bank. (Courtesy of John Harquail.)

branches are complemented by a network of automated banking machines, called Green Machines, permitting customers to perform most banking functions using a specially encoded card.

MONO LINO TYPESETTING COMPANY LTD.

Like many other successful entre-preneurs, William Robert Adamson, the founder of Mono Lino Typesetting Company Ltd., recognized a market vacuum and quickly filled it.

It was the early 1900s and Adam-son, a young printer, believed that Toronto printing houses faced limited choices in typesetting services. Most typesetting firms supplied linotype—a solid "slug" of type containing a line of connected characters. Adamson felt there were advantages to monotype, in which each character is a separate piece of type.

Along with two friends, William Addison and Henry Mainprice, Adamson formed Toronto's first monotype trade shop. It opened for business in 1912 with three employees at 154 Pearl Street—now the site of First Canadian Place in Toronto.

Besides monotype typesetting, the shop provided linotype service as well as the complete makeup of pages. It could also supply printers with a wider variety of typefaces than they customarily carried themselves.

Adamson became the sole owner of the business, now called Mono Lino Typesetting Company Ltd., in 1920. The firm, forced to relocate because of increased accommodation needs, occupied space in the Brigdens

---

Below: A scene at Mono Lino's plant at 160 Richmond Street West in 1920. Employees sit at keyboards while the monotype casters in the background turn out type.

Bottom: Today Mono Lino utilizes a data-processing department where traditional typographic knowledge is incorporated with modern computerized systems.

Building at 160 Richmond Street West. In 1928 it moved to a facility on Adelaide Street West.

William Adamson died in 1929 at age 52, a loss deeply felt in his com-pany and in the typographic trade. His widow, Ethel May Adamson, became president and plant superintendent Jimmy Howe was appointed general manager.

In 1936, as the Depression was winding down, the founder's son, Walter Adamson, joined the organization as assistant to the foreman. When Jimmy Howe died in 1948, Walter became vice-president and general manager. Ten years later he succeeded his mother as president—a position he still holds. Ethel Adamson served as chairman of the board until her death in 1967 at age 83.

Mono Lino participated in Canada's postwar boom, and in 1949 moved into the Garden City Press Building at 263 Adelaide Street West. But increas-ingly heavy traffic in the downtown core forced a shift in 1963 to its current premises at 420 Dupont Street.

Its market was changing, too. Until the 1950s, Mono Lino primarily served printers and lithographers. But it gradually came to rely on business from the advertising industry or directly from clients such as Sears and Canadian Tire.

The firm acquired its first photo-typesetting equipment in 1967, a move followed in 1969 by the introduction of computerized typesetting. These innovations required extensive staff retraining, but produced tremendous efficiencies. Today more than 90 percent of production is by computer-ized phototypesetting.

From sales of $5,700 and three workers in its first year, Mono Lino had grown by the early 1980s to $8 million in annual sales and 140 employees. It is considered one of the five largest trade typographers in North America.

VTR PRODUCTIONS LIMITED

VTR Productions' two television studios and three sound studios at 47 Scollard Street, Toronto, are active day and night producing and providing facilities for TV commercials, specials, and series.

Back in the 1950s, when television programmes were produced live or on film, a small group of visionaries was experimenting with a revolutionary new medium, videotape.

Much of the pioneering work was done in an old movie theatre on Woodbine Avenue in east-end Toronto. By 1959 the theatre had been converted into a videotape production centre by Meridian Films, an independent film producer, and its president, Ralph Foster.

Meridian Films and the Woodbine Studios are gone but videotape has become a well-established method of television production. And VTR Productions Limited, a direct corporate descendant of Meridian, is the largest videotape production company in Canada.

Its two television studios and three sound studios at 47 Scollard Street, Toronto, are active day and night producing and providing facilities for TV commercials, specials, and series. It also has advanced equipment for post-production, duplication and transfer, stereo recording, and computerized optical effects.

In 1959 Jerry Zaludek, now VTR's president, was part of Ralph Foster's videotape crew. Zaludek recalls that in those early years he was working up to 24 hours a day with no overtime pay—and loving it.

Meridian found itself in financial difficulties, and in 1963 merged with York Television, a competitor, to form VTR Productions Limited.

Colour invaded Canadian television in the late 1960s and VTR needed fresh financing; in September 1970 Bushnell Communications Limited of Ottawa (now owned by Standard Broadcasting Corporation Limited) bought the company. Reconstruction began immediately on VTR's Scollard Street premises, and by early 1971 the firm was in full-colour production.

The early 1970s saw a major turnaround in the company's fortunes, as the technical problems of videotape were overcome and the production industry embraced it as an efficient medium.

Today VTR Productions is part of Yorkville Studio Centre Limited, which also operates Eastern Sound with its three sound studios and CTA Video Distributors Limited, a distributor of video products. Yorkville, wholly owned by Standard Broadcasting, employs about 120 people.

VTR opened an expanded duplication facility for home video cassettes at 121 Railside Road in Don Mills in September 1982. The centre's 600 duplicating machines turn out 70,000 cassettes a month, making it Canada's largest duplicating facility.

This integrated approach to videotape production and marketing has spurred VTR and its sister companies to a 30-percent annual growth rate over the past 10 years.

COCA-COLA LTD.

In the late 1890s soda fountains in Canadian cities along the U.S. border began to sell a tasty-fizzy beverage called Coca-Cola.

The new drink caught on instantly, just as it had throughout the United States. In 1905 the trademark "Coca-Cola" was registered in Canada, and The Coca-Cola Company of Atlanta, Georgia, commenced to build a Toronto plant in which to manufacture syrup and bottle the drink.

With Canadian production imminent, Coca-Cola had come a long way since 1886, when an Atlanta pharmacist named John Pemberton created the syrup (using an iron tub and a boat oar, legend says) and sold it to a local soda fountain operator.

The Toronto plant at 65 Bellwoods Avenue opened in April 1906 with about 10 workers. By the end of the year two salesmen had sold 3,400 gallons of syrup, which, when mixed with water and carbon dioxide, forms the final product.

This head office was located in a new ultra-modern three-storey plant at 90 Broadview Avenue—"the last

In 1905 the trademark "Coca-Cola" was registered in Canada and The Coca-Cola Company of Atlanta, Georgia, built this plant on Bellwoods Avenue.

word in sanitation and efficiency," exclaimed a company newsletter from that period.

The fledgling venture expanded by establishing its own plants and by contracting authorized bottlers across the country. Company syrup plants opened in Montreal in 1910, Ottawa in 1912, and Winnipeg in 1915. By 1920 there were about 75 Canadian bottlers of Coca-Cola.

When the Winnipeg plant opened, the Canadian "home office" moved to that city from Toronto. But in 1923 the Canadian operation, until then a branch of the U.S. company, was incorporated as The Coca-Cola Company of Canada, Ltd., with headquarters in Toronto.

Coca-Cola Ltd.—which became the corporate name in 1945—experienced strong continuity in leadership. Eugene Kelly served as managing director from 1926 to 1952, when he retired. Ralph E. Sewell became managing director in 1954, and three years later was elected president of Coca-Cola Ltd., the first Canadian to serve in that capacity. Sewell retired as president in 1970 to become chairman of the board.

Under Sewell's stewardship, Coca-Cola Ltd. underwent great change and expansion. Until the mid-1950s the product had been available in retail outlets only in the distinctive 6.5-ounce bottle. A 10-ounce bottle was added in 1957, followed in later years by a variety of package sizes, shapes, and materials.

By 1965 Coca-Cola Ltd. had become a sprawling national enterprise with products from more than 140 plants sold through 165,000 outlets. That year it moved into a head office and bottling plant at 42 Overlea Boulevard in the Thorncliffe Park area of Toronto's Leaside. This is still headquarters for Coca-Cola Ltd.'s national operations, which employ about 2,800 people.

From the few glasses of Coke sold in border cities in the 1890s, Coca-Cola Ltd. and its bottlers have become an enduring, ubiquitous part of the Canadian scene.

Today Coca-Cola Ltd.'s Toronto plant is in this modern facility at 42 Overlea Boulevard.

FIRAN CORPORATION

Following a period as president of the Canadian subsidiary of the Firestone Tire and Rubber Company, in 1969 Morgan Firestone decided to leave the company, become a Canadian citizen, and start his own business here.

"Canadians were not risk capital-oriented in the early 1970s," says the youthful-looking 51-year-old Firestone. "I saw a need for someone willing to start up a business and risk their own capital."

In 1971 Firestone discovered Graphico Precision, a manufacturer of printed circuit boards for electronics systems, located at 1100 Bellamy Road in Scarborough. Graphico, founded in 1960 by Austrian-born Rudy Scherenzel, had excellent technical capabilities, but was experiencing financial troubles because of a cyclical slump in the electronics market.

Foreseeing vast growth potential in electronics, Firestone acquired Graphico, and in 1972 made it a division of his newly incorporated company, Firan International Ltd. Firestone, in effect, married Graphico's technical expertise with his own business management skills. He poured millions of dollars into capital equipment and vigorously pursued export business, particularly in the United States.

A Canadian citizen since 1972, he has built Graphico into a major producer of high-technology circuit boards for the military, telecommunications, and computer industries. Graphico was honored in 1980 as supplier of the year by Hughes Aerospace, the large California-based military contractor, in recognition of the Canadian company's ability to provide a high-technology product in volume to Hughes' specifications.

A second company has been established beside Graphico on Bellamy Road in order to build prototype circuit boards. Its president is none other than Rudy Scherenzel,

Morgan Firestone, president of the Firan Corporation, executes a final inspection of a circuit board.

Graphico's founder, who like most of his former employees had remained with the firm.

In 1978 Firestone amalgamated his private company, Firan International Ltd. (which included Graphico), with Glendale Corporation of Strathroy, Ontario, a recreational vehicle

manufacturer in which he had purchased a controlling interest in 1975. Graphico and Glendale are now the major divisions of Firan Corporation, a public company based in Oakville, west of Toronto. Morgan Firestone, chairman and president, owns about 85 percent of Firan. Firestone's strategy is to help feed Graphico's appetite for cash with funds generated by Glendale, which requires no new capital.

Graphico employed about 300 people and generated about $15 million in sales in 1982—a substantial increase over Graphico's 100 employees and $3-$4 million in sales in 1971.

More important, the company has kept abreast of the technological revolution in electronics—particularly the miniaturization and concentration of components into smaller, more efficient packages. Building on this solid base, "We're going to grow in the future, that's for sure," Firestone says.

Morgan Firestone and an employee with a machine for drilling holes in electronic circuit boards.

WAGNER SIGNS INC.

As a boy growing up in Toronto, George Wagner would observe a neighbour roaring off to work in an elegant Pierce Arrow car and dream about operating his own successful business.

After years of hard work Wagner has fulfilled that dream. His company, Wagner Signs Inc., is the country's largest, most diversified sign service— with accounts across Canada and other countries of the world.

The firm originated in 1936, when George's father, Herbert, retired from his company, Star Signs Studio, located at 220 Mavety Street in the Toronto Junction area. Herbert wanted to devote more time to a field in which he was gaining increasing recognition, as a landscape artist.

After acquiring the business George changed the name to Wagner Signs, and ran a one-man operation producing hand-painted signs at the rear of 2863 Dundas Street West. He eventually hired a sign painter, then additional personnel.

In 1947 George achieved a longtime goal by purchasing a competitor, Cunningham Signs, for $8,000—a $1,000 down payment with the rest

Wagner Signs Inc. has been at its current address, 15 Milford Avenue, since 1952.

financed by promissory note. The purchase resulted in Wagner operating from two locations: Cunningham's location at 61 Elm Grove Avenue in Parkdale, as well as his own.

By the time Wagner Signs obtained its charter in 1949, becoming Wagner Signs Ltd., the company had three departments: commercial signs, spray, and silk screen. The employees earned from $38 to $40 a week, while the proprietor's own wages were pegged at $18 a week for some time.

There were two other key moves that year: the purchase of equipment

George Wagner, president of Wagner Signs Inc.

to do direct labelling on glass and plastic containers for the cosmetic industry, which led to the formation of Wagner's container decorating division; and the move to larger facilities in a renovated building at 208 Weston Road.

Two years later a second location was acquired at 1114 College Street. However, consolidation soon became necessary, and in 1952 the firm relocated to its present site in a new subdivision at 15 Milford Avenue. Continuing growth led to the addition of a carpenter shop in 1955; then, in 1956, a metal shop; in 1959, a second floor for office space; in 1963, a sign shop and shipping area; and in 1964, the art, creative, and engineering divisions.

The evolution of Wagner's products and services resulted in the emergence on January 1, 1973, of a reorganized company, Wagner Signs Inc. Its products include illuminated signs (fluorescent and neon), and non-illuminated painted signs for use in areas such as land development, safety, real estate, and supermarket interiors. Among the organization's national sign services are installation and removal, rental and maintenance, and art and design.

As well as conducting a successful commercial sign operation, the direct labelling division of Wagner Signs has become the country's largest independent container decorator— supplying the cosmetic, pharmaceutical, automotive, distilling, and wine industries.

251

TORONTO TRUST CEMETERIES

Ideal burying places should be "worthy of the living, and beautiful resting places for the dead."

In these words, the Trustees of the Toronto General Burying Grounds in 1905 described what cemeteries should be. And in the 78 years since then, the nonprofit organization, now known as Toronto Trust Cemeteries, has come as close to fulfilling this ideal as is realistically possible.

The Trust's eight cemeteries, comprising almost 1,200 acres, are landscaped green spaces, filled with many varieties of trees—native and exotic—and sprinkled with flowering shrubs and other plants. They serve as informal, outdoor horticulture classrooms and quiet retreats from the bustle of a major city.

But when the Toronto General Burying Grounds trust was conceived in 1825, its purpose was utilitarian. Toronto, then York, was a fast-growing town of 1,700 people, more than double its population of 10 years earlier. And the only two burying grounds in the village were consecrated cemeteries of the Church of England and the Roman Catholic Church.

Care of the sick was inadequate—a general hospital wasn't opened until 1829—and, because of the poverty and poor living conditions that many York residents experienced, disease and epidemics were commonplace. The need for a general nondenominational burying ground was evident.

At that time, Upper Canada—as Ontario was then called—was a turbulent society. Many in the province were calling for a wider democracy and an end to domination of government by the establishment, "Family Compact." One of the leading voices for reform was the small, fiery William Lyon Mackenzie who published the *Colonial Advocate* newspaper.

But these differences were temporarily shelved on November 14,

The chapel at The Necropolis in downtown Toronto.

1825, when people of all political stripes met in the Masonic Hall on Colborne Street to discuss a new burying ground. Secretary of the meeting was Mackenzie, who reported it all in the December 8 issue of the *Colonial Advocate*.

One of the founding Trustees, Thomas Carfrae, Jr., reported that he had found an appropriate property, a

six-acre section of the John Elmsley farm on what is now the northwest corner of Bloor and Yonge streets. At that time, the land was one mile north of York's town limits; today, it is one of Toronto's most bustling intersections, an area distinguished by its elegant

Above: The entrance to The Necropolis is a distinctive Toronto landmark.

Left: Mount Pleasant Cemetery in the wintertime.

The Eaton Mausoleum in Mount Pleasant Cemetery on a winter day.

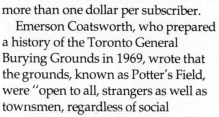

The Michael Shepard House in York Cemetery was built in the early 1850s.

boutiques and restaurants.

On January 30, 1826, the government of Upper Canada incorporated the six acres as York's first public burying ground. The cemetery was purchased for $300, raised by public subscription of no more than one dollar per subscriber.

Emerson Coatsworth, who prepared a history of the Toronto General Burying Grounds in 1969, wrote that the grounds, known as Potter's Field, were "open to all, strangers as well as townsmen, regardless of social standing or religious persuasion. The field was fenced and graced with marble columns—and 'a house to receive the departed.'"

A brief glance of the first board of Trustees reflects the political division in Upper Canada. Carfrae was an establishment figure, a Tory, who took a strong interest in the improvement of health facilities, particularly the care of cholera victims. But another Trustee, Dr. Thomas D. Morrison, was vociferously radical, and, on this platform, became the third mayor of the city of Toronto in 1835.

Like others of his political bent, Morrison supported William Lyon Mackenzie in the Rebellion of 1837, and later was arrested on a charge of high treason. Although acquitted, he feared being arrested again and fled to Rochester, New York, until 1843, when he returned to Toronto to spend the rest of his life.

Two other Mackenzie sympathizers, Samuel Lount and Peter Matthews, were executed in 1838 for their part in the rebellion, and their bodies were interred in the burying grounds that their leader helped found. The remains were later moved to another Toronto burying place, The Necropolis, where their monument stands today—not far

253

from the tombstone of Mackenzie, who, incidentally, died a natural death in 1861. The development of The Necropolis, overlooking the Don Valley between Winchester and Gerrard streets, was an outcome of Toronto's rapid growth in the 1840s to 1850s.

By this time, Potter's Field was no longer far outside the city limits, and the Trustees petitioned the legislature to allow them to buy new land. In 1855 the legislature agreed to close Potter's Field, allowing the Trustees to sell the land as soon as the remains were removed and buried elsewhere. The small burying ground was closed in 1875.

Another group of prominent Torontonians had in the late 1840s purchased and developed The Necropolis with its "commanding and picturesque position" above the Don. The Trustees of the Toronto General Burying Grounds purchased the 15-acre site from the group on July 11, 1855, for $16,000. Because the Trust had only $1,000 to spend, three Trustees personally guaranteed the remaining $15,000 debt.

About a decade later several areas were acquired on the south side of Winchester Street, and the land was prepared for use as a cemetery. However, the city subsequently bought the land from the Trustees and created what later became Riverdale Park and the former city zoo.

As The Necropolis reached its capacity in the 1870s, the Trustees found a suitable property in the

Mount Pleasant is a place that the living can enjoy.

township of York, which was to become Mount Pleasant Cemetery. Purchased in 1873, the grounds were put into shape, a fence constructed, walls and drives laid out, bridges built, a vault erected, and a series of small lakes, waterfalls, and rapid creeks designed. At that time, the cemetery extended a quarter of a mile along Yonge Street, and one and one-quarter miles eastward to the Second Concession, township of York.

This property has remained a highly visible Toronto landmark. It houses impressive monuments and private vaults—memorials to some of the city's most prominent families and individuals, such as Timothy Eaton, who built the department store chain; Sir Oliver Mowat, a father of Confederation; Drs. Banting and Best, co-discovers of insulin; Mackenzie King, former prime minister of Canada; and hockey great Charlie Conacher, to name just a few.

The Necropolis also reflects Toronto's history, with its monuments to Ned Hanlan, the world-class oarsman; George Brown, founder of *The Globe* (now *The Globe and Mail*) and a father of Confederation; and John Ross Robertson, founder of *The Telegram*. Toronto's architectural heritage was enhanced by the graceful gothic portal and buildings on either side of the entrance.

The Trust, of course, could not stand still after Mount Pleasant was developed. With the city's expansion to the north and west, in 1887 it purchased a 105-acre farm halfway between Dufferin and Keele streets, extending from St. Clair Avenue north to Eglinton Avenue. This farm was to become Prospect Cemetery.

A 1905 historical sketch describes the property: "Looking southward and westward from the rising ground in the Cemetery, the Lake for miles can be seen, and the valley of the Humber, with an immense extent of beautifully wooded land extending away to the distant horizon."

With a splendid natural site to work with, the Trust commissioned Joseph Earnshaw of Cincinnati, Ohio, to lay out the new grounds and Toronto architect W.G. Storms to design the red-brick mortuary. Both were highly praised for their work.

By the time the 20th century arrived, Toronto Trust Cemeteries' approach had evolved—a merging of the utilitarian requirement for burial places and a need for beautiful places for the living to enjoy. For example, there's York Cemetery, north of Sheppard Avenue between Bathurst and Yonge streets. The cemetery's office is the attractively renovated Michael Shepard House, whose owner, like Lount and Matthews, supported William Lyon Mackenzie in the Rebellion of 1837.

After imprisonment and a pardon, Shepard operated a mill north of Toronto, then began farming on what is now the York Cemetery site. He built this Georgian-style house in the early 1850s, and lent his name— although it's misspelled—to Sheppard Avenue.

Other cemeteries developed in the 20th century are Beechwood on Jane Street, Pine Hills on Birchmount Road at St. Clair Avenue East, Elgin Mills in Richmond Hill, and Meadowvale in Brampton. Several others are in various stages of planning and development.

Older even than the city of Toronto, and considered to be the oldest continuing corporation founded in Toronto, Toronto Trust Cemeteries has been, and will continue to be, an integral part of the fabric of this great community.

HALLMARK CARDS CANADA

By the second decade of the 20th century, two enterprising young men were establishing themselves in the burgeoning stationery and greeting card business. One, Joyce C. Hall, lived in Kansas City, Missouri; the other, William E. Coutts, was 1,000 miles away in Toronto.

These entrepreneurs eventually became close friends and business associates. From this relationship emerged Hallmark Cards Canada, the country's major supplier of greeting cards and other "social expression" products.

The greeting card industry was fostered by the 19th-century evolution of widespread literacy and affordable postage. Coutts learned the business while working at Ryrie Brothers (now Birks Jewellers) in Toronto for 12 years, then founded his own company, William E. Coutts Company Ltd., in early 1916. He had 10 employees.

The founder of Hallmark Cards Canada, William E. Coutts, with the happy winner of the annual doll and toy contest—Christmas 1968.

Demand was so strong that Coutts set up a printing press in his shop on Wellington Street. Later he recalled: "My small staff worked day and night to get the cards out for Christmas selling. I even pressed friends and relatives into service to help out with the packaging and shipping. We were a bit late, but the cards got out by the end of October."

Coutts visited Hall, founder and president of Hall Brothers Inc. of Kansas City (forerunner of Hallmark Cards, Inc.) in 1931. There was a strong rapport between them, and a handshake agreement allowed Coutts to reproduce Hall's designs in Canada.

In 1958 Coutts, in his mid-seventies and without children, was concerned about his company's continuance of its traditions of quality workmanship and sense of family. He decided the one solution that would preserve what he had built was to sell the firm to his old friend, Joyce Hall.

After the sale Coutts continued working until a year before his death at 91 in 1973, and today his imprint remains evident in the Painters of Canada Series. Members of the Group of Seven and other famous artists had their work reproduced on Coutts' cards, perpetuated by many artists who still contribute to this series.

As the firm expanded it had a number of Toronto locations, ultimately settling in 1973 into its present head office complex in Willowdale. This site houses office, manufacturing, creative, and distribution functions as well as the International Graphics Division— which provides all graphic requirements for 110 Hallmark companies around the world (with the exception of the United States). An additional distribution centre was opened in 1982 in Aurora, a few miles north of Toronto.

Hallmark Cards Canada today employs 1,450 people across the country. Looking to the future, the company emphasizes its objectives to maintain high standards of quality and to expand its Canadian creative content—an outlook reflected in the Hallmark Cards' slogan, "When you care enough to send the very best."

A member of Hallmark's creative design staff.

COMMUNITY NURSING HOMES LTD.

In 1959 Fred Lafontaine was inspecting a rambling old summer resort—called Rosebank—near the Rouge River, beyond the eastern boundaries of Toronto. The 36-year-old Toronto builder thought he might convert the structure into an apartment building, but was not sure that was a suitable choice.

"You could build a nursing home," suggested Rosebank's former owner—a recommendation that convinced Lafontaine and his wife, Marie-Paule, to enter that fledgling industry. Today the family company, Community Nursing Homes Ltd., operates 1,000 beds in its nursing and retirement homes across Ontario.

Lafontaine, who came to Toronto in 1945 from northern Quebec, explains his career shift: "I liked catering to people and the elderly are nice people to cater to."

Converted into a 40-bed nursing home, which was filled within three months of opening, the facility was commended with approval by the Ontario Hospital Commission to receive patients discharged from hospital for convalescence.

Two years later the Lafontaines purchased the 24-bed Rouge Nursing Home on Highway 2 at Altona Road, east of Toronto. They moved farther afield in the '60s and '70s, acquiring properties in other Ontario communities—Port Hope, Sunderland, Port Perry, Warkworth, and Alexandria.

The 70-room nursing home, Birkdale Villa, located at 1229 Ellesmere Road, Scarborough, also houses Community Nursing Homes Ltd.'s main office.

The industry has moved toward a greater professionalism, with small "mom-and-pop" operations in converted buildings becoming outdated. The Ontario Ministry of Health is now involved in licensing, subsidizing, inspecting, and upgrading conditions. Few converted buildings are left, and new homes must meet high standards. Having perceived a gap in services to the elderly, Community Nursing Homes in recent years has developed "retirement homes" for those who do not require extensive nursing care.

In the Toronto area the organization operates Birkdale Villa, a 70-suite retirement home built in 1977 at 1229 Ellesmere Road in Scarborough. In 1980 an apartment building at 1035 Eglinton Avenue West was converted into Pine Villa, a 70-suite retirement home serving a Jewish clientele.

Other facilities include the 26-bed Maple Nursing Home, north of Toronto, the 209-bed Village Retirement Centre, a combined nursing and retirement home in Pickering; as well as other facilities including the 1969 addition in Rosebank, now a 60-room retirement home.

Community Nursing Homes today employs a work force of 775 persons in Ontario, compared to approximately 30 in 1960. At that time Rosebank's 40 beds generated about $240 a day in revenues; in contrast, the 1,000 beds now in the company's various facilities produce $34,000 in daily revenues. Predictably, costs also have increased. Aides are now paid more than six dollars an hour—quite a raise from six dollars a day in 1959!

Community Nursing Homes' future seems assured. As 1982 ended, two new projects were on the boards; and, even more encouraging, four of the Lafontaines' six children were active in the business.

Rosebank, a former summer resort on the Rouge River, was converted into a 40-bed nursing home. Opening in September 1959, it was the first Community Nursing Homes facility.

REAL TIME DATAPRO LTD.

Gerry Meinzer came to Canada in 1957 with an optimistic outlook and a German business administration diploma. Both have served him well, and today he is president of Real Time Datapro Ltd., a leader in the highly competitive data-processing industry.

Meinzer has been at the helm of Real Time Datapro since 1973 after joining the business in 1970, following experience with IBM and another computer firm. One of his first policy decisions was to replace the company's aging data-processing equipment with state-of-the-art Sperry Univac computers and to specialize.

This vastly increased the firm's data-processing capabilities. From information systems developed for clients in the insurance industry, it was a natural step to expand to the municipal government market. Specialized programs now permit municipalities to maintain records on everything from taxes to truck fleets to recreation facilities.

Now the organization is poised to expand into markets in Europe and the United States. Expansion into the United States will bring Real Time Datapro full circle, for it was there in 1876 that the Library Bureau, a company specializing in mechanizing information on library index cards, was formed.

In 1911 the Library Bureau, which at that time provided statistics stored on punch cards to insurance companies, opened a Montreal office and the following year a downtown Toronto office. A major reorganization took place in 1929, when the name Recording and Statistical Corporation was adopted. In 1963 this firm became a division of Sperry Rand Corporation and later part of the Univac Division of Sperry Rand.

The Canadian branch of the company moved to its present Don Mills location in 1968, and Real Time Corporation took over the Univac Information Services Division of

Gerry Meinzer (left), president of Real Time Datapro, reflects with Brian Greenslade (right), president of Pilot Insurance Company. The business relationship between the two firms goes back 50 years.

Sperry Rand in Canada three years later. In 1974 Real Time Corporation Ltd. merged with Datapro Ltd., a London, Ontario, enterprise formed in 1962 to provide statistical services for accountants. The merged venture became known as Real Time Datapro

In the 1930s, when these photos were taken, the firm was called Recording and Statistical and provided statistics stored on cards to companies.

Ltd., a Canadian-owned public company.

In 1981 Real Time and GEAC Computers Ltd., of Markham, Ontario, created a joint-venture corporation, Real Time Insurance Systems, located in London, England.

The person most responsible for the recent expansion is Meinzer, an affable man active in community affairs. He currently serves as chairman of the Canadian Consultative Council on Multiculturalism, and is president of German House, a Toronto ethno-cultural group. He also is an international senator in the Jaycee organization and the immediate past president of the Canadian Association of Data Processing Service Organizations (CADAPSO)—his second term. In addition, he finds time to operate a thoroughbred horse-breeding and -racing stable and says the firm's track record is better than that of the horses!

But Meinzer doesn't gamble when it comes to Real Time Datapro. "There are other companies in the data-processing industry that can demonstrate a more spectacular growth," he says. "Our approach has always been to expand only when the bottom line justified it."

SINCE 1912—FOR COMMERCE, INDUSTRY, & GOVERNMENT

ALLSTATE INSURANCE COMPANY OF CANADA

When Allstate introduced a drive-in claim office to assess automobile damage over 20 years ago, it raised some eyebrows in the industry. However, that was not unusual for the Good-Hands company—which had established its reputation on a willingness to do business differently if it was advantageous for customers.

Doing business differently meant that Allstate was among the first insurance companies in Canada to computerize customer-service records. It was a pioneer participant in research to improve highway safety—by looking to upgrade automobile protection equipment, as well as campaigning against drunken drivers. Other endeavours include an instrumental role in putting Lock-it-and-Pocket-the-Key campaigns into Canadian cities, resulting in fewer stolen cars, and persisting in its campaign for better bumpers.

Nonetheless, automobile insurance is only one aspect of the company's services. It also maintains a complete line of home and industrial insurance in most provinces, and participates in jumbo manufacturing and industrial coverage through large commercial brokerage houses.

The philanthropic firm is active in helping a variety of social, educational, and charitable organizations through the Allstate Foundation, established with a $2-million grant in 1977.

Founded by the United States retail giant, Sears, Roebuck & Company, during the Great Depression, Allstate came to Canada in 1953—selling automobile insurance from offices at 9 Richmond Street East, Toronto. By 1959, when it expanded its underwriting scope to include coverages for residential fire, boat-owner, and health, it had moved its offices to 790 Bay Street.

The year after its incorporation in 1960 as a Canadian company, Allstate added life insurance policies, and in 1963 it introduced commercial insurance.

Moving to its current head office at 255 Consumers Road in Willowdale in 1971, the Corporation has since grown steadily to its present ranking as the fifth largest in Canada providing

The headquarters of Allstate Insurance Company of Canada is located at 255 Consumers Road, Willowdale.

property and casualty insurance.

The Allstate Insurance Company of Canada (jointly owned by Allstate Insurance Company of the United States and Simpsons-Sears Ltd. in Canada) employs approximately 1,700 people across Canada, including more than 450 sales agents in 65 locations.

Company officials emphasize that Allstate's enviable growth record is the result of an innovative yet consistent approach to business—an approach that rewards doing things differently if it results in better service.

Allstate foresees a necessity to move its head office again in the future, this time to a new facility built to its specifications. If the organization's past record is any indication, it may be sooner than later.

As one corporate executive stated, "We may have been newcomers on the block, but we're here to stay."

KING EDWARD HOTEL

On June 23, 1981, one of Toronto's glittering jewels reopened its doors after two years of restoration and rejuvenation costing in excess of $30 million. The King Edward Hotel, erected in 1903, was the realization of George Gooderham's bold dream to build a grand hostelry for the rich, powerful, and famous from every corner of the world.

Gooderham belonged to one of Toronto's most prominent families. He was president of Gooderham & Worts (the large family distillery), the Bank of Toronto (later merged into the Toronto-Dominion Bank), and Manufacturers Life Insurance.

By 1900 King Street East, traditionally the home of major businesses and elegant shops, was seeing its status threatened by areas west of Yonge Street. Gooderham hoped that the new hotel would preserve the prominence of that part of the city.

Architect E.J. Lennox designed the hotel's exterior in French Renaissance style, using terra-cotta trimmings. The interior was sumptuous, including massive marble columns and a sky-light in the lobby.

Construction costs totalled $6 million. In addition to that sum was

The massive renovation in 1979 1981 included letting the sunshine in by scraping the tar off the skylight. Said one United States writer, "The centre (of the hotel) is the joyful, exhilarating lobby, reminiscent of a Mediterranean villa's courtyard."

When constructed in 1903 the King Edward Hotel was an eight-storey structure, as in this early photograph. By 1922 a new wing had been added, which included a nine-storey tower.

the expense of the antique furnishings—17th-century tapestries, a Constable painting, Greek statues, a life-size gold Buddha, and, allegedly, the jewel box of Diane de Poitier, mistress of King Henry II of France.

In 1922 a new wing was built, including a nine-storey tower rising above the original eight-storey structure. This added 450 guest rooms, a convention room, and a ballroom on the two top floors. The hotel at one point advertised 1,000 rooms. But the Depression of the 1930s inflicted its wear and tear on the grand old lady. Ownership passed from hand to hand; financial troubles often threatened to close it down.

Many attempts were made to revitalize the building. But waves of thoughtless renovation eroded much of the hotel's distinctive charm:

Marble columns were painted and skylights and windows tarred over. Still, the King Edward managed to attract the world's luminaries. In the 1960s Elizabeth Taylor and Richard Burton carried on their scandalous romance there, while picketers outside denounced their defiance of public morality.

Trans-Nation Inc. purchased the hotel in 1979 for $6 million and commenced painstaking renovations that restored the building to its former glory. Years of grime and soot were sandblasted away, revealing an architectural gem that now boasts some of the most luxurious hotel suites in Canada. Guests can relax in the fine dining rooms, the modern health spa, or enjoy an evening of Old World elegance in the revitalized ballroom. The hotel is now owned and operated by Trust House Forte, the world's largest hotel management company.

The restoration of the King Edward is just another important stage in the revival of the downtown area east of Yonge Street, a quarter now brimming with theatres, restaurants, and shops. George Gooderham would be pleased.

M.S. ART SERVICES LTD.

M.S. Art Services Ltd. has been operating for just two decades, but in that time it has established an enviable reputation in Canada's film and advertising industries.

The company, founded in 1965 with four employees, operated out of rented quarters on the city's fashionable University Avenue. Revenue that first year totalled about $100,000; today the firm boasts sales that are rapidly approaching the $2-million mark, employs a staff of 19, and has spacious production facilities and offices at 410 Adelaide Street West.

M.S. Art Services produces film and audiovisual campaigns to introduce new products, create new and powerful corporate images, and to motivate sales forces. With a staff of expert graphic designers, illustrators, and production supervisors, the company has the capability of putting together 16- and 35-millimetre film and slide presentations for its corporate customers. M.S. Art Services also can produce sound tracks for audiovisual productions and can stage audiovisual presentations with up to 36 synchronized film projectors.

Clients of the firm range from large corporations in the consumer products field to smaller industrial and retail operations. Important customers include automotive, food, beverage, cosmetic, and pharmaceutical corporations. As well, the company serves a number of leading advertisers across the country and has become active in the production of graphics and other programme material for education television.

Originally established in 1965 to produce film credits, M.S. Art Services was purchased in 1967 by Manolo Corvera, its current president. Corvera, who emigrated from Spain in 1961, was educated as design draftsman and had worked for a brief period for the Spanish telephone system.

Film animation, however, was Corvera's first love. By 1957 he had founded a venture in Madrid to develop his interest in animation, and one of the larger projects he undertook was the translation of many Walt Disney children's books into Spanish.

In Canada, Corvera has become known as an animator whose creations appear daily on television screens across the country. "The Little Sprout," used in advertisements for many Green Giant products, is one well-known character who dances to Corvera's tune.

In 1982 M.S. Art Services joined forces with John A. Olsen Communications Limited, a corporate communications company with an international reputation for excellence in multi-image productions.

M.S. Art Services Ltd. animated the Canadian well-known "Little Sprout" character for Green Giant advertisements.

RELIABLE FUR DRESSERS AND DYERS LTD.

A few years after arriving in Canada in 1926, Harry Topper made a two-dollar investment that he was later to call the best he had ever made.

Virtually penniless and without a trade, the Russian immigrant applied for a shearer's job at a now-defunct Toronto fur dressing and dyeing firm. Not knowing anything about shearing, Topper paid a fellow worker two dollars to stay long after the day's end to teach him the basics. Topper landed the job, and launched a 50-year career in the fur business.

Today Reliable Fur Dressers and Dyers Ltd., founded in 1932 by Harry Topper and several partners, is a multimillion-dollar corporation with 150 employees at its downtown Toronto location and 500 customers worldwide. The firm prepares pelts for manufacture and dyes skins to imitate more expensive furs or to create fashion colors.

First located at Simcoe and Pearl streets in the heart of the city, Reliable was an immediate hit. In those tough, post-Depression days, rabbit fur was popular, mainly because it was relatively inexpensive. The company found a big market in overshoes, which were trimmed with rabbit fur.

In 1935 Reliable brought out a revolutionary product, called Two-Tone Beaver, which was actually rabbit fur dyed to resemble much more expensive beaver. Unfortunately, though there was strong demand initially, problems with the dyeing process forced many retailers to return the product, pushing Reliable to the brink of bankruptcy. With characteristic determination, however, Harry Topper found the money to overcome the difficulty and stay in business.

The firm continued to prosper during World War II. Not only did Reliable products wind up in the uniforms of Allied personnel, Harry Topper worked hard to raise money for the war effort.

Reliable moved to the present

The late Harry Topper founded Reliable Fur Dressers and Dyers Ltd. in 1932.

location at 400 Richmond Street West in 1941. Six years later Topper bought out his last remaining partner to become sole owner of the firm. About 10,000 square feet were added to the Richmond Street facility in 1963, and five years ago Reliable acquired an adjacent building for executive offices and for potential expansion.

Harry Topper's nephew, Joe Mann, became active in the business in 1947 and in 1952 Topper's son, Victor, joined the management team. Harry Topper remained in control of the firm until his death in 1981, when Victor and Joe Mann took over. A third generation—David Topper, Lawrie Mann, and Bobby Mann—have started up the management ladder.

Over the past 50 years the company

established a reputation for reliability, high-quality workmanship, and technological innovation. Harry Topper was recognized not only as a fur expert who took particular care to look after small customers, but as a considerate employer.

He treated his employees as family and the firm became known as the Reliable "mispoche," a Yiddish word meaning family. Harry Topper also was active in many charitable fundraising activities, primarily relating to Toronto's Jewish community. As well, he was one of the leading exponents of Yiddish in Canada, and financially supported Yiddish authors worldwide.

NATIONAL TRUST COMPANY LTD.

When National Trust Company Ltd. was born in 1898, Canada was 31 years old, with a population of just over five million, and a gross national product of one billion dollars. Eggs cost 14 cents a dozen, poultry was 11 cents a pound, and boys' suits were priced under three dollars.

Canada was also a rapidly developing country with seemingly endless prospects. Railroads and telegraph lines were being built, companies were being formed, and a branch-banking network was spreading.

With this business expansion, private wealth was accumulating, creating the need for institutions to manage this wealth and provide certain services for corporations. The result was the emergence of the trust company, a corporation which for a fee acts as a fiduciary—that is, it holds assets in trust for someone else. This is a particularly Canadian phenomenon because in most other countries this role is handled by banks.

The inspiration for National Trust—today one of Canada's major trust companies—came from George A. Cox, a financier who began his career as a telegraph operator in Peterborough, Ontario. He became a powerful figure in Canadian business, heading Central Canada Loan and Savings Corporation (a firm he had built), Canada Life Assurance Company, and the Canadian Bank of Commerce. Cox, a senator, served on the boards of about 50 corporations.

He saw the need for a trust company to serve the individuals and businesses around the corner of King and Victoria streets in Toronto, where Central Canada had its head office. So in 1898 the National Trust Company of Ontario was formed, with its office on the northwest corner of King and Victoria—a site occupied by the firm until 1962 when it moved across the street to a new complex at 21 King Street East.

National Trust's shares were traded

National Trust was first located behind the Central Canada Loan and Savings Corporation office at 26 King Street East. It was not until 1962 that the firm moved across the street to its 21 King Street East location.

on the Toronto Stock Exchange in 1898—one of 60 companies and about 12 banks listed. It is one of only five original members still listed today.

In that first year, National Trust employed about 10 people and its assets amounted to fewer than one million dollars—a far cry from the 1,950 employees and $2.5 billion in assets indicated in the 1981 annual report. In 1898 National Trust's manager was paid $50 a month and other staff members $10.

Even then, National Trust attracted people of talent. J.W. Flavelle—later Sir Joseph Flavelle—was its first president and served in that post until 1931. Flavelle, also from Peterborough, became one of Canada's leading businessmen and during World War I was chairman of the Imperial Munitions Board.

The firm's main typist that first year was Harry Gundy, later a founding principal of Wood Gundy Ltd., a leading Canadian investment dealer. The first general manager, W.T. White, also carved a niche in Canadian history. The story goes that he was with the city of Toronto's assessment office when two senior directors of National Trust attended an assessment appeal on behalf of another company

White was so impressive in presenting the city's viewpoint that he was offered the National Trust position.

White, later Sir Thomas White, temporarily left the firm to serve as Minister of Finance in the government of Sir Robert Borden during World War I. In that capacity he became the father of income tax in Canada (a "temporary" measure that was to die after the war but remains distressingly healthy to this day.)

In the early years, National Trust's work was largely to act as a trustee or transfer agent for companies. It was, for example, appointed trustee in a bond issue to raise capital for the Canadian Northern Railway—the first of many railway associations.

This role of trustee thrust National Trust into unusual situations. The firm once administered a circus and was concerned for some time that it might have to become a circus impressario.

By 1899 it was apparent the company's operation would not be confined to Ontario and, therefore, its name was changed to National Trust Company Ltd. In the same year, the firm became transfer agent for the Dominion Iron and Steel Company, on the condition that it open an office in Montreal—its first outside Toronto.

National Trust took over the Manitoba Trust Company in Winnipeg in 1900, and by the end of the year had one million dollars invested in farm mortgages in

Manitoba. It expanded to Edmonton in 1902, to Vancouver in 1947, to Victoria in 1950, and to Calgary in 1951.

Its scope wasn't limited to Canada, however. Dr. F.S. Pearson, a U.S. engineer who had helped build electric utilities in Latin America, came to National Trust for help in financing a project in Sao Paulo, Brazil. The money was raised in Toronto, with National Trust as bond trustee. In time, the firm assisted other businesses in that part of the world.

National Trust's net income had grown to $540,000 by 1929, and assets amounted to more than $250 million. However, according to former president E.H. Heeney, the years from 1929 to 1949—through the Great Depression and World War II—were largely a matter of "hanging on." Not until 1957 did profits return to 1929 levels.

The 1950s provided new opportunities as personal incomes rose, and Canadians, always serious savers, were looking for new places to put their money. A housing boom was on, and there was a growing demand for mortgages.

The company had always been empowered to accept deposits in trust. While still relying heavily on its fiduciary business, National Trust developed a satellite approach, opening retail offices in the major urban centres in which it was established. Hamilton's Centre Mall shopping centre was its first satellite office, opening in 1957 to offer savings accounts. A 1955 advertisement, for example, promoted savings account interest rates of 2.5 percent and first mortgages at 5.5 percent.

Despite increased activity in consumer services, the firm hasn't forgotten its bread and butter, the trustee function. Assets of estates, trusts, and agencies administered by National Trust exceeded $9.4 billion in 1982, compared with $8 million back in 1908.

BENJAMIN FILM LABORATORIES LTD.

From a modest family business started in 1953, Benjamin Film Laboratories Ltd. has grown into a multimillion-dollar wholesale photo-finishing establishment.

During its first full year of operation, sales totalled $50,000, primarily from Toronto area customers. Today, however, the company founded by Dr. George J. Benjamin and his wife Johanna, serves about 700 outlets in Ontario, mainly independent camera stores, and has a staff of more than 160.

One of the first privately owned colour film-processing companies in Canada, Benjamin Film Laboratories Ltd. has maintained a solid reputation for service and reliability, and consistently has been ranked at the top in recent surveys of photo-finishing quality. The firm always has been the first to embrace and develop new photographic technologies designed to improve product quality.

Originally from Riga, Latvia, Dr. Benjamin developed a passion for photography at an early age. Before graduating from the University of Latvia, he had produced some of the earliest colour photography in the country. After World War II he worked as a chemist with Imperial Chemical Industries in Manchester, England, specializing in colour film research.

When he and his family arrived in Canada in 1952, Dr. Benjamin's reputation as a photographer, explorer, and lecturer was well-established. He was made a Fellow of the Royal Photographic Society and a member of the elite Honorary Pictorial Society. He was recognized for his unique cave and snow photography, and for his active pursuit of excellence in everything he did.

The Benjamins' colour slide- and print-developing business established at 51 Duchess Street (later changed to 247 Richmond Street) in downtown Toronto was an immediate success.

From the earliest years, members of the Benjamin family have been active in the business.

By 1957 the company found it had to expand to handle its growing sales volume. An addition to its existing building was constructed and processing equipment was updated to handle colour negative film. The firm continued to grow in the 1960s and 1970s, during which time four adjacent facilities were acquired. The most recent expansion was in 1977, when the building at 287 Richmond Street East was remodelled for sales, executive, and accounting offices.

During the rapid expansion of the firm, Dr. Benjamin enthusiastically pursued his own photography. He has become well-known for underwater exploration and films, primarily of the Bahamas, and was honoured by the Underwater Society of America in 1978. His underwater work has been featured in a number of magazines, including *National Geographic*. Over the years he has crisscrossed North America on many lecture and exhibition tours, and in 1980 he was granted an honorary doctor of laws degree by York University in Toronto.

Today the family tradition remains strong. Dr. Benjamin is the chairman of the company he and Mrs. Benjamin founded, Johanna Benjamin is vice-president, and a son, Peter, has become president and general manager.

HUMPHREY FUNERAL HOME—A.W. MILES CHAPEL

The Humphrey Funeral Home—A.W. Miles Chapel, now well into its second century of service, remains very much a family firm. Located at the geographic centre of metropolitan Toronto at 1403 Bayview Avenue, the current president is Thomas A. Humphrey, third generation.

The original Humphrey Funeral Home dates back to 1879, when the sons of Louisa and Edmund Humphrey opened a funeral service establishment in the area of Yonge and Dundas streets. Julius A. Humphrey had carried on the firm for 29 years when he was joined by his son Albert.

The Humphrey family's business had been in operation for 22 years when Arthur W. Miles opened his first funeral home on College Street in 1901. While they were competitors in the early years, Humphrey and Miles shared inventories and assisted each other wherever possible. A great innovator among funeral directors, Miles operated the first motorized ambulance and funeral coach in Canada and also established the first formal funeral chapel.

Miles also was known as a philanthropist and established a 200-acre park—complete with a fully stocked zoo—at Erindale, now known as Mississauga. Perhaps motivated by memories of a childhood when he could not afford a trip to the zoo, Miles offered free admission and complimentary ice cream for the children of many Toronto church congregations who were invited to use the park for church school picnics. Sadly, on the coldest night in January 1944, Miles Park and most of its animals were destroyed by fire.

As Toronto expanded northward, Humphrey's moved from the Church Street location to Yonge Street. In 1927 Miles moved to St. Clair Avenue West, where he was joined by his son Bill. The business continued at the St. Clair location until 1981.

Albert E. (Bert) Humphrey, second

Top left: Julius A. Humphrey established the family business in 1879.

Top right: Albert (Bert) Humphrey became president of the firm on his father Julius' death in 1924.

Above left: Thomas A. Humphrey, president, took charge of the family business in 1935.

Above right: Bruce T. Humphrey, vice-president, represents the fourth generation of the family in the business.

generation, became president of the firm on his father's death in 1924. He presided over a move farther north on Yonge Street and also opened an additional Yonge Street location at Lansing.

When A.E. Humphrey died suddenly in 1935, Thomas A. Humphrey took charge. He operated the firm in a more central location at Yonge and Eglinton and finally, in 1955, moved to the present Bayview Avenue location. Bruce T. Humphrey, fourth generation, became active in the business in 1970 and is currently vice-president.

The Humphrey and Miles firms joined in 1981, following the purchase of Miles' St. Clair Avenue West property by a real estate developer and the acquisition of the A.W. Miles business by the Humphrey family from then-president J. Rennie Graham, who had served Miles in various capacities for 40 years.

During its many years of service, Humphrey Funeral Home has been noted for its innovative practices. Though quite common today, the prearrangment and preplanning of funerals were unusual when Humphrey's pioneered them.

Humphrey Funeral Home—A.W. Miles Chapel carries on today under the management of the Humphrey family and Rennie Graham.

ONTARIO MILK MARKETING BOARD

Toronto is Ontario's largest milk market, therefore it is appropriate the city should be host to the marketing organization for the province's milk producers. It was chosen for that site because the founders of the Ontario Milk Marketing Board (OMMB), established in 1965, initially wanted the headquarters to be near the seat of government from which it received its marketing powers.

The OMMB came into existence as a result of a report prepared by a committee appointed by the Ontario government in 1963 to inquire into the problems of the milk industry, including the boom-and-bust cycles of shortages and surplusses that made milk marketing so difficult. The report pointed out the need for "one producer-controlled marketing agency in the province."

As a result, the Milk Act of 1965 stipulated that all milk produced for sale on Ontario farms must be sold to one buyer, and all milk purchased by Ontario processors must be obtained from one seller. And that buyer and seller would be the Ontario Milk Marketing Board. The Board, in consultation with the processing sector, created an orderly system, such as uniform pricing, to replace the one in effect. To ensure stability the Board implemented a system of supply management, the scheduling and matching of production with demand, with its primary tool being the quota assigned to each producer.

The government appointed George R. McLaughlin, a well-known dairy farmer from Beaverton, Ontario, as the Board's first chairman. Head office was a leased building at 31 Wellesley Street East.

Initially all Board members were appointed by the government; today milk producers elect one from each of 12 regions of Ontario, and a 13th is named by the government to represent cream producers. In addition, 54 local milk committees serve as liaisons between the Board and producers. The activities of the OMMB are monitored by the Milk Commission of Ontario, and it is subject to decisions of the Farm Products Appeal Tribunal— which is empowered to hear appeals from parties who consider themselves aggrieved by decisions of the Board.

Officials of the Board note that because it has ensured farmers a fair return and security from the extreme price fluctuations of a "free market," producers are able to adopt modern practices in management and are more confident to invest in their operations. As a consequence, consumers are assured of increased production and marketing efficiencies, improved milk quality, stable prices, and a wide variety of products.

In 1969 the OMMB moved to 50 Maitland Street; by late 1983 it expects to relocate to offices in the Meadowvale area of Mississauga. About 90 of 135 permanent employees work at the head office.

After guiding the Board through its infancy, George McLaughlin retired as chairman in 1977. He was succeeded by another prominent dairy farmer, Kenneth G. McKinnon of Port Elgin, Ontario.

As the challenging 1980s unfold, McKinnon is still chairman, and therefore ultimately responsible for coordinating milk marketing in Ontario—producing one-third of Canada's milk.

George R. McLaughlin was appointed the first chairman of the Ontario Milk Marketing Board in August 1965.

Kenneth G. McKinnon, a Port Elgin, Ontario, dairy farmer, succeeded George McLaughlin as OMMB chairman in 1977.

INGLIS LIMITED

Inglis Limited, a company whose history has been closely entwined with that of Toronto, was not established in that city, but in Guelph, some 60 miles to the west.

It was there in July 1859 that Thomas Mair and John Inglis, two machinists from nearby Dundas, Ontario, leased a foundry and some water rights, and started producing machinery for grist and flour mills.

In 1881 the enterprise, now called John Inglis & Sons—five sons worked in the family business—bought land on Strachan Avenue in Toronto, and moved the operation to that site.

The company today is a major Canadian appliance manufacturer with about 2,400 employees and 1982 net sales of more than $222 million. Besides the Strachan Avenue site, it operates plants in Mississauga, just west of Toronto; Stoney Creek and Cambridge, Ontario; and Montmagny, Quebec. Among its products are washers and dryers (both domestic and coin-operated), refrigerators, dishwashers, dehumidifiers, and ranges.

There have been some rough detours along the way. In 1904 fire swept through the firm's wood-frame premises, and the business had to be rebuilt. But Inglis recovered under president William Inglis, the founder's son, and in the early decades of this century produced diverse machinery for mines, mills, power plants, factories, and ships.

It built engines for the Canada Steamship Lines passenger steamers, the *Hamonic* and the *Huronic*, which were the first engines of their kind in Canada. In 1935, Inglis constructed the Toronto Island ferry, named the *William Inglis*.

During the world wars, the company laboured mightily in Canada's defence effort. In World War I, thousands of shells and shell forgings were produced on Strachan Avenue, as well as more than 40 steam

The Toronto Island ferry, William Inglis.

marine engines for the government.

In World War II, Inglis turned its industrial muscle to the production of Bren guns and other armaments, in addition to marine boilers, engines, pumps, and various equipment. At one time over 5,000 machine tools and nearly 18,000 people were employed in the plants.

Solid-state electronic touch-control laundry appliances, first introduced in Canada by Inglis.

After the war, Inglis focussed again on its industrial product lines, including boilers and steam and hydraulic turbines. But it also moved strongly into home appliances, manufacturing laundry equipment and later refrigerators and freezers, under licencing agreements with the U.S. Whirlpool Corporation.

In 1966 Inglis closed down its equipment division to devote full attention to appliances. From 1969 to 1971 Whirlpool purchased 43 percent of the firm's shares, making it the largest shareholder. Simpsons-Sears Ltd., a major customer, owns 20.3 percent.

In March 1982 Inglis acquired certain assets of the former Canadian Admiral Corporation, Limited. Soon afterward, it resumed production in Admiral plants in Montmagny and Mississauga, largely with former Admiral employees.

Today Inglis, with its head office in Mississauga, markets its products under the Inglis, Whirlpool, and Admiral trademarks through its sales offices across Canada, as well as supplying Simpsons-Sears with appliances under the Kenmore label.

TORFEACO INDUSTRIES LIMITED

Queen Victoria was on the throne when the Toronto Feather and Down Company Ltd. was incorporated in 1894. The firm specialized in the manufacture of pillows and comforters—all made with the finest down and feathers.

Nowadays there are fewer feathers; the materials most often used are synthetics—polyester and blended fabrics for covers, and polyester for stuffing. The product line also has broadened, and Torfeaco—the name was shortened in 1960—now manufactures five major products: bedspreads, comforters, drapes, pillows, and mattress pads.

Torfeaco is a mid-size manufacturer which is a major supplier of these products to the large department and chain stores that have been its principal customers. To survive, the company has had to be equal to the challenge of change in both merchandising and production.

The latest challenge is meeting the quickly changing tastes of today's consumer. This means many patterns have a short life. Torfeaco is investing in new computer-assisted manufacturing equipment to allow the firm to change designs quickly, and already has a substantial computer installation to monitor its daily operations.

As indicated earlier, Canada's major department stores traditionally have been Torfeaco's biggest customers. For many years the stores have sold its products from coast to coast, and most Canadians have seen one or more of the company's products illustrated in a color catalogue or a newspaper supplement.

Torfeaco boasts a dedicated work force, with a minimum of turnover. Five employees have been with the firm for more than 25 years, and one for 44 years. When this man was hired in 1938, it was because he swung a good bat—the company fielded a competitive baseball team then.

The major shareholders of this enterprise were Joshua Ronn of Montreal, a Czech-Canadian textile entrepreneur, and the late Harry Warner of Toronto. In 1983 their interests were purchased by Harold Hafner, the firm's president and chief executive officer for the past nine years, and three of his key officers.

This document, dated October 4, 1894, consists of the "Letters Patent" incorporating the Toronto Feather and Down Company Ltd., now called Torfeaco Industries Limited.

Torfeaco Industries Limited, located at 545 Trethewey Drive, Toronto, includes a retail outlet for its comforters, bedspreads, draperies, and pillows.

Torfeaco was located for many years at Dundas and Ritchie streets in downtown Toronto but since 1977 has been in the borough of North York in northwest metropolitan Toronto. Its leased premises in a modern, well-lighted plant include a factory retail outlet.

CONSOLIDATED FASTFRATE TRANSPORT GROUP

"There aren't enough people making commitments," asserts Donald W. Freeman, the 46-year-old president and majority owner of the Consolidated Fastfrate Transport Group. "I'll make the commitment."

Hard work, aggressiveness, positive thinking: That's how Freeman explains the rapid emergence of Consolidated Fastfrate since 1966 into a major transportation company with more than 650 employees (about 325 in Toronto) and annual sales of more than $45 million.

Consolidated Fastfrate's main business has been freight forwarding—moving freight in rail car containers to its company terminals in other cities across the country for delivery through its extensive road truck network. Recently, the company also has become an interprovincial road transport business through ownership of McNeil-McGrath Transport Inc.

In early 1983 Consolidated Fastfrate moved out of its home of 12 years at 1100 King Street West and into a new 25,000-square-foot facility at 2525 St. Clair Avenue West, along the Canadian Pacific tracks. From this building extends a freight-handling facility that is 65 feet wide and 1,400 feet long—the equivalent of six city blocks.

All this must have seemed impossible to Donald Freeman in 1953, when he was hired as dockhand for a Toronto transport company. He was working 12 hours a day at $1.16 an hour. Freeman moved on to other jobs, gaining experience that would serve him well in later years. In the 1960s, he became terminal manager of a large transport company, only to see it sold to an outside group.

Freeman and partner Sophie Weimert persuaded Canadian Pacific to let them operate a forwarding operation between Toronto and Vancouver. Freeman recalls: "They rented us a tiny office at $25 a month and said, 'There's a little boxcar. Show us how good you are.'" And so, Consolidated Fastfrate was born, with just six employees.

The commitment to customer service exhibited by Freeman and Weimert—now the firm's secretary/treasurer—paid off. The firm soon took over the entire space in the old Parkdale railroad station. By 1969 plans were afoot for a new Toronto terminal at 1100 King Street West. On July 1, 1971, this much larger facility opened for business.

Consolidated Fastfrate expanded, opening terminals in Calgary and Edmonton in 1968, Winnipeg in 1969, Saskatoon and Regina in 1970, and

Thunder Bay and Victoria in 1975. In 1980 the company entered the road transport business by acquiring the 50-year-old McGrath Transport Inc. of Burlington. This was followed by the purchase in 1982 of another long-established road carrier, McNeil Transport Inc., of Brockville, Ontario, which was licensed to haul goods into Quebec. The two transport companies were merged in July 1982.

But Donald Freeman is not resting on his laurels. As 1983 began, plans were being finalized for the Consolidated Fastfrate Transport Group to expand its participation in the developing lucrative markets of the future.

Donald W. Freeman, president, reflects the confidence and commitment that is synonymous with the Consolidated Fastfrate Transport Group.

The "C.F. Action Team" concept is proudly placarded on the firm's fleet of special pictorial trailer units.

O'KEEFE CENTRE

*Don't let it be forgot
That once there was a spot
For one brief shining moment
That was known
As Camelot*
　　　Camelot, by Lerner and Loewe.

Twice in 20 years, Richard Burton took to Toronto's O'Keefe Centre stage to play the role of Arthur in Lerner and Loewe's romantic musical, *Camelot*—first for the glittering world premiere in October 1960, then for the centre's 20th-birthday celebration in June 1980.

Those fortunate enough to have attended either of those watershed performances left the theatre with something as intangible as tomorrow yet as real as yesterday—memories.

And memories—the big-stage, show business kind—are what the O'Keefe Centre is all about. In its 24-year history the O'Keefe Centre has become known as the heart of Toronto's big-stage show business productions.

That's the way its founder, industrialist E.P. Taylor, wanted it. And from the beginning the O'Keefe Centre has lived up to expectations that it would be one of Canada's most important performing arts centres. It has for many years provided a home for the National Ballet and the Canadian Opera Company.

But a home for ballet and opera was only part of E.P. Taylor's original plans for a multipurpose civic centre designed to "put Toronto on the map." Then chairman of the O'Keefe Brewery Company, Taylor became convinced in the mid-1950s that Toronto needed a centre for theatre and drama the equal of those in New York or London.

O'Keefe provided $12 million for the project, and architects Earle C. Morgan and Page & Steele were told to go first-class all the way. They used expensive granite and marble, brass and bronze fittings, and rich-hued cherry-wood walls in the auditorium.

With 3,500 seats and a huge stage, the O'Keefe was able to handle even the largest Broadway shows.

But staging high-quality shows is expensive and despite good intentions, the brewery never could make the centre pay. Faced with mounting deficits, O'Keefe finally sold the building to Metropolitan Toronto in 1968 for $2.7 million, the value of the land alone.

The financial posture looked up briefly after Metro took over, but soon the slide continued. The lowest point came in 1979, when the centre chalked up its biggest loss. That year, the shake-up came. Toronto agreed not to assess municipal taxes, and installed a cost-conscious board of management which set to work to make the centre commercially successful.

The O'Keefe Centre now plays on its traditional strengths. Along with ballet and opera, it emphasizes big shows, first-run musicals, and top entertainers.

Management also has undertaken an ambitious seven-year renovation programme designed not only to

O'Keefe Centre, the home of the National Ballet and the Canadian Opera Company, also provides an arena for first-run musicals and top entertainers.

preserve the original high-quality materials, but to add to them a new sense of glamour. The $5.2-million refurbishment will be completed in 1987.

Now that the O'Keefe Centre is on a solid financial footing, it looks ahead with confidence and aims to retain its place as an internationally known centre providing memorable big-name entertainment.

NATIONAL BALLET OF CANADA

In 1981, the year the National Ballet of Canada celebrated its 30th anniversary, some of its best young dancers were awarded medals in the prestigious International Ballet Competition in Moscow—and of the 26 countries represented, only the Soviet Union itself reaped more awards than Canada.

The coincidence of the two events signalled that in 30 short years—short, that is, when measured against the 200-year-old Russian ballet tradition—Canada's National Ballet had come of age.

The company is known today for its own special blend of cool, classical choreography and its vibrant, physical dancers. It also is known for welcoming new currents into its repertoire, drawing from the best traditions of Russian, British, and Danish choreography to create its own unique style.

The National Ballet of Canada was founded in 1951 in Toronto by Celia Franca, formerly the ballet mistress of London's Metropolitan Opera. She had been invited to Canada by a small group of dedicated ballet enthusiasts.

Franca introduced her dancers to a receptive Canadian public on November 12, 1952, and since then the company has never looked back. The ballet gave regular programmes in the Royal Alex from 1953—in addition to national tours starting in 1952—before moving to the larger stage of its current home at the O'Keefe Centre in 1964. Today the ballet spends 13 weeks a year on Toronto stages; much of the rest of the time it tours nationally and internationally.

Franca remained artistic director for 24 years. After the company's character was firmly established, she stepped aside in favour of her former co-director, David Haber. He was followed in 1976 by Alexander Grant, former principal dancer with London's Royal Ballet. Grant was succeeded by current artistic director, Erik Bruhn, in July 1983.

Gizella Witkowsky as Mercedes in the National Ballet of Canada production of Don Quixote, *choreographed by Nicholas Beriozoff after Marius Pepita and Alexandre Gorsky.*

CANADIAN OPERA COMPANY

In 1950 the Royal Conservatory Opera Company presented 10 performances of three operas to a total audience of 14,641 people. During the 1983-1984 season the Canadian Opera Company will present 46 performances of seven operas to approximately 126,500 people.

These statistics tell in a nutshell the story of the Canadian Opera Company. From its modest beginnings 33 years ago, it has blossomed into the largest opera company in Canada and, in terms of its budget size and scope of operations, the sixth largest in North America.

The growth of the COC has been gradual and steady. Dr. Herman Geiger-Torel, general director from 1959 to 1976, steered the COC from a regional company to a national institution. Under the leadership of Lotfi Mansouri, general director since 1976, the COC has embarked on many innovative and ambitious endeavours that have brought it international recognition.

Over the years many exciting operatic works have been introduced to Canadian audiences by the COC, including three world premieres of Canadian operas. The COC also has undertaken numerous community programmes and has led the way in nurturing the growth of Canadian talent through the creation in 1980 of a year-round resident artist corps, the Canadian Opera Company Ensemble.

In the fall of 1983 the COC will launch its first series of radio broadcasts, bringing opera to millions of Canadians across the country. And presently, plans are in progress for the opening of an opera house that will serve as the permanent home of the COC and the National Ballet of Canada.

Elisabeth Soderstrom and Alan Titus in the Canadian Opera Company's 1980-1981 season production of The Merry Widow *by Franz Lehar. Designers: Murray Laufer (sets), Suzanne Mess (costumes). Directed by Lotfi Mansouri. Photographer: Robert C. Ragsdale, F.R.P.S.*

CANADIAN PACIFIC LIMITED

It was a cool November 7 morning in 1885 when a small crowd gathered at Craigellachie, British Columbia, to watch as a Canadian Pacific Railway director, Donald A. Smith, made history. With the final blow from his hammer, Smith drove the spike that completed the CPR—five years ahead of schedule.

In Toronto, on June 28 of the following year, workers began stoking the boilers of a train that eventually linked with one coming through from Montreal. It became part of the first scheduled transcontinental trip, and shunted Canada into the railway age.

Toronto since has grown into a major railroad centre, and the CPR has grown along with it. Today CP Rail and all of the associated companies grouped under the Canadian Pacific Limited and Canadian Pacific Enterprises organizations, comprise Canada's largest private employer, with 2,400 employees in Toronto and approximately 129,000 across Canada working in rail, air, trucks, ships, telecommunications, oil and gas, mining, trucking, air travel, forest products, iron and steel, real estate, agriproducts, and hotels.

All of these activities make Canadian Pacific Limited Canada's largest investor-owned corporation, with revenues in 1982 of more than $12 billion and total assets of more than $17 billion.

But the story of Canadian Pacific's corporate success begins with the story of the railway—of how businessmen and politicians invested their entire fortunes or public careers on a project that few believed in.

The CPR story began around the time of Confederation, with a dream of linking all territories north of the United States by an iron road. And it was this promise to build a transcontinental railway that enticed British Columbia to join Canada in 1871. The need for a trans-Canada railway became a cause célèbre with Sir John A. Macdonald, Canada's first Prime Minister, who knew one would be needed to keep British Columbia from pulling out of Canada and joining the United States.

Macdonald also believed private enterprise should lead the way. Eventually a group of private investors, known as the Canadian Pacific Syndicate, emerged and, on October 21, 1880, was awarded the contract to build the westward extension of the railway.

These men, including Donald Smith and Sir George Stephen, the railway's president from 1881 to 1888, also were farsighted businessmen. When Royal assent officially incorporated the Canadian Pacific Railway Company on February 15, 1881, to build the railway, included in the contract were provisions for 25 million acres of land along the route as compensation for the risks involved. Today only 300,000 acres of the CPR lands connected with railway construction remain in the hands of Canadian Pacific. Most had been sold, returned to repay a government loan, or in some cases, given away, by the mid-1930s.

Company directors knew they needed more than just a route to the West to make the CPR a success—they needed direct access to the lucrative Central Canada market that was dominated at the time by rival Grand

The Canadian Pacific Building, on the southeast corner of King and Yonge streets, was Toronto's second tallest skyscraper at the time of its construction in 1904. This view from the northwest corner looks south down Yonge Street.

At 9:22 a.m., November 7, 1885, Donald Smith, later Lord Strathcona and Mount Royal, drives the last spike to complete the CPR's transcontinental main line. Immediately behind, with the white beard, is Sanford Fleming; to the left, with the black beard, is W.C. Van Horne.

Toronto's original Union Station, at left, in the early 1900s, with the York Street Bridge crossing over the rail yards. In the rear is the Cyclorama Building, now the side of University Place.

Trunk Railway. So began a programme of buying existing railways and building new spur lines in Eastern Canada.

On January 4, 1884, the CPR made a pivotal acquisition when it leased the Ontario & Quebec Railway. This line was seen by William Van Horne, CPR's vice-president, as essential to gaining access to the Toronto-Montreal corridor, as well as a good part of southern Ontario.

The Ontario & Quebec Railway, which had absorbed the Toronto, Grey & Bruce Railway and the Credit Valley Railway a year earlier, gave the CPR access to Ottawa, Peterborough, the Georgian Bay district, Woodstock, St. Thomas, Orangeville, and Galt. As a result, the CPR bought into a ready-made rail network based in Toronto.

By the time the last spike was driven, the CPR was poised to benefit from the economic boom that soon followed. In 1882, with the acquisition of the Toronto-based Dominion Express Company, the CPR put down the roots of its future road-trucking enterprises. By 1887 it had a direct line between Toronto and Montreal, and with the opening of the West the CPR hauled vast numbers of new immigrants and freight to the new territories.

The turn of the century saw the

Marathon Realty's University Place, at the foot of University Avenue, is one of the more recent additions to the Toronto skyline.

CPR's presence in Toronto grow large. It constructed a new building on the southeast corner of Toronto's King and Yonge streets in 1904. It was the city's second-tallest structure at that time, and still occupies the site today.

This period also saw the CPR involved in steamship services. In 1883 it had taken delivery of two 2,000-ton lake steamers to help transport railway construction supplies from Montreal to the Lakehead, and by 1887 it was operating services from Vancouver to the Orient. This activity led to the creation of Canadian Pacific Steamships Ltd.

The CPR continued its expansion into the 20th century, and it had a double track between Toronto and Montreal by 1914. The two world wars put the CPR's service to use as a transporter of men and supplies. By the 1950s the company began to shift its focus to other activities, and in 1971 Canadian Pacific Limited—of which CP Rail is a division—was incorporated to oversee the company's transportation activities. The resources-based and manufacturing activities already had been grouped under Canadian Pacific Enterprises Limited.

Today CP Rail owns or operates close to 15,000 miles of rail lines in every province except Prince Edward Island and Newfoundland. It also owns the Toronto, Hamilton & Buffalo Railway Company and controls the Soo Line Railway Company in the United States.

Canadian Pacific's future plans in Toronto include a continuing programme of upgrading and stream-lining its facilities as well as participation, through Marathon Realty, in a major redevelopment of railway lands south of Union Station.

COLOR YOUR WORLD INC.

"My father was a man of foresight and initiative," says Bruce Strongman, and judging by the current success of Color Your World Inc., these are characteristics Bruce and his brothers also possess.

With Bruce at the helm as president, Color Your World Inc. is today Canada's largest manufacturer, wholesaler, and retailer of paint and home decorating products, with over 200 outlets serving paint contractors and do-it-yourself home decorators in both Canada and the northeastern United States.

This phenomenal success began in the early 1900s when Bruce's father, W.A. Strongman, opened a paint and wallpaper store on College Street. It soon became one of the largest wallpaper wholesalers in Toronto.

As the business grew, Bruce Strongman put aside his thoughts of a professional hockey career and joined his father and older brothers in the firm. On the suggestion of a friend, they began to manufacture their own paint and expanded into the wholesale paint market, too. "In our first year we sold $50,000 worth of paint," Bruce proudly explains. "That was 1949. From that point on, the business took off."

To accommodate the burgeoning manufacturing operation, the Strongmans purchased land at their present Carson Street, Etobicoke, location and built a small plant. The company grew and opened stores from Halifax to Vancouver, necessitating a second manufacturing facility in Vancouver.

Seeing a unique opportunity to serve the growing market in home decorating, Bruce and his brothers then conceived of a novel "supermarket paint store" format and, through franchising, developed a totally new concept in paint marketing under the name Color Your World.

Today large, free-standing retail stores with a distinctive image and

A

B

C

D

merchandising concept service both the retail and wholesale paint and wallpaper markets across Canada. To support this national operation, Color Your World maintains three of the most sophisticated manufacturing warehouses and distribution facilities in their product line.

Through two generations of delivering the highest quality product possible and through the same

The Strongman family, founders of Color Your World Inc.: (A) W.A. Strongman, (B) Bruce Strongman, (C) Del Strongman, and (D) Morley Strongman. (Courtesy of Ashley & Crippen.)

initiative and foresight displayed by their father, the Strongmans have made Color Your World a Canadian success story.

KELLOGG SALADA CANADA INC.

Readers of the *Toronto Evening Telegram* of September 30, 1893, opened their newspapers to discover a half-page advertisement for a new brand of prepackaged tea called Salada. The advertisement emphasized two characteristics that have become synonymous with Salada Tea: quality and eye-catching packaging.

Salada soon became a market leader, earning its founder Peter Larkin the reputation of "the tea king of America." Montreal-born Larkin was a prominent Toronto businessman and staunch supporter of Sir Wilfrid Laurier's Liberals.

Salada merged in 1957 with the Shirriff-Horsey Corporation Ltd., itself the product of a 1955 merger: Shirriff, Ltd., founded in Toronto in the 1870s, and the J. William Horsey Corporation Ltd., originally a citrus fruit processor established in Florida in 1946 by a group of Canadians.

Today the tea king's company is part of Kellogg Salada Canada Inc., one of Canada's largest diversified food manufacturers with 1,560 employees.

While Salada Tea was becoming established in Canada, the Kellogg Company opened its first Canadian cereal plant in Toronto in 1914—in what corporate officials believe was an old jail. Kellogg's Corn Flakes have been a favourite of Canadian families ever since.

That Toronto plant became part of the Kellogg Company of Canada Ltd., with headquarters in London, Ontario, in 1924. Fifty years later the company moved back to the Toronto area, to its present head office in Rexdale. Its plant there produces the market-leading Mrs. Smith's pies, Eggo waffles, Neo Citran cold remedies, and Shirriff Good Morning marmalade. The London plant is Canada's largest ready-to-eat cereal facility, and a $150-million expansion targeted for completion in 1984 will keep it that way. Called Project 2000, it represents Kellogg Salada's promise to have the

capacity to the year 2000 to provide Canada with nutritious, wholesome, ready-to-eat cereal products so that the familiar "Snap! Crackle! Pop!" elves will continue to symbolize Kellogg Salada's tradition of providing Canadians with consumer products that achieve the highest standard of quality and value. From providing educational programmes in schools and consumer material, to funding medical research and holding comprehensive biennial seminars for experts in nutrition, Kellogg Salada has become a leading corporation in educating the nation about the benefits of good nutrition.

During the 1960s the combined company forged ahead in the market, riding on the strength of popular products and memorable marketing campaigns. Many consumers remember Salada's premiums, such as pictures of Canadian game fish, bone china cups, and popular records. There was even a booklet on how to tell fortunes—where else?—in a teacup.

Kellogg also had become a market leader, depending on similar strategies to those used by Salada Foods. In 1969 Kellogg merged with Salada. Many

Peter C. Larkin founded the Salada Tea Company in 1892. When this photo was taken in 1928, he was High Commissioner for Canada to the Court of Saint James.

Canadians are surprised to learn that this combined company not only makes Canada's most popular cereals and tea but also such products as Shirriff scallopped potatoes, Pop Tarts, and Rise N Shine beverage crystals.

With more than 100 years' experience in manufacturing quality food products, and with Project 2000 leading technology, corporation officials believe that the future will be a "snap" to suit them to a "tea."

The Salada Tea Company's headquarters on King Street West, as it appeared in 1928.

SOUTHAM MURRAY PRINTING

For many companies, the true test of their mettle is how they perform during a crisis—the loss of an important client, a drastic drop-off in sales, or simply weathering difficult economic times.

For Southam Murray Printing, the crisis came in 1976, when its single largest client, the T. Eaton Co., closed the cover on an era. That year, Eaton's annual catalogues, mainstay winter reading for generations of Canadians, rolled off the Southam Murray presses for the last time.

It was a hard blow for Southam Murray to sustain, and it took some severe measures to offset the loss of that important business. But the company took a hard look at itself and came back in better form than ever.

Today, while the number of employees has been halved since Southam Murray's halcyon days—to 600, down from the peak of 1,200 before 1976—the firm presents a new, leaner look designed to meet the challenges of staying at the forefront of printing technology. Southam Murray remains the largest printer under one roof in Canada, however, with a 342,080-square-foot printing plant in Weston, northwest of Toronto.

The company still specializes its printing services, printing numerous store catalogues and special-interest magazines, annual reports, newspaper flyers, and inserts. It also offers a full range of personalized printing services, including creative design, photosetting and composition, pre-press camera work, and platemaking, as well as a complete bindery and mailing service. Most of the work is done on high-speed web-offset presses, although Southam Murray still operates letterpresses and rotogravure presses.

Southam Murray expects that the presses of the future will mostly use the web-offset method, and since 1979 it has purchased seven large high-speed web-offset presses, the last of

William Southam, founder of the newspaper empire Southam Inc., took over a printing business in Toronto in 1880.

James Murray established his printing company, much later to become part of Southam Murray, in Toronto in 1884.

which will cost $4.3 million for total installation. Computer technology also is becoming important to the modern printer, and here, too, Southam Murray is adapting new technology to traditional printing services.

Southam Murray Printing is a division of Southam Printing Limited, one of several autonomous companies that compose the communications giant, Southam Inc. A completely unionized operation, it traditionally has enjoyed good labour relations and is proud of its highly skilled, often long-term employees.

The firm is the result of the merger of two printing companies, each of which traces its history back to before the turn of the century in Toronto.

James Murray and Co., printers and bookbinders, got its start in Toronto back in 1884, at 26-28 Front Street West. By 1893 the firm had moved to 31-33 Melinda Street and changed its name to the Murray Printing Co.

Murray Printing specialized as printers of railway timetables and folders and in printing for theatres—everything from posters to shredded paper for snow scenes. James Murray was joined in the business by his son,

John, and, on John's retirement, by brothers Douglas and Joseph. Douglas eventually became president. After Douglas' death in 1945, Joseph served as president until 1957, when his own son, John D. Murray, became president.

In 1932 Murray Printing Co. purchased Canadian Gravure Limited, whose gravure presses were added to Murray's letterpresses. The firm's name was changed to Murray Printing and Gravure Ltd.

By 1952 Murray was printing 40 percent of Eaton's catalogues, using its gravure presses. A year later it agreed to produce them all, and took over three Eaton printing plants. The whole operation—the staff from Murray's and Eaton's plants, 700 employees in total—moved in 1954 to new facilities in Weston.

About a third of the shares in Murray Printing were sold to the Southam Company Limited in 1961, and three years later Southam purchased the remaining shares. The Weston plant was enlarged and in 1966 the Southam operation, including its offset lithography equipment, was moved to Weston, which is still home to the company's printing facility and head office.

Roughly 85 years after the separate foundings, the two firms became Southam Murray Printing.

Printing has come a long way since the days of William Southam and James Murray, as reflected in the company's new high-speed, web-offset presses.

Southam's Toronto business started in 1880 when William Southam, founder of the vast communications empire that still bears his name, bought out a printing firm and moved it into two floors of the *Toronto Mail* Building.

Southam had only just then gotten his start: In 1877 he and a partner, William Carey, had purchased the financially troubled daily newspaper,

the Hamilton *Spectator.* Southam was quick to realize that a printing company could be a profitable complement to his newspaper, and for years his printing business made more money than his newspapers.

For many more years the two companies pursued their separate paths. By 1909 the Mail Job Department, as Southam's firm was known, changed its name to the Mail Job Printing Co., and then to Southam Press Limited, when the firm moved into a five-storey building on Duncan Street, on land it acquired from Upper Canada College.

In 1913 Southam secured a contract to print the colour pages of the Robert Simpson Company Limited fall and winter catalogue. The next year, and until 1930 when Simpson's started its own rotogravure plant, the entire catalogue was printed by Southam.

Southam established a group insurance plan for employees in 1920, the first printing company in Canada to do so. In 1940 it established a contributory pension plan, and in 1945 a Quarter Century Club. Murray Printing also formed a long-service group, and, in keeping with the family atmosphere, the president's mother served tea to shareholders prior to annual meetings.

By the time the two companies finally joined forces, they had pursued remarkably similar developments. Both were family-oriented organizations that had carved niches for themselves by specializing in high-speed, long-run printing contracts—especially department store catalogues. And both had a commitment to reinvesting a large proportion of their profits in capital expenditures.

With the crunch of 1976 behind them, officials at Southam Murray Printing predict that the future will hold plenty of good news that's fit to print—in sufficiently long press runs, of course, to get their newer presses warm.

ELIZABETH ARDEN OF CANADA LIMITED

Few people today know that the founder of one of the world's largest cosmetic companies was born in Woodbridge, Ontario, just north of Toronto. But Elizabeth Arden, founder of the business that was to bear her name, was just such a small-town girl.

Born Florence Nightingale Graham, she was, like her namesake, trained to be a nurse. But she soon became convinced that her destiny lay in New York City, then as now the centre of the fashion world in North America.

Young and alone, but gifted with an extraordinary beauty and a perfect complexion—both rare in those days before skin care was practiced—she opened a small storefront beauty salon in New York. The year was 1910.

Beauty care products in use at that time hadn't changed for centuries. Women were still using little more than rose water and glycerine to tone their skin and cold cream to relieve dryness. Those with "painted faces" were frowned upon, and for therapeutic treatments there were obnoxious-smelling depilatories.

Convinced of a need for skin care products that would actually improve women's complexions, Florence approached a young chemist and together they developed her plan for care of the skin: a cleansing cream and astringent skin lotion that today remain the keystones of her skin care regimen.

She then took her next big step: a bank loan that would allow her to make her products more widely available. She was able to repay the loan in just six months. She chose the name "Elizabeth Arden" by combining the titles of two books she had been reading, and the rest is history.

Gifted with extraordinary business sense, she personally shepherded her company's rapid expansion, first throughout the United States, then into Great Britain in 1922. Her first Toronto manufacturing facility opened

about 1930 in the Terminal Warehouse on the waterfront, where it remained for many years. Finally, over the winter of 1974-1975, the firm moved into its current headquarters in Agincourt in the northeastern part of metropolitan Toronto.

Elizabeth Arden also had an innate sense of drama and glamour, and was at ease with the great families of the United States and Europe. She was an ardent horsewoman—a legacy of her childhood—and her horse, Jet Pilot, won the 1947 Kentucky Derby. Elizabeth Arden died in 1966. It was consistent with her life of romance and mystery that no one really knew how old she was.

Eli Lilly and Company, a major U.S. pharmaceutical company, in 1971 acquired the worldwide operations of Elizabeth Arden, Inc., from the founder's heirs. And in 1981 Eli Lilly Canada Inc., its Canadian affiliate, consolidated with Elizabeth Arden of Canada Limited after the two corporations had operated separately for a decade.

The present owners intend to remain faithful to Elizabeth Arden's belief that good skin products should be therapeutic—and the firm's research laboratories are developing Elizabeth Arden products for the 21st century.

Florence Nightingale Graham, better known as Elizabeth Arden, as she appeared in a Harper's Bazaar *magazine feature.*

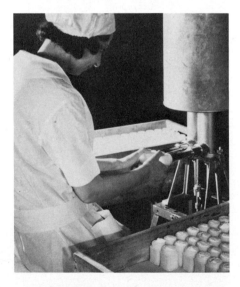

An employee fills bottles of cream in the Elizabeth Arden plant in the Terminal Warehouse, Toronto.

Terminal Warehouse, 207 Queen's Quay, was the home of Elizabeth Arden of Canada Limited from 1930 to 1974. The building is still part of the waterfront scene.

FAIRBANK LUMBER COMPANY LIMITED

When they rolled up the sidewalks in York Township in 1912, John T. Watson could be forgiven for being proud. After all, his firm, Fairbank Lumber and Coal Co., founded that year, supplied all the wooden planks needed for the job.

Today John T. Watson is still remembered—there is a small park named after him in what is now the city of York—and Fairbank Lumber is still going strong. Watson's son, Gordon M. Watson, an active and fit 85, now controls the company, and the founder's grandson, John H., is secretary/treasurer.

Fairbank Lumber was founded in the distant wake of the optimism accompanying the election of Prime Minister Wilfrid Laurier in 1896. All around Toronto, mothballed projects were dusted off. The Grand Trunk Railway revived plans for its Old Belt Line Railway, which would run across west Toronto to Union Station. The railroad stretched past John T. Watson's land, a 100-acre farm near what is now the Eglinton-Dufferin intersection in the city of York.

Watson sold 87 of the 100 acres of his family's farm to a local developer in 1909, retaining the 13 acres that contained the home and farm buildings. (The company now owns about 3.5 acres.) In 1910 he applied to the railway for a siding.

By 1912 the immigrants who had come to take up the land in that part of the Toronto area could purchase their coal and lumber from Watson's firm.

That year, Watson hired as his manager Dave Riddell, a knowledgeable lumberman. The men became partners in 1914 and a limited company was formed in 1921. Both men were active in community affairs in those days—Riddell served on council, and Watson was reeve of York Township in 1911-1912 after five years on council.

There were five employees that first year; today Fairbank Lumber has 92

Fairbank Lumber and Coal Co. as it appeared in 1932 on Dufferin Street at Old Belt Line.

John T. Watson (1858-1945), founder of Fairbank Lumber Company Limited, and his wife Isabel on their 50th wedding anniversary in 1941.

Gordon M. Watson, son of the founder, presently controls Fairbank Lumber Company Limited.

employees, a figure that rises to 100 during the busy summer season.

Horses were kept at the stable on the family farm until 1919, when a stable was built at the yard. The firm also bought its first truck that year, a flatbed Ford.

Fairbank Lumber survived some mighty challenges—from the crushing Depression of the 1930s to two fires in adjacent companies' yards. But there were never any layoffs, not even in 1930, the only year the business lost money—a total of $500. And no needy family was ever refused coal.

Eight varieties of coal were sold in the 1930s, ranging in price from $10.50 to $14.25 a ton. (Coal was phased out

in the 1940s.) And in 1934 Fairbank Lumber would build a client a four-room summer cottage with porch for only $295. The firm offered many other specialty services, and today it continues to cut custom mouldings and trim.

In late 1982, after nearly three-quarters of a century in one place, Fairbank Lumber was planning a second location—a combination traditional lumberyard and home-centre outlet—north of Toronto, in the township of Vaughan, where it has owned a parcel of land since 1965. Company officials vow to maintain the high standard of quality and service responsible for so many years of success in the past.

CANADA CARTAGE SYSTEM LTD.

It wasn't difficult to total the assets of Canada Cartage System Ltd. back in February 1914: one horse, one wagon, one driver. The driver, a hard-working young Scot named Robert Leslie, was the founder of what today is one of the largest privately owned trucking companies in the country.

One lone horse has grown to over 700 trucks — 900 including the company's truck leasing subsidiary, Premier Truck Leasing Ltd. — and the original payroll of one has grown to 550 in three Toronto-area locations.

It took more than Scottish frugality and hard work to get it there, though. From the earliest days of horses and wagons, Canada Cartage specialized its services by providing contract trucking — operating and servicing the entire cartage needs of its clients.

Contract trucking still constitutes a large part of the firm's business. Canada Cartage's services make sense to many large corporations. It provides reliable, experienced drivers, and services the trucks as well. Scheduled maintenance and repairs are completed overnight, in the company's 24-hour garage, so trucks can be back to work the following day.

Canada Cartage's growth was slow and steady. By 1917 Robert Leslie's original horse had 13 more to keep it

This was Canada Cartage System Ltd.'s mode of transport in 1931.

company, as well as one of the first trucks in Toronto.

Trucks gradually began to take up more of the firm's parking places, and by 1931 the shift to trucks had been completed. But a retired employee who started with Canada Cartage in 1926 remembers that even in those years the horses — teams of Belgians — sometimes worked during the day, then were curried up for evening competitions at the Royal Winter Fair, where for many years they took ribbons.

With the hardest years behind him, Leslie devoted attention to other activities. Times were difficult in the 1930s, and in 1931 he ran a soup kitchen at Queen and Shaw streets in Toronto. He became active in civic politics, serving as a Toronto alderman and twice running for mayor.

Those years also saw the company settle into its first real home, when

Leslie purchased the premises at 65-67 Shaw Street. By the 1940s his organization had expanded to Cross Street, in the Dufferin-Dundas streets area. And in 1954 it moved to newly built facilities on the Queensway in West Toronto, Canada Cartage's current head office. A Scarborough office was opened in 1964-1965, and office and service facilities were opened in Rexdale, west of Toronto, in the late 1960s.

Robert Leslie built the firm's solid foundation, but his son, Rodger, directed its greatest period of expansion. He assumed the managerial reins in 1936 and stayed at the helm until his retirement in 1974.

On his retirement, Rodger Leslie sold the venture to his son, Fred, and Fred's partner, William Lindsay, who between them had over 35 years' service with the company. Along with a smoothly running trucking business, the current owners took over a management philosophy that has served the firm well. They have continued to direct Canada Cartage and its growth since 1974 and have been successful in expanding into the cartage and leasing markets in the Montreal region with the establishment of Sonar Transport Limited and Premier Truck Leasing Ltd.

One of Canada Cartage System's current fleet of trucks parked in front of the firm's headquarters in Toronto.

RICHARDSON-VICKS LIMITED

What sick child has never had his chest rubbed with soothing Vicks VapoRub? This familiar home remedy has been around so long, it seems to be a real tradition for most of us. VapoRub was the innovation of a young druggist from Greensboro, North Carolina, named Lunsford Richardson, who developed it in the 1880s. Its principal ingredient is menthol prepared in an ointment—a little-known commodity in the late 19th century.

Today Richardson-Vicks Limited, based in Weston, is much more than a cough and cold products company. With a wide range of personal health and personal care products, R-VL is a diversified manufacturing and marketing operation.

Products such as Vicks VapoRub, Vicks Throat Drops, Vicks Cough Syrup, and Vicks Formula 44 and 44D continue to be a significant portion of the firm's business, accounting for about one-half of sales. What many people don't realize is that Richardson-Vicks has evolved as a sophisticated and advanced company with a much broader line of products. Its personal care products include Oil of Olay, Clearasil and Topex medications, Lavoris mouthwash, and Fixodent and Fasteeth denture products, accounting for the remaining one-half of company sales.

Richardson-Vicks continues to diversify its product line with selective acquisitions within the area of personal and health care products. The Pantene line of high-quality hair care products was acquired in January 1983, and Vidal Sassoon shampoos and hair treatments were recently added to the firm's hair care product lines.

The company is an autonomous Canadian subsidiary of Richardson-Vicks Inc., a Connecticut-based international corporation. Its fully integrated, 220,000-square-foot manufacturing, sales, and

administration facility is located in Weston. Staffed by approximately 250 employees, it serves the entire Canadian market.

Richardson-Vicks first came to Canada in 1952, when the Vick Chemical Company purchased a plant in St. Thomas, Ontario. It remained there until 1960, when the expansion of the Canadian business created a need for larger facilities, and Toronto was chosen because of its strategic location.

In June 1960 Vicks broke ground at its present location, and a modern, 66,000-square-foot plant opened for business in January 1961. Fifty-four people were employed that first year, and sales amounted to between $3 and $4 million.

Then followed the period of the company's greatest growth, and the

From 1952 until 1960 this St. Thomas plant was the home of Richardson-Vicks Limited in Canada.

Since 1960 Richardson-Vicks' headquarters has been situated at 2 Norelco Drive, Weston.

Weston facilities were enlarged several times, most recently in 1981. The current plant, warehouse, and office facility boasts a new high-rise, semi-automated warehouse, modern production facilities, and a pleasant working environment. And though the surrounding area has been built up considerably over the past 20 years, the Weston site remains an agreeable location with easy access to suppliers,

customers, and employees.

For the future, Richardson-Vicks plans to build on its respected name, with new products in the health and personal care area, and through selective acquisition of companies in related fields. The firm is dedicated to the manufacture of high-quality, highly effective products, and a positive working environment for its employees.

As the Canadian market continues to grow, so will the ability of Richardson-Vicks to serve it.

ROYAL YORK HOTEL

One of the first sights greeting generations of visitors to Toronto has been the Royal York Hotel, a beacon on the Toronto skyline.

And while the Royal York may not dominate the skyline quite as much as it used to—for there is a new generation of landmarks that define Toronto—this distinguished hotel has kept its place as a landmark, maintaining old friends and making new ones.

Built in 1929, the hotel reflects the ambitious scope of large Canadian companies during a period of great economic expansion. Its vast scale and tasteful materials mark it as the last flourish of an era known for extravagant gestures.

Architects Ross, Patterson, Townsend & Fish pulled out all the stops to make it the showpiece for their client, Canadian Pacific Hotels Ltd., an autonomous division of the Canadian Pacific Railway Company (it still is CP Hotels' flagship and houses the firm's head office). Only a giant corporation such as CP Hotels Ltd. could have afforded the cost of the venture—an unprecedented $16 million.

What CP Hotels received for its money was the largest hotel in the British Commonwealth, a 400-foot-tall limestone show place—and a fitting partner to Union Station across the street, opened only two years earlier.

In two years Toronto had seen two of its fondest dreams fulfilled: a great hotel and a great railway station. This was tangible proof of the sort that Toronto was hungry for—proof that visitors could not only arrive in the city in style, but stay in a world-class hotel.

A local newspaper editorial read, in part: "A city within a city reaches the zenith of human achievement . . . [this] signifies to the world that Canada is on the move again." The editorial writer had probably been to see the hotel's exciting opening-night ceremonies on June 11, 1929, and like everybody else, he came away suitably impressed.

His Excellency, Viscount Wellington, Governor General of Canada, addressed a glittering crowd of 2,000 which included such luminaries as Prime Minister William Lyon Mackenzie King; the Honourable R.B. Bennett, leader of the opposition; the Honourable G.H. Ferguson, Prime Minister of Ontario; E.W. Beatty, CPR president; and other well-known Canadians.

In the 1950s when Toronto was enjoying another period of prosperity, the hotel undertook a $15-million expansion, adding 400 rooms to the hotel, bringing the total to 1,600.

Part of the reason for its continued success is its location in the heart of downtown. It is served by underground connections to adjacent highrise office towers and Toronto's three-mile underground merchant mall system, as well as by an underground passage to Union Station.

A visit to the Royal York is a memorable experience. Despite the teeming hive of activity typical of a hotel its size, the Royal York preserves an aura of dignity—and the atmosphere this imparts to the hotel is the real key to its success.

The ambiance has its effect as soon as one enters the lobby. Traditional decor is richly appointed and tasteful. Carpets were specially woven for the Royal York, and paintings and murals were commissioned. Antique furniture, crystal chandeliers, and murals all add up to an atmosphere of elegance and luxury.

And the Royal York has no intention of resting on its laurels, however great its tradition. Recently renovated rooms keep the hotel at a world-class level. Convention facilities are equipped with the latest electronic equipment.

Other improvements are not visible to the public but they help the hotel operate like a well-oiled machine. For instance, at the centre of the hotel now beats a heart of pure silicon—a compact computerized communication system replacing the old manual switchboard.

To accommodate the hotel's visitors—in an average year, nearly .5 million registered guests—the Royal York employs 1,400 people, who work to serve its 28 conference rooms, 42 meeting rooms, and the largest room

The main lobby area of the Royal York.

in the hotel, the Canadian Room, which seats 1,400 people for a meal and 2,200 for a meeting. The hotel even has its own painters and locksmiths on staff, as well as 20 musicians.

The Royal York's immense kitchen, running the full length of the hotel, employs an extensive staff which prepares up to 10,000 meals per day.

Among the dignitaries who have stayed at the hotel are Her Majesty, Queen Elizabeth II, and other members of the Royal Family; Sir Winston Churchill; General Charles de Gaulle; and Baron Rothschild. From the entertainment and fashion world, visitors have included Noel Coward, Tallulah Bankhead, Perry Como, Gina Lollobrigida, Ingrid Bergman, Elizabeth Arden, Helena Rubenstein, Cary Grant, Bob Hope, Helen Hayes, and Raquel Welch.

Tradition has it that when the hotel opened, the keys to the front door were thrown away, signifying that the Royal York would never close.

That implies a commitment to service worthy of the tradition of the world's great hotels.

The Royal York Hotel, a familiar sight on the Toronto skyline.

The Concert Hall on the Royal York's convention floor in a schoolroom setup.

ASSOCIATION OF IROQUOIS AND ALLIED INDIANS

In 1759, as the Battle of Quebec was being fought, a battle over the future site of Toronto also was drawing to a bloody close. After nearly 100 years of deadly skirmishes, the combative Iroquois were fought to a standstill by the Mississaugas, who were part of the Ojibwa tribe and originally from the Ohio Valley.

To avoid mutual annihilation, the two Indian nations agreed to become allies, and undertook a policy of intermarriage. The Mississaugas gained control of most of southern Ontario, including the site of what is today Toronto, and the Iroquois took territories elsewhere.

This spirit of cooperation continued into the 20th century, and today the Iroquois and Mississaugas are members of the Association of Iroquois and Allied Indians, a political voice for eight southern Ontario bands. Its member bands are Walpole Island, Moravian Town, Oneida, Batchewana, New Credit, Gibson, Hiawatha, and Tyendinaga.

However, it is the New Credit band, descendants of the Mississaugas, that has the closest links with the early history of Toronto. Their ancestors once owned all the land on which Toronto is now located, and they have left their name on a Toronto-area suburb.

The association was established in 1971, and its first headquarters was the Mohawk Cultural Centre on the Six Nations Indian Reserve in Brantford, Ontario. The head office is now in London, Ontario, where an all-Indian staff of 20 administers an annual budget of over one million dollars.

In Toronto, the organization's office is shared with the Chiefs of Ontario, and the association sits on a joint council of three other Indian groups. In addition to such activities as lobbying for Indian rights in the Canadian Constitution, the association is actively researching possible future land claims.

Gordon Peters, president.

Chief Earl Hill, vice-president.

For example, it has long been recognized that the so-called Toronto Purchase—which in 1787 saw the Mississaugas cede to the British Crown all of Toronto and much of its surrounding lands for £1,700 in cash and goods—was never a valid deed. It never even specified the exact amount of land involved in the transaction.

Even so, the increasing number of settlers in the Toronto area put inexorable pressure on the Mississaugas to sell their remaining land—so much so that by 1847 the band found itself with no land at all.

Fortunately the Mohawks, a traditional ally and part of the Iroquois nation, stepped in with an offer of a fertile tract in the southwest corner of their Six Nations Reserve near present-day Brantford, where the Mississaugas still live. They call themselves "New Credit" to distinguish themselves from their old home on the Credit River, closer to Toronto.

Actually, the Mohawks had been given their own land by the Mississaugas during their more prosperous days, and were pleased to return the favour. In a magnanimous gesture, the Mohawk chief of the Six

Nations Council said in 1847 that the Mohawks "felt great pleasure in returning the compliment to their [the Mississaugas'] descendants."

Not many associations can boast members who have been as cooperative as this—and for such a long time. This bodes well for the future—which will surely include legal claims for compensation for the Mississaugas' land.

Wilcy Kewayosh, executive treasurer.

MITSUI & CO. (CANADA) LTD.

Just as Toronto's skyline has changed dramatically over the past few years, the face of Toronto business has been transformed, as well.

No longer is Toronto the centre of only local or even national business interests. Increasingly, it plays host to important international companies, connecting the city to the vital pulse of world business activity.

One of these important international corporations is Mitsui & Co. (Canada) Ltd., which celebrated 25 years in Canada in 1981.

Mitsui & Co. (Canada) Ltd. is part of the giant Japanese family of companies grouped under the parent organization, Mitsui & Co. Ltd., one of the world's largest general trading companies. It promotes trade and development through its head office in Tokyo and a network of some 200 offices around the world. The overseas investments and loans of Mitsui—exceeding one billion dollars—are the largest of any Japanese firm.

With Canadian head offices in Toronto since 1956, Mitsui & Co. (Canada) Ltd. directs commodity trading of iron and steel, coal, nonferrous metals, uranium, machinery, chemicals, foodstuffs, textiles, pulp and paper, lumber, and general merchandise. Mitsui also has committed investment capital to Canadian industrial development and commercial activity, chiefly through minority positions in joint ventures with Canadian and other companies.

Back in 1956, though, it was unusual for a Japanese trading company to locate its Canadian head office in Toronto. Most chose Vancouver, closer to Japan. Mitsui's choice of Toronto, however, has been justified by the growth of its business community since then.

Under the name Daiichi Bussan Kaisha (Canada) Ltd., Canadian operations began in 1956 with offices in Toronto and Montreal; a few

Mitsui exports Canadian high technology, such as the Telidon videotex system pictured here, to Japan and other Asian countries.

months later a branch office was established in Vancouver and in 1965 a liaison office was opened in Edmonton (later relocated in Calgary).

Sales have grown from a modest $178,000 in 1957 to nearly $1.7 billion in gross trading transactions in 1982, ranking Mitsui 39th in sales for all Canadian companies. In fact, Mitsui now accounts for 20 percent of all trade between Canada and Japan. To commemorate the company's 25th anniversary in Canada, Mitsui established the Mitsui Canada

Foundation with a $250,000 grant.

Toronto may be a long way from the Pacific Ocean—or even from Vancouver's Japanese cherry trees—but Mitsui plans to expand and diversify its operations in Canada, not only in its traditional role as an international trader, but also as an investor in Canadian resource and industrial development.

COMMODORE BUSINESS MACHINES LTD.

When Jack Tramiel founded Commodore Business Machines Ltd. back in 1958, it was a small typewriter sales and repair company located in downtown Toronto.

From the vantage point of Commodore's 25th anniversary in 1983, however, Tramiel saw a venture that had outgrown its local roots to become one of North America's leading manufacturers of microcomputers for business, educational, and personal uses. With world headquarters now in Wayne, Pennsylvania, its Canadian head office and two production plants are located in Scarborough, a city that is part of metropolitan Toronto.

From the firm's earliest years, Tramiel, a hard-working Polish immigrant who still is Commodore's vice-chairman and chief executive officer, had a gift for anticipating future business needs—and the ability to move quickly to fill them. For instance, during Commodore's first decade, he recognized that a lucrative future lay in business equipment, and so moved into the manufacture of office furniture.

Then, during the 1970s, Tramiel changed directions once more, moving into electronics. Commodore began to produce Liquid Crystal Display (LCD) watches, as well as personal and desktop calculators. The year 1977 marked another watershed for the company, for this was when it produced its first microcomputer. Also that year, Commodore introduced microcomputers into Ontario schools—the first company in Canada to do so.

Today most Toronto-area youngsters are learning at least some of their "3 Rs" on a microcomputer. Of the 50 percent of Ontario schools that have installed microcomputer systems, 80 percent of these use Commodore equipment, making it the market leader.

Its growth in the area of home computers has been equally impressive. Its popular VIC-20 model

is the largest-selling personal computer in North America. In the highly competitive market for business computer systems, Commodore is among the top four manufacturers.

Meanwhile, Tramiel had moved the firm's financial head office to the Bahamas and the operational headquarters to the United States in the late 1970s, after first gaining a

Commodore's popular VIC-20 is a versatile home computer/video game machine used by the whole family for entertainment, education, finances, and a host of other activities.

Commodore's newest addition to its business systems features 128 or 256K RAM, expandable to 896K. Another of Commodore's excellent business systems to assist managers and executives.

foothold by the acquisition of several American electronics companies.

Commodore is listed on the New York Stock Exchange. The Canadian organization, still called Commodore Business Machines Ltd., became its operating subsidiary.

The firm has not forgotten its Canadian roots, however. Canadian activity calls for Commodore's further expansion into the national educational, business, and home markets.

Commodore also is the only international microcomputer corporation to manufacture its equipment in Canada. Two of its most popular microcomputers—the VIC-20 and the 64—are produced exclusively in its Scarborough plants. The production figure for these two models in 1983 was about 450,000 units, producing revenue of nearly $100 million. Canada exports these microcomputers to more than 25 countries worldwide.

AMERICAN-STANDARD

Seventy-five years ago, in Pittsburgh, Pennsylvania, an enterprise called Standard Sanitary started producing plumbing fixtures, especially bathtubs. And on August 23, 1907, the owners of Standard Sanitary opened a facility in Toronto.

By the end of its first decade in Canada, Standard Sanitary employed 300 people, including a Canada-wide sales force. (Today known as American-Standard, the firm has nearly 1,000 Canadian employees.)

Apart from the bathtubs and plumbing fixtures, the company undertook a certain amount of custom work. In 1911, when Sir Henry Pellatt built for his wife a mansion known as Casa Loma—with 98 rooms and 30 bathrooms—Standard Sanitary supplied the fixtures and baths, including one bathroom's gold fixtures.

In the 1920s, with renewed residential construction and a boom in the commercial sector, Standard Sanitary experienced its single most profitable decade. In this atmosphere, corporations had to expand or lose ground.

It was at this time that Standard Sanitary Manufacturing Company consolidated with American Radiator Company to form American Radiator and Standard Sanitary Corporation in the United States. The Standard Sanitary and the Dominion Radiator & Boiler plants operated by these two firms in Canada continued to carry on business as separate ventures in this country. They would not become one enterprise until 1940.

Despite the Great Depression, Standard Sanitary continued to plan for the future. In 1932 it introduced modern toilets with lower water tanks—the kind we know today. The firm also was among the first to offer an alternative to cumbersome cast-iron fixtures. In 1934 Standard Sanitary erected a new vitreous china pottery plant in Toronto.

In 1940 Standard Sanitary in Canada merged with Dominion Radiator & Boiler, forming a new venture called Standard Sanitary & Dominion Radiator, the company known today as American-Standard.

Standard Sanitary & Dominion Radiator moved to a new head office and spacious facilities in 1948. More than 100 additional employees were hired. This modernization put the organization in excellent shape for the 1950s.

Management determined that the company would have to be innovative, more aggressive in sales, and more efficient in manufacturing if it was to continue growing. As a result, plants and facilities were again updated to meet the new challenges. On January 1, 1956, Standard Sanitary & Dominion Radiator absorbed two more companies and became American-Standard in Canada.

Having just celebrated its 75th anniversary in 1982 with the introduction of several new product lines—notably products made with acrylics—American-Standard is confident about the future and looks forward to the year 2007, when it will celebrate its first century of operation in Canada.

This sofa bath, part of the American-Standard collection of antique plumbing fixtures, was used in the late 1700s and early 1800s when homes didn't have bathrooms and bathtubs were concealed in sofas, chests, and under beds.

Before the 1930s, when American-Standard introduced toilets with low water tanks, this style was in wide use.

BLAKE, CASSELS & GRAYDON

Before he became a world leader, young Winston Churchill visited Canada on a speaking tour. But he might have walked out on his contract had he not first consulted Sir Walter Cassels, a prominent Toronto lawyer of the day. "You may have a great future ahead of you," Sir Walter told Winston prophetically. "Don't begin it like this."

Such forthright counselling has made Blake, Cassels & Graydon one of Toronto's most successful law firms— and, at 126 years old, it also is one of the oldest. Since 1857, when Edward Blake first opened his practice, the firm has taken part in the shaping of Canada's political and economic history, including the creation of modern Ontario.

And it was Edward and his brother Samuel, who joined in 1858, who set the firm's early course. Samuel served briefly as Vice-Chancellor of Ontario from 1872-1881 and was a respected judge, but he spent most of his time running the law firm while brother Edward applied his advocacy skills in politics.

Edward held a federal seat in Ottawa at the same time that he was briefly Premier of Ontario (1871-1872), until Sir Oliver Mowat assumed that post. In 1883 Edward, a constitutional expert, helped Sir Oliver convince judges at England's Judicial Court of the Privy Council (then Canada's final court of appeal) that the mineral-rich northern territories, which now comprise nearly 80 percent of the province, should be annexed to Ontario instead of Manitoba.

Edward also served as federal Minister of Justice in Alexander Mackenzie's Liberal government of 1873-1878, then as his party's Opposition leader from 1880-1887. In 1892 he returned to London for 15 years, where he sat as a member of the Irish Nationalist party in the Imperial Parliament.

The firm has had a number of distinguished partners in its time. Henry Cawthra, son of a prominent 19th-century Toronto family, eventually became director of the Bank of Toronto (now Toronto Dominion Bank), Consumers' Gas Company Ltd.,

and Canada Permanent Mortgage & Loan Co. Sir Walter Cassels was appointed a judge of the Exchequer Court (now Federal Court of Canada) in 1908 and was knighted in 1917. Allan R. Graydon, who gave his name to the firm, served in World War I as a lieutenant with the Royal Field Artillery.

In 1912 members of the Blake firm helped put the final touches on what was then Canada's largest foreign investment: the Brazilian Traction Light & Power Co.—today known as Brascan.

Now occupying nearly four floors of Toronto's 57-storey Commerce Court West, Blake, Cassels & Graydon is one of Canada's largest law firms, with a staff of 410, including 77 active partners. The firm's diverse legal activities and its international clientele would make Edward and Samuel Blake proud.

Samuel H., Edward, and Hume Blake (left to right).

SHIPP CORPORATION

Gordon S. Shipp (1891-1981), founder of Shipp Corporation Limited.

In 1923, when Gordon S. Shipp built a home for his family on Coxwell Avenue in East Toronto, he had little formal training as a builder. But as a farmer from Ridgetown, Ontario, near Chatham, he knew fine craftsmanship when he saw it, and he applied what he knew to house building.

That first Shipp-built house still stands—along with thousands of others constructed since then—and today the company Gordon Shipp founded is one of Canada's largest privately owned builders. The founder's grandchildren are active in the company today.

In recent years the Shipp Corporation has become a developer of commercial office buildings, and its head offices and 127 employees are located in one of these projects, the Mississauga Executive Centre, a 40-acre business complex comprising four office towers, a hotel, and three high-rise apartments. It is a joint-venture project with Mutual Life of Canada.

But if the scale and nature of the firm's typical projects have changed somewhat, the Shipps' attitude to quality in building hasn't. Says Harold G. Shipp, the son of the founder and current chief executive officer and chairman of the board, "We don't want to be known only as one of the bigger Toronto-area builders. We take more pride in being known as one of the best local builders, with strong family ties."

Having survived the Great Depression, Gordon decided in the 1940s to try his fortune in the borough of Etobicoke and in 1951 moved to what is now the city of Mississauga, just west of Toronto—then, as now, one of Canada's fastest-growing areas. It was there that Gordon and his son and partner, Harold, had an opportunity to build not just houses but an entire community.

The name Applewood Acres was coined—Applewood since has become synonymous with the business—and

as a symbol of the Shipp Corporation's pride in craftsmanship, to the right of each front door was a brick incised with "Shipp-built" on its face.

The company continued to grow along with the sprawling community which eventually became Mississauga. Applewood Village Shopping Centre opened in 1954, and this was followed by the development of Applewood Heights and Applewood Hills.

The 1960s saw the Shipp Corporation undertake similar projects elsewhere, including communities in Martingrove Gardens in Etobicoke, Riverview Heights in Streetsville, and Forest Heights in Sault Ste. Marie. In the 1970s the firm switched to high-rise apartments and office buildings.

The Shipp family is active in community affairs and belongs to the Kiwanis Club and United Church. Harold is past president of the Mississauga City Board of Trade, and both father and son are past presidents of the Toronto Home Builders' Association and the Housing and Urban Development Association of Canada.

Shipp Centre, located at Bloor and Islington streets, is a commercial office building developed by Shipp Corporation Limited.

Following Gordon's death in 1981, Harold assumed his father's role as chairman of the board in addition to the presidency. Stuart H.B. Smith, formerly the executive vice-president and treasurer, has been president and chief operating officer since 1983. June C. Shipp, wife of Harold, is now deputy chairman.

Other major commercial developments are now being negotiated and a return to building single-family homes is near, with the Shipp Corporation's 900 acres, Milton Woods Estates, nearing the development stage.

As Harold Shipp puts it, "We can now turn to anything we set our minds to. And as long as we continue to approach our projects with enthusiasm and zeal, the rewards will automatically come."

THE CONSUMERS' GAS COMPANY LTD.

When a young Charles Dickens visited Toronto in 1842, he observed that "The streets were well paved and lighted with gas." Torontonians were proud of their new gas lighting, which had only been introduced to the city the previous year.

Several companies wanted to supply gas to the growing community of Toronto, but in 1848 certain local consumers decided to operate the system themselves and joined together to form The Consumers' Gas Company of Toronto.

The founders and first directors of Consumers' Gas were prominent local merchants. Consumers' first president was Charles Berczy, who also was the local postmaster and son of Toronto's co-founder William Von Moll Berczy. Over the years, many important and colorful Torontonians have served as directors and officers of the company, including Sir Henry Pellatt, Sir Casimir Gzowski, William and George Gooderham, Sir Edmund Osler, and James and Albert Austin. In more recent times, Oakah L Jones headed the firm during the initial 20 years of expansion that followed the introduction of natural gas in 1954.

For more than 100 years—until the mid-1950s—gas was produced by heating coal in large retorts. For this Consumers' required large acreage near railroad lines and shipping docks to store the thousands of tons of coal and coke. Many Torontonians will recall these yards in the Front and Parliament streets area and farther out on Eastern Avenue, and at Front and Bathurst to the west.

The company's head offices were constructed in 1852 at 19 Toronto Street, "By all odds the finest street in Toronto." In 1876 architect David B. Dick designed a Renaissance-revival style building adjacent to the original structure, both of which stand today as a designated historical site.

Consumers' enjoyed steady growth as the city of Toronto grew, but in the

The construction of the Eastern Avenue-Don Roadway pipeline by Consumers' Gas in 1926.

postwar years of the late 1940s, the rising cost of coal pushed up the price of gas and resulted in lost customers and declining revenue. The decision to build the TransCanada Pipeline, and bring abundant supplies of natural gas from the west to Toronto and many other Ontario communities, revitalized the company and set it on a new course of expansion.

Today, 135 years after its incorporation, Consumers' is one of the oldest public utilities in North America and serves 750,000 customers in south central and eastern Ontario, western Quebec, and northern New York State. There are 3,200 employees in the Consumers' Gas System and during the fiscal year 1982 the corporation delivered more than 8.7 billion cubic metres of natural gas to its customers through an underground network of 17,000 kilometres of pipe.

One other achievement that is worthy of note: the firm has paid uninterrupted dividends since 1849.

In 1968 Consumers' moved the majority of its Toronto region and corporate operations to new facilities on a 15-acre site at Victoria Park Avenue and Highway 401. In 1977 most of the remaining staff at 19 Toronto Street moved to the Victoria Park Centre. The longtime "home" of the Gas Company was sold

This building, at 19 Toronto Street, was the headquarters of Consumers' Gas from 1852 to 1977. Photo circa 1880.

and the firm's head office moved to First Canadian Place in Toronto.

Consumers' became part of a large diversified corporation in 1981. The newly formed Hiram Walker Resources Ltd. holds all the shares of Hiram Walker-Gooderham & Worts Ltd. and Home Oil Company and 90 percent of the common shares of the gas utility whose official name is now The Consumers' Gas Company Ltd.

LAVALIN INC.

Lavalin's Ontario regional headquarters in downtown Toronto.

Although its origins are in the province of Quebec, Lavalin, one of Canada's largest engineering firms, has one of its three major regional headquarters at 33 Yonge Street in Toronto—in a new 13-storey office complex jointly owned with A.E. Lepage Ltd.

For more than 30 years, Lavalin's divisions have participated in high-profile public works and industrial projects in Toronto.

This privately owned enterprise is the product of the vision, ambition, and drive of Bernard Lamarre, Lavalin's president since the 1960s, who expanded the company beyond Quebec. Since its origins in 1936 as Lalonde Valois Associates, a Montreal engineering firm, Lavalin has grown to a multidisciplined engineering giant with more than 40 divisions active around the world.

Lavalin's Ontario organization was launched in 1975, when the company acquired Foundation of Canada Engineering Corporation Ltd. (Fenco) and Geocon Ltd., the engineering and geotechnical arms of the Foundation Company of Canada.

Fenco, established in 1953, is the largest Ontario division, providing expertise in three technical areas—transportation, minerals and metals, and industrial. In addition, it offers complete MEPC services. It has been associated with such projects as the Don Valley Parkway, the Toronto subway system, major interchanges on Highway 401, and the Terminal 2 parking structure at Toronto International Airport.

Geocon, founded in 1954, has provided geotechnical services for such projects as the subway system, major thoroughfares, plant expansions, and high-rise developments. It also has conducted a detailed study with recommendations for stabilizing the Scarborough Bluffs.

Ebastec added thermal-powered engineering to Lavalin's expertise as a result of the acquisition, in 1977, of the assets of the Canadian arm of Ebasco Services of New York, one of the world's largest engineer-constructors in electrical utilities.

MacLaren Engineers Inc. became a Lavalin division in 1980, bringing its reputation as one of the top organizations in the environmental field. For 30 years MacLaren has been identified with engineering investigations and design of local works such as the Humber Treatment Plant, Easterly Water Purification Plant, Bermondsey Solid Waste Transfer Station, and the district heating system for downtown Toronto—as well as environmental planning monitoring studies for the Toronto waterfront development.

Lavalin consolidated its Ontario operations at 33 Yonge Street in the summer of 1982. The Ontario family by that time included Partec Lavalin Inc., an engineer-contractor in petroleum and petrochemicals; Shawiningan Energy Consultants Ltd., a firm with a proven record in hydroelectric power generation; and Warnock Hersey Professional Services Ltd.

Warnock Hersey is a highly diversified testing and inspection company founded in 1888. Canadian-owned and -operated since then, the firm has worked on the Toronto subway, Toronto International Airport, Roy Thompson Hall, the Ontario Science Centre, and various downtown high-rise complexes.

Lavalin has also contributed to the Toronto cultural scene. It was one of the corporate sponsors which, with the Ontario government, commissioned the giant fantasy retro-mural gracing the outside wall of the Gooderham Building, one of the last North American examples of "flatiron" architecture. The mural faces the Scott Street entrance of Lavalin's new Toronto headquarters across from Berczy Park.

The Gooderham Building's Flatiron Mural— unveiling ceremony, September 1980.

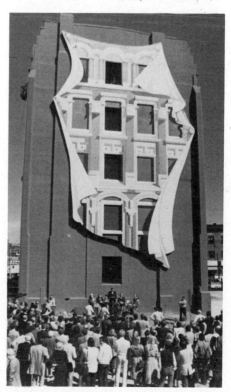

APPENDIX

MAYORS OF TORONTO AND METRO CHAIRMEN

— Died in Office R — Resigned

I   MAYORS OF TORONTO

William Lyon Mackenzie
1834

Robert Baldwin Sullivan
1835

Thomas D. Morrison
1836

George Gurnett
1837, 1848-1850

John Powell
1838-1840

George Monro
1841

Henry Sherwood
1842-1844

William Henry Boulton (R)
1845-1847, 1858

John George Bowes
1851-1853, 1861-1863

Joshua George Beard
1854

George William Allan
1855

John Beverley Robinson, Jr.
1856

John Hutchison
1857

David Breckenridge Read
1858

Adam (later Sir Adam) Wilson
1859-1860

Francis H. Medcalf
1864-1866, 1874-1875

James E. Smith
1867-1868

Samuel Bickerton Harman
1869-1870

Joseph Sheard
1871-1872

Alexander Manning
1873, 1885

Angus Morrison
1876-1878

James Beaty, Jr.
1879-1880

William B. McMurrich
1881-1882

Arthur R. Bosewell
1883-1884

William H. Howland
1886-1887

Edward F. Clarke
1888-1891

Robert J. Fleming (R)
1892-1893, 1896-1897

Warring Kennedy
1894-1895

John Shaw
1897-1899

Ernest A. Macdonald
1900

Oliver Aikin Howland
1901-1902

Thomas Urquhart
1903-1905

Emerson Coatsworth
1906-1907

Joseph Oliver
1908-1909

George R. Geary (R)
1910-1912

Horatio C. Hocken
1912-1914

Thomas Langton Church
1915-1921

Charles A. Maguire
1922-1923

William W. Hiltz
1924

Thomas Foster
1925-1927

Samuel McBride*
1928-1929, 1936

Bert S. Wemp
1930

William J. Stewart
1931-1934

James Simpson
1935

William D. Robbins
1936-1937

Ralph C. Day
1938-1940

Fred J. Conboy
1941-1944

Robert H. Saunders (R)
1945-1948

Hiram E. McCallum
1948-1951

Allan A. Lamport (R)
1952-1954

Leslie H. Saunders
1954

Nathan Phillips
1955-1962

Donald Dean Summerville*
1963

Philip Gerald Givens
1963-1966

William Dennison
1967-1972

David E. Crombie (R)
1973-1978

Frederick J. Beavis
1978

John Sewell
1979-1980

Arthur Eggleton
1981-

II METROPOLITAN CHAIRMEN

Frederick G. Gardiner
1953-1961

William R. Allen (R)
1962-1969

Albert M. Campbell (R)
1969-1973

Paul V. Godfrey
1973-

SUGGESTED READING

The following list of books has been divided into five sections for the convenience of the reader: sources of further information; general works on Toronto and studies of a special period in its development; specialized studies on such fields as architecture, education, labour etc.; biographies of municipal political figures; and histories of the various municipalities that now form part of Metro Toronto or are located near its borders.

The vast wealth of material on Toronto precludes more than a short selection of books, but both scholarly and popular works have been included, based partially on their availability. Articles, theses, and the innumerable biographies of Torontonians other than municipal politicians have been omitted.

1. BIBLIOGRAPHIC SOURCES

Aitken, Barbara B. *Local Histories of Ontario Municipalities: A Bibliography: 1951-1977.* (Toronto, 1978)

Armstrong, Frederick H., Alan F.J. Artibise, and Melvin Baker. *Bibliography of Canadian Urban History. Part IV: Ontario,* in Vance Bibliographies. (Monticello, Ill., 1980)

Artibise, Alan F.J., and Gilbert A. Stelter. *Canada's Urban Past; A Bibliography to 1980 and a Guide to Canadian Urban Studies.* (Vancouver, 1981)

Bishop, Olga B. *Bibliography of Ontario History, 1867-1976.* (2 vols., Toronto, 1980)

Morley, William F.E. *Canadian Local Histories to 1950: Ontario and the Canadian North.* (Toronto, 1978)

Neary, Hilary Bates and Robert Sherman. *Ontario Historical Society: Index to the Publications, 1899-1972.* (Toronto, 1974)

Toronto Public Library. *Early Canadian Companies.* (Toronto, 1967)

Urban and Regional References, 1945-1969. (Ottawa, 1970)

2. GENERAL WORKS

Adam, Graeme Mercer. *Toronto: Old and New.* (Toronto, 1891, reprinted 1972)

Firth, Edith G. *The Town of York, 1793-1834.* (2 vols., Toronto, 1962-1966)

Glazebrook, George P. de T. *The Story of Toronto.* (Toronto, 1971)

Goheen, Peter G. *Victorian Toronto, 1850-1890.* (Chicago, 1970)

Guillet, Edwin C. *Toronto from Trading Post to Great City.* (Toronto, 1934)

Hale, Katharine. *Toronto: Romance of a Great City.* (Toronto, 1956)

Hathaway, Ernest J. *The Story of the Old Fort at Toronto.* (Toronto, 1934)

Illustrated Historical Atlas of the County of York. (Toronto, 1878, reprinted, 1969)

Kerr, Donald and Jacob Spelt. *The Changing Face of Toronto.* (Toronto, 1965)

Kilbourn, William, ed. *The Toronto Book.* (Toronto, 1976)

Kyte, Ernest C., ed. *Old Toronto: A Selection of Excerpts from "Landmarks of Toronto" by John Ross Robertson.* (Toronto, 1970)

Masters, Donald C. *The Rise of Toronto, 1850-1890.* (Toronto, 1974)

Middleton, Jesse E. *The Municipality of Toronto, A History.* (3 vols., Toronto, 1923)

_____ . *Toronto's 100 Years: The Official Centennial Book, 1834-1934.* (Toronto, 1934)

Mulvany, Charles Pelham. *Toronto: Past and Present.* (Toronto, 1884, reprinted, 1970)

Pearson, William H. *Recollections of Toronto of Old.* (Toronto, 1914)

Robertson, John Ross. *Landmarks of Toronto.* (6 vols., Toronto, 1894-1914, reprints, Vol. I, 1976, Vol. III, 1974)

Robinson, Percy J. *Toronto During the French Regime, 1715-1793.* (Toronto, 1933, reprinted, 1965)

Scadding, Henry. *Toronto of Old.* (Toronto, 1973, abridgement by F.H. Armstrong, 1966)

Spelt, Jacob. *Toronto.* (Toronto, 1973)

_____ . *Urban Development in South-Central Ontario.* (Assen, the Netherlands, 1955, reprinted, 1972)

Taylor, Conyngham Crawford. *Toronto Called Back.* (Toronto, 6 editions, 1886-1897)

Timperlake, J. *Illustrated Toronto, Past and Present.* (Toronto, 1877, reprinted)

Walker, Frank N. *Sketches of Old Toronto.* (Toronto, 1965)

West, Bruce. *Toronto.* (Toronto, 1967)

3. SPECIAL STUDIES

Arthur, Eric. *Toronto: No Mean City!* (Toronto, 1964)

Cauz, Louis. *Baseball's Back in Town; From the Don to the Blue Jays.* (Toronto, 1977)

Clark, Christopher, St. George. *Of Toronto the Good, a Social Study.* (Toronto, 1898, reprinted, 1970)

Dendy, William. *Lost Toronto.* (Toronto, 1978)

De Volpi, Charles P. *Toronto a Pictorial Record, 1813-1882.* (Montreal, 1965)

Filey, Michael. *A Toronto Album; Glimpses of the City That Was.* (Toronto, 1970)

Glazebrook, George P. de T. *A Shopper's View of Canada's Past: Pages from Eaton's Catalogues, 1886-1930.* (Toronto, 1969)

Jones, James Edmund. *Pioneer Crimes and Punishments in Toronto and the Home District.* (Toronto, 1924)

Kealey, Gregory S. *Toronto Workers Respond to Industrial Capitalism, 1867-1892.* (Toronto, 1980)

Lorimer, James. *The Ex: A Picture History of the Canadian National Exhibition.* (Toronto, 1973)

McAree, J.V. *Culled From Our Columns.* (Toronto, 1962)

Mann, W.E., ed. *The Underside of Toronto.* (Toronto, 1970)

Martyn, Lucy Booth. *Aristocratic Toronto: 19th Century Grandeur.* (Toronto, 1980)

———. *The Face of Early Toronto: An Architectural Record: 1797-1936.* (Sutton West, 1982)

———. *Toronto 100 Years of Grandeur: The Inside Story of Toronto's Great Homes.* (Toronto, 1978)

Obodiac, Stan. *Maple Leaf Gardens: Fifty Years of Hockey.* (Toronto, 1981)

St. Lawrence Hall. (Toronto, 1969)

Thom, Ron, and others. *Exploring Toronto.* (Toronto, 1972)

Thompson, Austin Seton. *Jarvis Street: a Story of Triumph and Tragedy.* (Toronto, 1980)

———. *Spadina: A Story of Old Toronto.* (Toronto, 1975)

Toronto Board of Education, Centennial Story, 1850-1950. (Toronto, 1950)

Transit in Toronto: The Story of Public Transportation in Metropolitan Toronto. (Toronto, 1982)

Wallace, William Stewart. *A History of the University of Toronto, 1827-1927.* (Toronto, 1927)

Zerker, Sally F. *The Rise and Fall of the Toronto Typographical Union, 1832-1972: A Case Study of Foreign Domination.* (Toronto, 1982)

4. MUNICIPAL POLITICAL FIGURES

Caulfield, Jon. *The Tiny Perfect Mayor* (Crombie). (Toronto, 1974)

Colton, Timothy J. *Big Daddy: Frederick G. Gardiner and the Building of Metropolitan Toronto.* (Toronto, 1980)

Flint, David. *William Lyon Mackenzie: Rebel Against Authority.* (Toronto, 1971)

Kilbourn, William. *The Firebrand* (Mackenzie). (Toronto, 1956)

Morton, Desmond. *Mayor Howland: The Citizens' Candidate* (William H. Howland). (Toronto, 1973)

Phillips, Nathan. *Mayor of All the People.* (Toronto, 1967)

Russell, Victor L. *Mayors of Toronto Vol. I, 1834-1899.* (Toronto, 1982; the second volume will appear shortly.) In addition to the above the completed volumes of the *Dictionary of Canadian Biography* for the 19th century, Vols. IX, X, and XI, covering the period 1861 to 1890, contain biographies of many of the mayors who died during those years.

5. LOCAL OR BOROUGH HISTORIES

Bonis, R.R., ed. *A History of Scarborough.* (Scarborough, 1965)

Boyle, David. *The Township of Scarboro, 1796-1896.* (Toronto, 1896)

Boylen, J.C. *York Township, 1850-1954.* (Toronto, 1954)

Byers, Mary, Jan Kennedy, and Margaret McBurney. *Rural Roots: Pre-Confederation Buildings of the York Region of Ontario.* (Toronto, 1976)

French, William. *Most Unlikely Village: An Informal History of the Village of Forest Hill.* (Toronto, 1964)

Given, Robert A. *The Story of Etobicoke, 1850-1950.* (Islington, 1973)

Hart, Patricia W., ed. *Pioneering in North York: A History of the Borough.* (Toronto, 1968)

Heyes, Esther. *Etobicoke: From Furrow to Borough.* (Etobicoke, 1974)

Johnson, James. *Aurora: Its Early Beginnings.* (Aurora, 1972)

Matthews, Hazel. *Oakville and the Sixteen: the History of an Ontario Port.* (Toronto: 1953)

Mitchell, John. *The Settlement of York County.* (Toronto, 1952)

ACKNOWLEDGMENTS

The writer and the picture researcher both would like to thank the staffs at the various repositories that were consulted, especially John Crosthwait at the Metropolitan Public Library; Ken Macpherson at the Archives of Ontario; Joy Houston and Jim Burant at the Public Archives of Ottawa; Henri Pilon at the Trinity College Archives; Linda Goodwin at the Ontario Ministry of Industry and Tourism; and Victor Russell, Linda Price, Karen Teeple, and Elizabeth Cuthbertson at the City of Toronto Archives.

We would also like to thank Jack Hyatt, Chairman of the Department of History, University of Western Ontario, for his many kindnesses and above all our long-suffering and once again very patient wives, Joan Armstrong and Sandra Martin.

In addition the writer would like to thank James J. Talman of the University of Western Ontario, Barry Gough of the University of Waterloo, and Dave Russell of the Archives of Ontario for their assistance. Colin E. Friesen, the bursar, and Desmond Neill, the librarian, at Massey College have gone out of their way during several summers' research to provide a perfect setting for my studies. Ron Stagg of Ryerson Polytechnical Institute has made helpful comments on the problems of the Rebellion of 1837 and Edward Phelps and John Lutman of the Regional Room, Weldon Library, University of Western Ontario, have assisted with endless small points. Lissa Sanders, Annette Igra, and Laurel Paley of Windsor Publications have combined to make the preparation of the manuscript and its editing a pleasure. Finally, Roger Hall and Maurice Careless have been good enough to read the manuscript and make many valuable comments. The writer, of course, takes full responsibility for any deficiencies.

Finding open country for running to the hounds was becoming increasingly difficult for Toronto's fox-hunting enthusiasts in the early 1900s. A hunt in progress in the Klondyke Ravine near Bathurst Street was photographed about 1912. CTA James 159

INDEX

General Index
Italicized numbers indicate illustrations.